To Bid Them Farewell

A Foot & Mouth Diary

Adam Day MRICS

HAYLOFT

First published 2004

Hayloft Publishing Ltd, Kirkby Stephen,
Cumbria, CA17 4EU.

tel: (017683) 42300
fax. (017683) 41568
e-mail: dawn@hayloft.org.uk
web: www.hayloft.org.uk

ISBN 1 904524 10 9

A catalogue record for this book is available
from the British Library

Cover photography Peter Koronka
with thanks to Kevin Wrathall.

Produced in Great Britain
Printed and bound in Hungary

This book is dedicated to my family and in particular my grandfather, Robert Jackson, farmer, coal merchant and special constable. It was he who introduced me to the farm and auction as a young boy. Happy days!

With special thanks to the chairman, board of directors and all of my colleagues at Mitchell's Auction Company. Also to so many farmers mentioned within the book who so readily gave me permission to tell the story, although some may never bear to read it, and I know my words can never adequately convey it....

The Deserted Village

Sweet smiling village, loveliest of the lawn
Thy sports are fled, and all they charm withdrawn
Amidst thy bowers the tyrants hand is seen
And desolation saddens all thy green
One only master grasps the whole domain
And half a tillage stints thy smiling plain...
Sunk are they bowers, in shapeless ruin all
And the long grass o'ertops the mouldering wall
And trembling, shrinking from the spoiler's hand
Far far away they children leave the land...

Oliver Goldsmith, 1770.

CONTENTS

'LAAL JOHNNY'

Written one evening in April when I was as low as could be. Johnny telephoned me. We finished our conversation and without thinking I put pen to paper. This is what I wrote:-

'Laal Johnny' is a friend of mine. Everybody in the livestock auction world knows 'Laal Johnny'. He lives for his day out at the auction.

Every Wednesday without fail he comes to Cockermouth mart with his brother and two nephews. When I sell his sheep he stands at the edge of the ring and writes down each price and the name of the buyer. When he has sold-up he walks into the mart office to prepare his luck money.

"Hey up lasses" he shouts as he walks around the counter. You cannot see Johnny behind the counter because he is in his own words "a bit short in t'leg."

When he comes back into the ring I get the thumbs up or thumbs down depending on the trade. Sometimes he rings me later in the evening.

"You were on form today," he will say if prices were good.

"Job's a bit steady," if the trade was bad.

In the autumn months he comes in to his own. He loves to travel around the auctions where he often collects luck money for buyers who cannot leave their ringside position. Johnny has a marvellous knack of being able to squeeze a touch more luck penny out of the most conservative seller.

When at home he rides around on a specially prepared tractor with raised pedals. He is an enthusiast. Everybody knows Johnny whether at home, in the auction or at the hound trails.

On the morning of my marriage Johnny rang me to wish me good luck. When my wife was heavy with child Johnny rang to enquire of her condition.

Tonight he has just telephoned me. We are in the middle of the foot and mouth crisis. He is genuinely concerned as to how it is affecting me personally. He tells me not to get depressed. We are, he says, doing a great job for farmers, knowing that we are valuers, councillors and social workers working seven days a week. He knows we are witnessing our own business being slaughtered down the drain. He asks that we be strong and keep going. Soon it will be over. Farmers will always need the auction. His words of support cheer me up from the low depths to which I have descended.

I realise how much I miss the auction and the tug on the back of my auctioneer's tunic as Johnny walks up behind me. Johnny is a friend of mine and tonight I am truly thankful for it.

INTRODUCTION

Foot and mouth is a highly infectious viral disease causing a fever followed by the development of vesicles (blisters) in the mouth and on the feet. It is one of the most infectious animal diseases known to veterinary science. It affects cloven-hoofed animals, domesticated and wild. It also affects elephants, hedgehogs and rats. It is believed that humans can catch it, although this has never been proved. The virus can be transported through the air, on infected meat, and by direct contact of animals. It can also be passed on through infected foodstuffs. It is believed that virus can be transported on vehicle wheels and can contaminate roads if infected organic matter (animal waste) is deposited.

The virus itself is present in great quantities within the blisters on an infected animal. It is also found in saliva, exhaled air, milk and dung. It is present in the blood and all parts of the body. Heat and sunlight can kill it, cold and darkness can help it thrive.

The particular strain of FMD that devastated our industry in 2001 was the pan-Asian type 'O'. This is a particularly virile strain especially in cattle many of which showed very obvious clinical signs, slobbering, licking of lips, sore feet, blistered muzzles, high temperatures and so on. Signs in sheep were far less clear if at all. Pigs were the most susceptible of all animals.

Had the infected animals been allowed to live, nearly all would have survived and recovered to varying degrees. Some would return to normal, others would suffer further health problems as a result of the foot and mouth. No studies have ever been undertaken into whether different breeds have different levels of susceptibility or an in-built genetic immunity.

In 1967 there was a major outbreak of foot and mouth in England. Later in 1980 there was a minor outbreak in the south of the country. That was all I knew about the disease until February 2001. Only when the public information fact sheet was issued by MAFF did I learn much more until, of course, I began to work on infected premises. Then I saw it for myself first hand.

Just how FMD came to our shores no one knows or no one is prepared to tell. The disease is endemic in many foreign countries and has been found on most continents. Whatever route it found onto our island still remains intact. The rules and regulations imposed on farmers since the end of the crisis is tantamount to an admission that the disease is expected to return. The vast amounts of legally and illegally imported meat coming into our country may well be a ticking time-bomb. Is that truly the fault or the responsibility of the British farmer whose business is the most highly regulated in all of Europe?

In the aftermath of FMD, just when the food producers of this country should be supported and encouraged back to production, we find ourselves hardly able to run our businesses and all in the name of good veterinary science. Meanwhile our doors remain virtually open to a FMD 're-match'. We beat it last time and we will again if we have to. But why should we even contemplate having to be the foot soldiers again in another unnecessary war against FMD. Could it now be in the name of good politics rather than good science?

I do not have the answers for I am only a Cumbrian auctioneer and proud of it. Like many others in the field I gave my very best. Later in the crisis I tried hard to inform the higher powers like DEFRA as to just what effect their policies of the time were having on farmers and related businesses. I attended stakeholders' meetings and wrote reports some of which you may read later. I do not know if they were studied or even read. I sincerely hope they were for there were many genuine people trying to offer help and guidance to get us out of a sorry mess. In any case, I do not feel that I could have done any more at that time.

Do not expect a ripping yarn or hearty tales of laughter. War stories are rarely comical. There is for the most part, little joy in this book until the final chapter for everyone likes a happy ending. If however, at the close, you are left with a clearer understanding of what happened to our county in 2001, and why, then my time has not been spent in vain. Many of the questions we were asking at the time still have not been answered. Those of us working on infected farms thought we knew some of the answers. Those in the high echelons of power either did not want to listen to us or did not believe us

I do not seek credit, praise or pity from this book, for I was but a small bit-player in this dreadful crisis. Other auctioneers have their own tales to tell. Many had to visit far more foot and mouth farms than I did. Some had to live out of suitcases, banned from going home if they lived on farms. Many auctioneers endured a protracted form of torture that even farmers whose holdings were struck down by disease fail to realise.

The farmers whose farms went down with the disease endured a nightmare that lasted but a few days. Then there was only silence and a time to grieve. For many it was almost a relief as the creeping death finally swept onto their farms and in to their buildings. Then the farmers began the long road to recovery, while we took the short road to the next farm and the next and the next. For those farmers the war was over, for us the battle continued to be fought day after day. We stood together, the vets, field officers, hauliers, pyre builders, slaughtermen and regular army. We saw so much of each other that we were on first name terms. On the farm we were valuers, advisors and councillors, each client needing a different approach. Always there were tears. Tears of sorrow, tears of anger and rage, tears of bewilderment and tears of hopelessness.

By day we maintained our professional guard, our face and our front. At night we went home and counselled to ourselves. We cried our tears behind closed doors and lay awake wondering if we were not valuing away our own existence. By morning we were ready again. Every morning we were ready again.

Millions of animals were killed by human hand but few died of foot and mouth. The cattle and sheep were culled but the farmers were not. They will breed their replacement herds and flocks. They will restock the fells with sheep and the pastures with cattle. They will sell their stock again with pride and continue to produce food of the highest quality for the populace. You may be sure of that. For farming is not a job. It is a way of life. Farmers and their stock make the Lake District the beautiful place that it is. So many of our animals have gone but our way of life continues although it has changed immeasurably. What effect this whole tragedy has had on all of us, only time will tell.

No lies have been told within these pages, only the truth. Every recollection, every tale, every emotion described is fact and truth. I would have far more to lose than to gain by making these chapters up. I truly wish that it could be a work of fiction. Sadly it is all too real.

So many people fought the disease and have their own horrendous tales to tell. I want to tell mine only because I am left with an enduring feeling that we, the people of Cumbria, were so very badly let down. By whom? I shall let you be the judge.

1
In the Beginning

Wednesday, 23 February
Total national cases: 6
Ban on all export movements announced

To many people the auction mart is a wonderful place. Is it the buzz of the ringside, the crashing of gates and the non-stop patter of the auctioneer imploring more bids? Is it the pleasure of seeing so many wonderful animals produced on Lakeland farms, some for meat, some for breeding? Maybe it is the happy atmosphere as the farmers laugh and joke enjoying one of the few social days within the week. I think it is all of these things and more.

So why is the auction mart so important to the farming community? It is of course a place to buy and sell but just as importantly it is a place to socialise. It is part of the fabric of rural life especially in the Lake District. We are well off the beaten track, far away from the major conurbations and yet much of our produce will eventually end up in butchers' shops and supermarkets in the city. Not only are we food producers, but just as importantly, we produce breeding stock that is bought by farmers all over the country. They are assured of the animals' health and thriftiness. That is why Cockermouth Mart has always been popular for buyers and sellers. We are justifiably proud of this.

From an early age I visited the auction mart with my grandfather. I was and still am excited by the buzz and even the smell of the place. Now when the bids come thick and fast I am in my element. It is like winning at the roulette table. There is no better place to be. And that is what makes the auction mart such a wonderful place. So it was on that fateful Wednesday afternoon in February 2001.

I cleared my throat and launched into selling mode. Prices were good and I had my 'eye in' from watching my colleague Alisdare who had been selling the sheep in the first half of the sale. All the usual buyers were there. These were meat buyers and dealers known to farmers throughout Cumbria for their weekly appearances in local auction marts. Our stock would be travelling all over the country. Abattoirs from Devon to Aberdeen would buy from us, assured of the quality of the animals and trusting in the way we handled the stock. Bruised or injured animals would be of no use to them. This system of purchase has worked well year after year. All the buyers without exception enjoyed buying in the Cockermouth ring. For it was a true farmers' market. All our animals came straight from local farms. Many were from the holding of birth. Ours was an uncomplicated market: probably the only ring in the county that maintained a steady congregation of watching farmers from start to finish. The atmosphere always made the old market at Cockermouth that little bit special.

Half an hour into my stint I was going well and prices were holding firm. The buyers were enjoying the recent lift in trade because they had good prices to give and a steady order to fill. Knowing that, I was able to engage in some banter to keep the sale flowing: "£45 bid and I've put you in," I said to Keith Ewbank a well known sheep buyer from Appleby.

"I hear you prefer it that way!" he gesticulated with raised fingers.

"Is that another twenty then Keith?" I laughed.

Everyone was having a good day, farmers, buyers and auctioneers alike. Even better was the fact that we were due to make a presentation to the company's shareholders that very evening to confirm that the new auction mart development was to go ahead. At last the green light was on. We had all waited many years for our new market. The fact that it was now going to happen was a credit to the local farmers who had supported us through thick and thin.

Then the buyers' mobile phones started to ring. Not just one or two as usual, but each and every one of them. Within 30 seconds every single buyer had retired to a quiet corner and was talking underneath cupped hands in to the phone. I stopped selling.

"What's going on here?" I quipped, "you're not talking to each other are you? That's called a cartel and it's illegal." My joke was in vain.

Neil Iveson from Hawes was first to respond. "I'm switched off," he said referring to the fact that his abattoirs had told him to stop buying.

"Why's that?" I asked knowing that his main order from Anglesey was very strong that day. He shrugged his shoulders and sat down.

All of the buyers were shaking their heads and making calls themselves. I decided to continue selling the sheep. Only two buyers even attempted to bid. There was Arthur Pooley from Lancashire who had been Cockermouth's mainstay for several years and Robert Skelton a young local buyer who was very much the new kid on the block. Every one else sat down. Prices plummeted quickly and there was nothing I could do. All the joking finished. I had no idea what new price levels the buyers had been given. I was punching in the dark.

My good friend Jimmy Craghill from Haverigg brought his heavy Suffolk lambs into the ring. They were bid to a price around six pounds per head less than just a few minutes ago.

"What the hell's going here?" enquired Jim using his extensive knowledge of Anglo-Saxon.

"Jim I just don't know," I replied "but whatever it is has got to be serious."

"It's foot and mouth," interjected Arthur Pooley quietly. I was dumbstruck. I thought FMD had disappeared in the 60s and couldn't get into this country.

"It's been discovered in Hexham," he continued "we don't know anymore than that." The other buyers nodded their heads in agreement.

"We are waiting for phone calls," said Neil Iveson "they've put a ban on exports" he continued.

I contemplated cancelling the sale there and then but Arthur Pooley said he would buy a few to lair over. Robert Skelton said he would carry on too. This was the beauty of having dealer buyers. They could buy sheep and hold them over in order to play the market. If demand in any week was poor and prices low, then sheep could be taken back to the dealer's own farm to be sent to market when the prices improved. This regime was very good for all farmers because it ironed out the highs and lows in the market place. Consequently there was far less fluctuation in the trade compared to the situation after FMD when the anti-competitive, anti-auction mart twenty-day rule was introduced by DEFRA.

I made a brief announcement to the farmers who were shocked and incredulous. Jimmy Craghill decided to pass his sheep out of the ring and take them home unsold.

"I'll bring 'em back next week," he said, "when this has all blown over they could be dearer," he said with a chuckle. No one knew if he was right or wrong.

The sale continued and many farmers accepted the lower prices as a disappointing and unusual turn of events. Many farmers do not like to pass stock out of the ring believing that the buyers are there to buy in both good times and bad. It is called taking the rough with the smooth.

Gradually the phone calls came in and most buyers began to bid again with caution. The sale was completed and most sheep were sold. Afterwards in the office there was much conjecture about the disease. There was however a strong belief that it could easily be contained and that things were going to get back to normal pretty quickly. Besides that, our friends at Longtown Mart, the biggest sheep market in the country were proceeding with their sale the next day as normal. The Government had not even stopped the movement of animals around the country so the outbreak could not possibly be serious. Anyone remotely connected with farming in Cumbria would know that sheep sold in Longtown and all the other markets would be all over the country within 24 hours.

That night, Peter Greenhill our company chairman, John Marrs, company secretary and myself gave a fighting presentation about the development plan for our new mart. We had heard that a contingent of shareholders who were not auction mart supporters were going to try and hijack the presentation to stop the development. We blew them away. The support from the farming shareholders was unequivocal. After six long years we were going ahead at last. We had an option to purchase some farmland on the outskirts of Cockermouth and after a long and protracted battle we now had planning permission to build. There were other agriculturally related businesses that also wished to occupy our site. We were going to create a business park for the farming community with a prestigious new mart as the centre piece.

The business plan stacked up and in my closing sentences to the shareholders I summed up by saying that nothing now could stop the company. We were going to take Cockermouth's livestock market into the 21st century. The only possible cloud on the horizon was a reported outbreak of foot and mouth disease in Northumberland.

"Surely," I said "surely, in this day and age such an outbreak will be controlled and eradicated quickly. Thank you for your kind attention ladies and gentlemen. We will now retire to the bar where the auctioneers will be delighted to offer you a drink or some other refreshment." That was to be the last drink we had with our farmer customers for many months. Already there were six cases reported around the country. The nightmare was about to begin.

Later that night I travelled the dark and quiet A66 road back to my home village of Greystoke. I felt a glowing sense of satisfaction that we really had achieved our goal in bringing the new auction mart plan to fruition. What I did not know was that I had brought the hammer down within the old Cockermouth mart for the final time. Never again would we fill the place with sheep and farmers. Never again would we strive to move and unload sheep through Kittyson Lane. 130 years of trading livestock at Fairfield in the middle of Cockermouth was over and we did not even know it.

That night James Mattinson and Robert Cowen our yardsmen loaded the last remaining sheep of the day onto a wagon bound for a Welsh abattoir. They turned off the lights, locked the doors and shut down the West Cumbria mart for the final time.

2
THE DAYS OF DENIAL

Tuesday 27 February
National cases: 27
First case reported in Cumbria

The days following our last sale were put to good use in planning the final stages of the new mart development. We kept a close eye on the national news still believing that the outbreak would be swiftly curtailed.

On Friday 23 February Nick Brown, the Minister of Agriculture announced that a total ban on livestock movements would come into force at 5pm that day. All around the country livestock hauliers and buyers who were lairing stock prior to slaughter, tried to ship them to abattoirs before the curfew. Some, including a local sheep buyer, did not make it and were stopped on the road after 5pm only to be turned around and sent home with the sheep.

The facts themselves were unbelievable. FMD had been found in some pigs waiting to be slaughtered in an abattoir in Essex. It was confirmed on the 19 February. Even by the Wednesday 21 February, the day of our last sale, it had not been publicly announced. Why we were kept in the dark is anybody's guess. Even worse was the fact that it was not until Friday 23rd that the decision was taken to suspend livestock movements around the country. There in front of us was the worst and most glaring mistake made throughout the crisis. It was tantamount to negligence and let every single farmer in the land down so very badly. The fact that stock continued to move around the country in a normal manner was not the fault of the farmers, the auctioneers, the abattoirs or the dealing fraternity.

By the end of the week there were outbreaks all over the land including Scotland and Northern Ireland. By now MAFF was faced with the impossible task of trying to trace the movement of every single animal around the country over the last few days. Of course the best source of information on animal traceability was the auction marts whose book keeping is always exemplary. Our friends at Longtown mart, who by their own success at what they do, fared so badly when FMD erupted, were able to provide complete information on the movement of many thousands of animals and all within two hours of MAFF's request.

On Saturday evening I travelled to Greenhill Hotel, Wigton. The occasion was a wedding reception for which my band the Soul Traders had been booked to play. It was a freezing cold evening as we trailed up the road in the old 'Tour Bus'. On the way I tried to explain to the band what foot and mouth was. I realised that my knowledge was very limited and totally based on past information related to what I had heard about the 1967 outbreak. At this point there had been no mention of the deadly pan-Asian 'O' strain.

Our bass player Jamie who is a road engineer made the comment that it wouldn't affect his line of work. How wrong he was, for within the month he was travelling from infected premises to infected premises to design huge lagoons that MAFF required to hold all stored slurry which was deemed to be a major infection and contamination risk. The cattle were gone but the disease could, in the right conditions, live on in the slurry. This was MAFF policy.

The wedding party was a real success and we performed well. A farmer friend of mine called Cyril Moore was a relation of the bride. I had a brief chat with him but we were both a little uncomfortable about the situation. I think we were both glad when it was home-time. In the early hours of Sunday morning I slid into bed beside Paula and was glad to cuddle up to the warmth of her body. I soon fell asleep.

The next day as I played with Olivia, our little girl not yet two years old, the first outbreak in the county of Devon was revealed. That night Paula and I sat in front of the glow from our open fire. She was heavily pregnant with our second child and being a little uncomfortable needed to sit away from the fire. On the TV screen we watched in silence the dreadful scenes of funeral pyres being lit in Devon. I began to waken from the state of denial that had clouded over the last few days. A shiver went through me when the presenter announced that the source of infection in Devon was most probably from an auction mart in Cumbria. It was Longtown, one of the most successful sheep marts in the country.

I said to Paula: "If the disease has got to Devon then it will be all over Cumbria."

"How do you know?" she asked

"Because everybody buys in Longtown," I replied. I then spent many minutes thinking about how many farmers and dealers I knew that had been to Longtown in the last couple of weeks to buy store lambs and store cattle. Sleep came uneasily that night.

3
On the Doorstep

Tuesday 28 February
Total national cases: 30

During the afternoon I walked into the office to see my colleagues gathered around a small portable radio.

"What's going on?" I enquired.

"Sssshhh! Listen!" I was ordered.

The local radio announcement told us that the first foot and mouth case in Cumbria was being investigated. Clinical signs of the disease had been found in livestock on a farm near Longtown. Blood-test results would reveal whether the animals would have to be slaughtered. We spent many minutes debating how far the disease might spread. We were reassured by the distance from Longtown to Cockermouth and remained hopeful that the disease could be stopped in its tracks. Even so, we knew many of the affected farms that were being slaughtered in the Longtown area.

What we had no conception of at that time, was the indescribable horror that many of those farmers were suffering in those early days. There was no contingency plan to put in to operation. The vets in charge, through no fault of their own were making it up as they went along. In some cases there were not enough bullets to shoot the animals. The only way to dispose of the dead animals was to burn them on pyres. Within a few days there were several pyres burning around the outskirts of Longtown. The people around the area suffered dreadfully, with no way of stopping the pungent stench of smouldering coal, sleepers and animal carcasses. Ash, skin and other debris from the pyre poured into the sky. It was described as 'hell on earth' and like 'Dante's Inferno'. Pretty soon there were too many bodies even for the existing pyres. As the disease took hold, MAFF were forced into importing bodies from other parts of the county. This was to happen much later in West Cumbria also. Meanwhile we lived in hope, totally ignorant of how awful the situatiowas in North Cumbria.

The following day the local newspaper visited our empty, silent auction and took pictures of Alisdare Bruce and myself, the company's two livestock auctioneers.

"Try and look glum," said the photographer. It was not difficult.

That night I discovered that Sockbridge Hall, a farm near Penrith run by the Errington family had succumbed to the disease. This was only three miles from my own home at Greystoke. John Errington had purchased thousands of store sheep from Cockermouth mart in past years. Now every sheep they owned and the whole large dairy herd would have to be slaughtered and burned. It was reported that John had around 9000 sheep in various locations all of which he had been in 'dangerous contact' with.

Dangerous contact applied to all animals with which a farmer had been in contact, if it could be proved that he had also been in contact with FMD infected stock. Dangerous contact meant the killing of each and every animal, healthy or not. The contiguous cull was to become Government policy. In time many dangerous contact farms would be contiguously culled out around the infected premises. In Cumbria a conservative estimate would be a ratio of four or five dangerous contacts to every infected premises.

I felt heartily sorry for the Erringtons whom I had known for many years. After some days a massive pyre was constructed and the bodies of the animals were piled high upon it. When the fire was lit it burned brightly for many nights eventually fading to a glowing mass. All trace of the bodies was gone. Only the stench of the burn remained together with a massive black scar across the pastures of Sockbridge Hall. Everybody in Penrith and beyond could smell the burning pyre. Nobody escaped. When the wind turned westward, the smoke drifted across Greystoke. I sat in my front room with windows closed tight but still the eerie stench crawled its way into my home. It hung there in every room. I thought for a moment about what it must be like for those persons living close to, or even next to the burning mass of bodies.

In their home village of Tirril some people's houses were so badly smoke damaged, they had to move out and have the places redecorated when the fires had burned out. This would be the case for most villages close to burning pyres. There were to be 147 burn sites in North Cumbria.

Around that time John Errington rang me to apologise for not sending a cheque for the last lot of sheep he had purchased in Cockermouth Mart just before we were closed down. He was hardly in control and it was difficult to know what to say to him. No words were adequate. I reassured him that payment could wait a little longer bearing in mind his predicament. He was very down.

"If I know you John, you'll bounce back again," I said and I meant it.

Later in the year our paths were to cross again when he was employed by DEFRA as a shepherd/gatherer on infected premises. Like everyone else he still had to make a living once all of his stock was gone. For the foot and mouth valuations only gave him a market price which in time might allow him to purchase replacement stock. No one knew when that might be and the valuations could make no allowance for living expenses or staff wages until that time.

Sure enough in time John would return to Cockermouth to purchase sheep once again. Sadly it was to be a long, long time in the future.

4
MARCH - IN LIKE A LION

1 March 2001
Total national cases 32

The first day of March was spent inviting tenders for an archeological survey that was required by the local council before we could develop the new mart site. I hoped and prayed that this would not uncover some hitherto unknown Roman relic or medieval burial pit. Nor I hoped would it end up being a foot and mouth burial pit or funeral pyre site. It did not, but sadly the farm was to lose its dairy herd and sheep as yet another dangerous contact. One of four contacts resulting from its neighbouring infected premises. That is for later.

Around the country there were now eleven infected counties. The disease had also slipped over the Scottish border into Dumfries and Galloway. Vainly we contacted all the abattoirs that were normally represented at our market on auction days. They all desperately needed stock but were unable to buy. The UK meat industry was in danger of going to the wall.

Abroad, many countries with licenses to export meat to the UK rubbed their hands together with glee. The British farmers were on their uppers but the supermarkets would make sure their shelves were not empty. There was talk of massive price rises due to the shortage of meat. This despite the increased level of imports. Meanwhile our own farmers begged us to try and sell their beef and lambs. The stock was either getting past its best or eating its way through what small profit might have been made had it been sold at the optimum time.

In the office we felt helpless, fielding call after call from farmers wanting advice or reassurance. We could not really give them either. At night the phone continued to ring at home.

Confirmed cases in Cumbria continued to rise with farms well known to me on Cumbria's east fellside going down with the disease. Longtown auction mart also succumbed and was actually named as an infected premises.

Through the first weekend in March the disease spread rapidly in the Carlisle and Brampton area. We held an emergency meeting of farmer directors to discuss the repercussions of the disease. I gave a short presentation about how most of our customer base would remain in tact if the disease spread no further west. The directors decided that as long as the disease kept away from West Cumbria then it would be safe to proceed with the new mart development. At least we still had some hope.

I wrote to Andrew Hayward, the Chief Veterinary Officer at Carlisle. My letter detailed the reason why he should allow Cockermouth mart to become a collection centre for slaughter animals to be collected on behalf of the abattoirs. Sadly events were to overtake us and the idea of a temporary collection centre at Cockermouth was put on hold until much later.

I ate my lunchtime sandwiches with James and Robert our yardmen and reassured them that the new mart was definitely still in the pipeline. Then the phone rang. It was local sheep buyer Robert Skelton whose farm was four miles from Cockermouth. I knew from a previous conversation that MAFF had blood tested his sheep recently due to the fact that he had purchased some out of Longtown Auction Mart and brought them home to Dearham. Robert had told me some of the sheep were lame and one had been off colour. He did not think that it was FMD. He was sadly wrong.

"Sorry Adam," he said quietly "we've got it and it's definite." For the first time throughout the early stages of the epidemic, my heart sank.

"What happens now?" I asked.

"They are going to burn them," he replied in a matter of fact tone "anymore than that I don't know." I put the phone down. Robert and James looked down at the floor shaking their heads.

"Now we are in trouble," I said. We ate our sandwiches and discussed what might happen next.

Throughout the remainder of the week we watched the disease spread throughout our county and beyond. From Gretna to Lazonby to Penrith, case after case was reported. Every afternoon in our office we listened to BBC Radio Cumbria giving updates and naming infected premises. Even in West Cumbria many of those farms were known to us. As we sat listening I was reminded of my Grandfather who told me about listening to the radio broadcasts during the Second World War. There were striking similarities to the broadcasts.

"Today there were nine cases and a further seventeen are awaiting blood test results." We were literally being slaughtered down the drain.

Apart from the one case at Broughton Moor, no others reared their heads in our area. We began to believe that we might get through alive.

On the afternoon of Thursday 8 March, Les Bouch a local trading standards officer visited our office. He was clearly distressed and agitated. He began with an apology.

"I am really sorry to have to do this," he said. "I have to visit all the auction marts to serve you with one of these." He produced from a plastic document holder a sheaf of papers which turned out to be a "D" notice effectively shutting down the auction mart building forthwith. We were instructed to place "Keep out - foot and mouth" notices on the doors. We were not allowed to hold our weekly car boot sale or let the general public through our doors.

We chatted for a short while to Les. He and his colleagues had been present at several infected premises and slaughter sites over the last few days. This had clearly been distressing. The trading standards officers had not had much rest and the strain was showing. Les shook with emotion. We offered him encouragement but he could not reciprocate. As he left he offered prophetic words.

"This disease is everywhere," he said, "we have not seen the last of it."

We did not know at the time but every single auction mart in the European Union had been shut down. More ominously over 96,000 animals had been culled but had not been disposed of. The Government simply had no contingency plan to dispose of carcasses in any number. Around the county the bodies of cattle and sheep lay rotting. In fields, farmyards and buildings there were stinking piles of corpses with plastic bags over their heads and feet to try and prevent the shedding of foot and mouth virus. Even the daily hosing with disinfectant did not prevent vermin and carrion picking at the bodies before flying back to their roost or disappearing into their burrows. It was a hopeless situation.

The following Christmas a few weeks after the FMD crisis had officially ended, I met an acquaintance in our local pub. He worked for a machinery contractor and his job had been to place the dead bodies on to the pyres with a loading machine. In those early days some of the bodies were so badly decomposed that they actually fell apart as he tried to lift them. Later when they lit the pyres they used to stay well away as thousands of rats, foxes and all manner of vermin fled their temporary abodes and escaped to pastures new.

"Worse than that," said my friend quaffing his Guinness, "worse than that was the smell, all day every day, in my hair and my clothes. I could even smell it at night lying in bed. I can still smell it now." I knew what he meant.

It was at this point in time when the Government introduced its contiguous farm policy. From now on any farm which was in direct contact with an FMD infected farm would have all livestock culled out, irrespective of whether that contact could be perceived as dangerous. The slaughter procedure was just the same on these farms, the pain no less for the farmers. The only difference was that these farms were never recorded on the Government's official foot and mouth listings. Remember the ratio, at least four or five to one.

It was now becoming apparent that through the firebreak policy of contiguous culling, thousands of healthy animals were now being slaughtered wholesale. The crisis was growing more desperate by the minute. To anybody involved in the procedure at field level it was an outbreak of disastrous and tragic proportions.

5
THE FIRST CASE SCENARIO

Sunday 11 March
Total national cases: 172

It was early evening and I was enjoying a relatively quiet family week-end. I had taken Olivia swimming although at less than two years of age she had not found her water wings. Paula was heavy with child and declined to enter the pool. She did however enjoy watching us splashing around. Later I even found the will to go for a three mile run around Greystoke. This was a vain attempt to get myself fit for an invitation game of rugby in April to celebrate a rugby acquaintance's 40th birthday. I was determined to prove to my old mates that at 36 years of age, I had not 'lost the plot'. The match was to be an old boy's game against Penrith's current first team. That was all the incentive I needed to go for a run.

Now, with Olivia tucked up in bed I rested my aching legs. The phone rang:

"David Owen here from Tirril." It was an unexpected surprise.

"Hello David what can I do for you?" I asked.

"Foot and mouth has just been confirmed here," he said quietly. "I've just talked to David Jackson and he suggested I called you." David Jackson was an old colleague of mine from Penrith auction days. We had both since left the company, but he still helped David Owen to sell his stock from time to time.

"I want you to value the animals before they shoot them." Although I had been expecting such a call at some stage it still hit me like a shock-wave.

"Thank you" I said, immediately regretting my urbane response, "I mean I would be honoured to do it for you." David continued to give me the details about his livestock. He asked me to arrive at the farm at 10.30am. That was an instruction from the MAFF vet. He had not left any other instructions and MAFF had not issued any other protocols to our office. I was, in effect, going in totally unprepared.

I put the phone down and explained the situation to Paula. She asked me what effect it would have on my immediate future. Would I be able to come home after being in contact with the virus? Could she catch the disease? Could the cat catch it? What about the sheep in the fields around our house? I knew some of the answers but not all of them.

That night I lay in bed wondering how I would feel walking on to the infected farm. Would I have to watch the animals being slaughtered? I had heard stories of animals losing their tongues and being so ill they could hardly walk. Would this be the case tomorrow? Sleep was difficult.

The next morning I made a quick dash to my office at Cockermouth. This was in case I was no longer allowed back there after the valuation was complete especially as farmers visited our offices every day. I soon learned that anyone visiting an FMD infected farm was classed by MAFF as 'dirty'. From that day forward I was a 'dirty valuer'. For seven days after every valuation I had to keep away from all susceptible livestock or their keepers. I was told that any traces of the virus on my body or within my nasal passages should die after one week. This was, according to a MAFF directive, proven scientific fact. As FMD continued to ravage the county, MAFF ran desperately short of 'clean' vets. After a few days the 'dirty' period was reduced to five days. When things got really bad it was reduced to three days. At the height of the disease I met some vets who were travelling from dirty to clean farms within 24 hours.

Later I was to 'enjoy' hearing the tales of MAFF staff meeting up at weekends for nights of partying and passion. A number of bars and clubs in Carlisle were the meeting places for many vets, field officers, slaughtermen and young valuers who all got together in the evening after difficult days in the field. I even heard of a points system ranging from maximum points for a night with a female vet to minimum points for MAFF support staff.

I made the return journey along the A66 to Penrith. Anybody who has driven from Penrith to Pooley Bridge will have passed through Tirril. It is a gateway to the Ullswater valley although I had no inclination to appreciate the scenery.

It was a bright but cold early spring morning. I am not ashamed to say that I was nervous and apprehensive. In no time at all I was at David Owen's farm gate. I climbed out of my car and was met by the official MAFF vet. I was relieved to find that it was Philip Watson whom I already knew as he too played rugby. We exchanged pleasantries and we both admitted that it was our 'first time'. He asked me if I had a disposable suit to wear. I did not, so he hunted a spare one out of his car boot. Suitably dressed and with the appropriate paperwork duly provided by Phil we set off to the sheep pens where David Owen was waiting with his sheep. There were no clinical signs of infection within the sheep. I felt relieved. It was almost as if I was undertaking a normal valuation of in-lamb mule ewes.

I proceeded to count and inspect every single sheep. Before visiting the farm I had contacted an auctioneer from another firm with whom I was on good terms. He gave me a genuine guide as to what basis of valuation the now-experienced F&M valuers were using. I offered my sheep valuation to David Owen and he seemed fairly satisfied.

Then we moved to the cattle sheds. Phil the vet showed me the cow that had produced the first clinical signs of the disease on the farm. That was several days ago but MAFF policy at that time was that no slaughter could begin until positive blood tests had been produced. Those results had only come through on Sunday. Now some five days since the first signs of the disease both farmer and vet commented that the cow seemed to be over the worst and looked a lot better than before the weekend. Despite the telltale nasal mucus, the cow had obviously eaten and was chewing her cud. She was not in any way distressed. Phil explained that this did not stop her from potentially shedding large amounts of live virus in to the atmosphere. I made my valuation and we moved on.

The next shed was full of young feeding bulls. Some were in prime condition ready for the abattoir. Others needed more time. However when David opened the shed door to let the cattle into the holding yard I got the shock of my life. Maybe I had been lulled into a false sense of security by the improving cow, but these animals were clearly distressed. Some were hardly able to walk because their feet were so sore. Others had huge amounts of mucus trailing in wisps from their mouths and noses. Others left tell tale drops of blood on the concrete from weeping sores within their mouths. I tried to detach myself from their condition in order to put a market value on them. There were a lot of cattle in the shed and I had to walk through them several times to make sure I inspected them thoroughly. David spoke up.

"I wish you would put them out of their misery now." It was a desperate plea and I know Phil Watson was thinking the same thing and wishing he could do so there and then. MAFF policy would not allow it.

By now it was lunchtime. As we sat in the kitchen I tried to lighten the atmosphere by recounting a chance meeting I had with David Owen the previous summer. For on a whim one fine June Saturday afternoon I set off to climb the famous Sharp Edge on Blencathra. Half way up the climb I could see a tall slim figure charging down at full kilter.

The phrase 'silly bloody idiot' went through my mind at the time. As the figure got closer I saw that it was indeed David Owen who being a keen fell runner was out on a short training run. He could get up Sharp Edge and down to the A66 main road in well under 40 minutes. My time would more than double that. My only excuse was that I wanted to enjoy the view, which you hardly can when running down Sharp Edge. What is the point of climbing mountains when you can't eat your sandwiches at the summit?

We moved onto David Owen's second farm at the other end of the village and performed the same routine. Thankfully there were no animals here showing any clinical signs of the disease but the animals were obvious dangerous contacts. The valuation was fairly straightforward. Afterwards we scrubbed down thoroughly and removed our protective clothing. I asked David how he thought the disease might have travelled onto his farm. He was convinced that it had either travelled on the wind or had been brought by vermin from Sockbridge Hall a few hundred yards away. This was one of the first farms in Cumbria to become infected. Their giant pyre was still smouldering away even after several days.

As I got into the vehicle to travel back to David's house a local resident approached me. "Well have they got it then?"

"No," I said.

"But you're still going to kill them aren't you?" There was more than a little venom in the person's voice.

"Not me personally," I replied.

"We can't stand another fire in this village you know."

"It's really nothing to do with me," I said lamely.

"You're all the same you Government people, always passing the buck."

I drove off feeling a little disgruntled but understanding the resident's feelings. Within a few days I would be thinking exactly the same way. Not about the people on the ground like Phil Watson who did a magnificent job all the way through in impossible and distressing circumstances, but the high level bureaucrats and politicians. The faceless, nameless often clueless people who came to be known by their office address,

'Page Street'. All decisions had to be made by Page Street. Every vet seeing clinical signs on a farm had to get a decision from Page Street. Borderline cases especially on contiguous farms had to be referred to Page Street. The answer was always the same: "Kill them." The only time a direct answer could not be gleaned from Page Street was on matters of policy.

The disease began to rage out of control but no one would make a decision on how to stop it. Everyone at ground level could see that infected animals had to be slaughtered as quickly as possible then disposed of immediately. The decision should have remained fairly and squarely with the vets in the field or at least in consultation with their superiors in Carlisle. Here again we were very badly let down.

I discussed this situation with Phil Watson as I completed the official valuation sheets in triplicate. In his opinion two things had to happen. Firstly the animals had to be slaughtered within 24 hours of showing clinical signs. Secondly the bodies must be disposed of within 48 hours. Also the contiguous culling of the dangerous contact farms should take place within 48 hours of discovering the disease. Without this policy in place the disease would spread right throughout the county and beyond.

"You can't be serious Phil?" I argued.

"It's bloody true," he said, "we need the army in now to make this happen. We are sitting on a time bomb."

I then sat for a few minutes listening with incredulity as the young vet tried in vain to secure a slaughter team for David Owen's animals. Then he made several attempts to plan a carcass disposal operation. Eventually he put the phone down clearly frustrated. He composed himself and then began to explain to David the problems that he and every other 'dirty' vet was facing. All the working slaughter teams, of which there were very few at that time, were booked up. It would be tomorrow afternoon before a killing crew could get there. The rendering plant operators were offering to pick up and take away the carcasses in around nine days time because they had not agreed an operating plan (payment terms) with MAFF. The local parish council were (quite understandably) opposing any further burning pyres in and around the village.

"What I really want to do," said Phil "is bury the bodies as soon as possible. I have enquired about sinking a pit in one of your pasture fields but the Environment Agency have blocked it in case there is any contamination of local water courses through land drains in the field."

Phil went back to the phone to try and find some way to dispose of the bodies. It was hopeless. More worrying was the fact that this was taking place on every single infected premises in the county. At this point my role was complete so I decided to leave and let them get on with it. I made my goodbyes and departed.

In the end after much argument and much wasted time, it was decided that the only real solution to the problem was in fact to build yet another pyre and burn the lot. Unfortunately this operation took several more days. The pyre was eventually lit on the following Sunday morning, some eleven days since the disease first showed itself on the farm. David Owen had to use his own loader tractor to pile the dead bodies in neat heaps in his farmyards where they lay for five days. Phil Watson's chilling warning came back to me, "dead in 24 hours, disposed of in 48 hours, or else!"

All around the county the same fiasco was being played out in full. It really is no wonder that the virus was able to spread from farm to farm at this time. What could any farmers do to prevent the spread when sheep and cattle can so easily rub noses through the fence?

By now it was mid-afternoon and I could not go back to the office. I hated the thought of taking the virus in to my own home so I decided to go to the local swimming pool where I reasoned that a few doses of chlorine up my nose would dispose of any FMD virus. The Government was recommending use of citric acid as one of the approved compounds to kill the infection. We had purchased buckets of it at significant cost. They later removed it from the approved list and we could not use it any more. Why was it on the list then taken off? I do not know. Scientific advice perhaps?

I thought the chlorine in the swimming pool might be as strong as the citric acid. I had a change of clothing in my car anyway. I arrived at the pool and was booking in when a female voice spoke up behind me.

"Hello Adam how is it going?" I turned around and froze. It was a local farmer's wife who had come to use the pool facilities in the late afternoon. What could I say? I mumbled a few words and walked straight out of the building. I was shocked and actually felt dirty.

"What if she has breathed in some virus from me?" I thought. I felt dreadful as I drove straight home. As instructed by the vet, I put my clothes into the washing machine and went straight into the bath. Within a few weeks this routine would not make me bat an eyelid although I was never to lose the feeling of being some sort of leper when amongst the general community. This stayed right through the crisis as long as I continued to value stock for slaughter.

The next morning I was force feeding soggy weetabix to Olivia when the phone rang. It was the vet Phil Watson.

"Adam you have to come back today," he said.

"What have I done wrong?" I asked immediately expecting the worst.

"Nothing at all" he said, "there are some sheep which David Owen has taken in for winter from a farmer near Appleby. Page Street says they have to be valued and slaughtered."

The farmer was Ernest Harker whom I knew from my selling days at Penrith and Kirkby Stephen.

"Surely he will want his local valuer to do the job," I said.

"No, I have spoken to him and he is happy for you to do it." Again I felt honoured to be given the job but it was not in any way a pleasant feeling.

So for the second time I returned to Tirril. This time to count and inspect away-wintered sheep. Mr Harker had no wish to come anywhere near the farm so it was agreed that David would act as his authorised agent. On that cold Tuesday in March we quickly completed our task and again I drove straight home. That night I rang Ernest Harker and discussed my sheep valuation. He seemed satisfied and thanked me for my efforts. I told him that I hoped to meet up with him during better times.

I reflected that I was now a fully-blooded foot and mouth valuer. It was a job title that I did not want. For the next six months it gave me no pleasure. At that time I had no idea of how much worse it was going to get. I should have paid more attention to Phil Watson for he knew exactly what he was talking about and was proved to be totally accurate. The 24/48 hour policy was talked about in Government circles. The Prime Minister actually referred to it once saying that they were almost achieving the target. In reality they didn't manage it. Worse still was the fact that they were nowhere near it in those crucial early weeks.

Why did Page Street not listen to the real experts? Why did they bury their heads in the sand? Was it the Government's scientific advisors, the Agriculture Minister or even as has been suggested, the Chancellor of the Exchequer who was unwilling to release funds to pay for it?

6
RIVAL VALUATIONS

Saturday 17 March
Total national cases: 295
155,000 animals awaiting slaughter

Following my first valuation requests we continued to monitor the spread of the disease throughout the county. Every day we listened to the three o'clock 'war' report on local radio. Silloth, Wigton, Carlisle, Penrith, it was relentless. We still believed that the virus would not find its way to West Cumbria and that we would be spared. With hindsight we were clinging to a forlorn hope.

On the evening of Friday 16 March I was contacted by the unfortunate Ernest Harker again. He had a large batch of Swaledale sheep on a farm to the north of Penrith. MAFF insisted that they had to be slaughtered as dangerous contacts to neighbouring infected premises. Once again I was in business. Soon after, the duty vet rang me and we agreed to meet early next morning.

Later that night I watched the news to see that the Prime Minister Tony Blair had visited Cumbria that day. He was warned that the disease would flare up considerably when cattle, which were housed for winter, were turned out during the spring. Unknown to us all, the fire was already well and truly alight. Worse still, the current slaughter and disposal policy was fanning the flames. Mr Blair did not stay very long in our county. It was more of a back door flit really. Perhaps it was understandable knowing that he must carefully plan his campaign trail leading up to the General Election.

Early next morning I drove through Unthank near Skelton to take a shortcut to the valuation farm. This was a bad mistake because it took me directly past Home Farm where the entire dairy herd had been slaughtered several days previously. The pyre was under construction and the decomposing bodies were piled high. The stench was overpowering and I wondered how the poor residents could stay in the vicinity even for a minute. Never mind the burning crews who had to lift and transport the bodies in a state of semi-putrefaction.

At the agreed time I arrived at the contact point and was met by the vet.

She was in fact a private practice vet who had been seconded in by MAFF. We walked into the fields and helped gather in the sheep. It was a fairly muggy and overcast morning. I was sweating uncomfortably in my oilskins and protective disposable suit. It took some time to count the sheep of which there were several hundred. Then I made my inspection and valuation. The vet had not seen many Swaledales before and I discussed the sheep with her, explaining that the owner had a very good reputation for his sheep going back several generations.

We completed the valuation papers that included the form of appointment from MAFF. By signing it the vet was appointing me on MAFF's behalf to undertake the valuation. It meant that although the farmer could choose who would value the stock, the valuer was actually hired and paid for by MAFF. The appointment form also detailed the scale of fees that would be applied for each valuation. This was loosely based on a percentage of the overall valuation total subject to a minimum and maximum fee for each individual valuation. In those early days I was only concerned with getting the job done. I had not even stopped to consider what level of fees I would be charging MAFF.

Again Ernest Harker could not leave his own farm near Appleby. David Owen being the gentleman that he is, agreed to act on behalf of Ernest by signing the papers. This, despite the distress of losing his own livelihood only a few days previously.

The sheep then had to be walked across the road to some temporary holding and slaughtering pens that the MAFF team had erected. I agreed to help shepherd the sheep across the road as a gesture of goodwill. The duty vet had informed the local constabulary who arrived soon after to put up a road-block as we transferred the sheep across the highway. Once the operation was done, I washed down and disinfected before going home to shower and get some lunch.

That afternoon I had just settled down to watch the six nations rugby matches when the phone rang. It was MAFF (Carlisle).

"Mr Day you have been requested to do a valuation of sheep on a farm east of Penrith." They gave me the full details. "Can you do it within the next hour?"

"Yes."

"Good, please ring the duty vet on this number who will give you directions. Goodbye." It was all rather clinical. It could have been Anne Robinson at the other end of the phone.

"You are the weakest link, goodbye." It most definitely would not have been true!

I rang the number that I had been given and was duly instructed by the vet. He was another seconded privateer. Within five minutes I was on the road wearing yet another clean set of clothes that by nightfall would be going through a 60-degree hot wash.

By the time I got to the farm the weather had turned appreciably colder. The fields were open and exposed. The in-lamb ewes were looking pretty miserable though they were well fed.

The vet informed me that one of the rams that had run with ewes showed clinical signs of the disease and had positive blood samples. None of the ewes had those signs. The farmer's brother guided me to the sheep. The farmer dare not come near the sheep because their home farm had a dairy herd. The brother had always fed the sheep and was here now to sign the valuation papers as the appointed agent.

I made my valuation and the brother was delighted with my findings.

"You've done him proud," said the brother giving me the thumbs up as I drove away.

Soon after I arrived home the phone rang. It was a valuer from a rival firm. He was valuing sheep for the very same brother who had just signed my valuation papers. The brother had not told me that he was going to value his sheep with his own valuer. Had I known, it would not have made any difference to me at all.

The other valuer had made his valuation of the brother's sheep, which he felt were better quality than the ones I had looked at. Unfortunately he could not value his sheep as high as I had valued my sheep.

"Are you telling me I'm wrong?" I asked.

"Well, err, no, but you might have to come back and do yours again," he retorted. I declined and said that I was not going to do that knowing that I definitely had not over-valued the sheep. The other valuer did not want to lose face. He had simply not valued the sheep high enough. Fortunately it was the same vet that I had just worked with. He had followed with the brother to meet his valuer. I spoke to him on the phone explaining the situation and that I was standing by my original valuation. The vet seemed to accept my stance.

Having put the phone down I began to fret. What if the other valuer put in an official complaint about me? Would I be blacklisted as a valuer? If that happened would I lose my job? What if there was an inquiry?

In a moment the phone rang again. It was the brother who had given me the thumbs up. He was not so happy now.

"This valuation you have done for my brother is wrong."

"Says who," I replied calmly.

"My valuer. I've got better sheep you know and I've taken him to see the sheep you've valued and he says you've given too much. You'll have to change your valuation," he said.

"Sorry I am not going to do that," I replied "I've done quite a few sheep recently and I know how much they are worth. I suggest you speak to your own valuer." With that I put the phone down. It did not stop me worrying about the whole situation. It prayed on my mind so much that I decided to ring the other valuer at home. We agreed that it was not good practice to be seen to be arguing about valuations. We agreed that it would be prudent to keep in more regular touch about valuation levels. We parted amicably.

Within a few days MAFF brought out a standard valuation which was a set of 'book prices' to be offered to farmers as a flat rate payment rather than employing a professional valuer. The book price for the sheep I had just valued was at a considerably higher level than my own valuation. I also learned from other sources that the other valuer had jumped his own valuations considerably too. So much for co-operation!

The book price itself was simply a way of cutting out the valuer. MAFF made excuses that valuers were slowing the operation down. This was a complete untruth for we were at MAFF's beck and call 24/7. They called me as early as 7.05am and as late as 11.55pm and I never turned a job down. I knew of other valuers who helped MAFF by working through the night to get the job done.

7
MARCH - OUT LIKE THE LAMBS

Thursday 15 March
Total national cases 253

March 15th was a pretty dismal sort of a day in the offices of Cockermouth Mart. I busied myself with a raft of paperwork, which had built up on me over the last few days. Numerous calls were made to solicitors, contractors and possible site purchasers at the new mart. We kept going in the forlorn hope that FMD would never rise up in West Cumbria.

At around lunchtime, Nick Brown, Minister of Agriculture, made a statement to the House of Commons. His pronouncements sent a shiver down the spine of every farmer in Cumbria. All hell broke loose with farmer after farmer ringing our office for advice. That is the very point that we could never get across to MAFF. When any new policy or set of rules that affect farming businesses are issued, the farmers often ring the auction companies for advice or information. It is us that they trust.

So what did Mr Brown say to cause such a mass panic? He said this: "The large focus on infection in the north of England and southern Scotland has been mostly concentrated in the sheep flock although there is now cattle to cattle spread in Cumbria. There are a considerable number of cases in this area with the potential for rapid spread to adjacent farms and even further afield. In this case we must still ensure that infected animals are removed as quickly as possible and in order to do this it will be necessary to destroy animals within the 3km zones on a precautionary basis."

Now every farmer within 3km of an infected premises was apparently going to be completely culled out. Farmer after farmer rang up asking the same questions. Did Mr Brown mean all stock per se? Was the definition of three kilometres from the centre of the farm or the furthest boundary? What if the same holding number applied to different parcels of land spread over a wide area? We had no answers.

I rang MAFF Carlisle but nobody could or would commit as to just what Nick Brown meant. I tried our local NFU officers with whom I had regular dialogue. They were as in the dark as we were.

I took a call from Mark Potter a young farmer in the Matterdale area near Penrith. Together we had enjoyed a magnificent day last autumn when I sold a Herdwick shearling ram of his breeding for a world record price. Now he was beside himself. As he tried to speak to me about Brown's statement he broke down. Mark's farm was definitely within three kilometres of an infected premises. The thought of losing every single one of his prized Herdwick sheep and all the rest of his cattle and sheep had completely overwhelmed him. I had to tell him to put the phone down and ring me back when he could speak. Meanwhile I would try to get to the bottom of what Mr Brown had meant in his announcement.

An hour later Mark Potter rang me back. He was composed but resolute. "I will not let them take my sheep" he said. "They will have to shoot me first." I could tell by his tone that he truly meant it. We never even discussed the possibility of valuing the animals. It was just not going to happen in his eyes. Sadly he was to be proved wrong.

Around the country a public furore built up. The media, particularly local broadcasters like Border TV's Fiona Armstrong who has close family links to farming, were now heavily involved demanding to know the extent of Nick Brown's statement. By late afternoon he was forced to make a public apology and retraction. He had not meant to say all animals, but should have qualified his statement to account for sheep only. It served only to show the ineptitude of his whole department. For Cumbrian shepherds it was still a major blow. Many hundreds of dairy and beef farmers breathed heavy sighs of relief and lived to fight another day.

So the 3km contiguous cull finally evolved. Even then there remained a total lack of guidance as to whether the 3km cull was voluntary or compulsory. This was to last for several days. No one knew what was going on. Only one thing was for sure, the 24/48 hour policy was still a long way from reality. Many were driven to desperation that day. Mark Potter was not the only man who thought that his world was going to collapse. This whole episode should never have happened. It was a warning to farmers as to what was to follow. Yet again we were badly let down.

That night I spoke to Mark Potter for the third time. He was slightly more calm and reassured but the writing was on the wall.

"I think I'm going to need you soon Adam," he said ruefully. He was not mistaken.

8
A TRIP TO THE COAST

Friday 23 March
Total national cases: 511

Friday morning was mild and overcast. I made an early journey across North Cumbria to Newtown near Allonby. It would be the first of many visits to the area. The cold grey waters of the Solway Firth and the Galloway hills beyond made an impressive backdrop to the scene. I was to value a number of breeding and store sheep that were away-wintered on a coastal dairy farm. I had spoken to the owner the previous night. He certainly was not going to make the 20 mile journey from Whitehaven to meet me. The dairy farm was a dangerous contact. The term was now becoming common place and meant that a neighbouring farm had been declared an infected premises.

The dairy farmer was in quite a distressed but stable state. He greeted me at the front door of his farmhouse and I noticed the packed suitcase waiting in the hall. We had not met before and it was quite an awkward moment.

"I can't stand this," he said. "I know I should stay and watch my cows die but I just can't face it. I'm leaving for a few days. The cows won't need me by tonight any way." He looked totally beaten and dejected.

"You don't have to stay and watch," I said. "You mustn't feel guilty. Don't put your self through it." He just shrugged and continued to stare at the carpet.

We both waited in silence. Eventually the duty vet rolled up together with a Land Rover containing a couple of soldiers who were from Merseyside. They were the first I had seen and it was not a moment too soon. Many days had passed since the vet on my first infected premises told me: "We need the army in now."

The role of the army was now increasing by the day. Brigadier Alex Birtwistle had been brought in to oversee the war against FMD. What greeted him was a massive chaotic unorganised battlefield called Cumbria. The casualties already on the ground numbered many thousands. Great heaps of cattle and sheep were lying in piles. Farmyards, buildings and fields were full of rotting carcasses with no means of disposal. More and more heaps were appearing by the day. There was no contingency plan for the Brigadier to implement. He had to make one himself which he did so over the bonnet of a car because he did not at that stage have a command centre. This short-time Brigadier (his own words) did an unbelievable job to even begin tackling the guerrilla virus that could not be seen, smelled or heard. I have heard first hand from Alex Birtwistle what he had to do and what he went through. That is his story and not mine. I know the experience has left him, like many more of us, blighted and sour. I know of no other way to put it.

It was a great honour for Mitchell's Auction Company when Alex Birtwistle agreed to officially open the new livestock mart at Cockermouth in 2002. Back in 2001 his appearance in Cumbria marked a ray of hope although from the outset his men were acting as street cleaners rather than front-line fighters, for the disease was already too far ahead of them. He was trying to shut a stable door after the horse had left the parish. The only problem in this case was that he had to make the stable door first. Eventually Brigadier Birtwistle was to succeed.

The MAFF vet who was a character by the name of Ian, the soldiers and I, set out to find the sheep which were to be valued. A slaughter team had apparently been located to commence their work on the dairy animals and the sheep during the afternoon. Eventually we found some of the sheep. At that point we realised that the farm did not have sheep proof fencing in any of the fields. The sheep took one look at us advancing across the field and took flight in all directions. They went through gaps in fences, gateways, across tidal streams and into many neighbours' fields. We had no dog or farm bike with which to round them up.

The soldiers were bemused especially as I had asked them to count the sheep as they ran. One soldier had got to about 40 then given up. One thought there were 96. I had counted 106. I was going to settle at that figure when around fifteen more sheep suddenly broke cover from a neighbouring field. We could not be sure that we had not counted them before. In the end I told the vet what number of sheep the owner had informed me there should be. We agreed that the number would suffice but if after slaughter the numbers were different we would have to revise the valuation. Thankfully the right number of sheep were eventually slaughtered.

As we completed the paperwork I jokingly said to one of the soldiers that Alsations were sheep dogs so why did the army not use their guard dogs to round up the sheep. He wrote the suggestion down to tell his superior. The suggestion was not as daft as it seemed. Within weeks the army had contracted-in local shepherds many of whom had already lost their stock to gather sheep for slaughter. I worked with some of them several times. It certainly made life easier for all of us, except the sheep that is.

By lunchtime I was scrubbed up, disinfected and on my way back to the Penrith area for my next call. As I travelled, I listened to the radio. The government was now saying FMD was getting out of control! Luckily for us Mr Blair had taken personal control of the out of control situation and the COBRA committee had been set up. I really hoped that Tony Blair would get into the field to see what was happening and support all of his troops. Not just the ones in combat fatigues, but the rest of the ordinary citizens who were battling to save their own businesses. The farmers, auctioneers, slaughtermen, hauliers and so many more. We were all caught in the downward spiral. Soon they would be declaring that FMD was following 'expected patterns'. The only pattern I could detect modelled the 'Big Bang' theory where the disease seemed to explode outwards… *ad infinitum.*

Within an hour I was parked at the side of the Wigton to Penrith road at Unthank. Here I was to value a batch of good quality young Swaledale breeding sheep that were away wintering to give them a good start prior to summering on the slopes of Blencathra. Now they would never see the fell gate. In fact they were penned in a yard which they would never leave alive. Only the previous evening I had valued some sheep for the same farmers at another location. Now John Lamb and his family were losing even more sheep.

The farm in question belonged to the Jackson family whom I knew from my training days at Penrith Auction. I was staggered by the generous hospitality and friendly welcome even at this time of trauma and distress. For they too were losing every dairy animal they owned. My valuation was done quickly. The sheep were easy to value. They were a wonderful level batch of well-bred sheep. I felt as I did many times after, that it was such a dreadful waste of breeding, shepherding and devotion. It is sad that I was often the last person to really appreciate the sheep alive. Actually it was rather upsetting.

Later as I sat in the farmhouse kitchen filling in the appropriate valuation forms I talked to Tanis Brough the duty vet. She was a lady I had known since she was a young girl. She was a local farmer's daughter who had qualified as a vet before settling down locally. Now she felt a calling to do her bit. She had responded to MAFF's request for vets old, young, retired or in practice to take up the call. In a way it was nice to be working along side people I knew. Over the next few months we were to work together several times.

Someone asked whether I was still singing with the Soul Traders. This led to an amazing conversation with Emerson Jackson. He was well into his eighth decade but knew all about my vocal talents or lack of them! He told me about his old family band The Jackson's who were well renowned throughout Cumberland and Westmorland.

"Were there five of you?" I asked jokingly.

"Sometimes," he said not picking up on my poor attempt at a pun, "and I was the drummer." He told us tales of having to submit a written tender for the Coniston Foxhounds Hunt Ball; of playing from eight o'clock in the evening until three in the morning then driving home to go straight out to work and milking cows without sleep.

I admitted that a schedule like that was not really for me.

"We did it," he said "because we enjoyed it." Then with a twinkle in his eye he added: "Mind £40 was a lot of money in those days." I laughed.

A little later I left the farm. The old man had cheered me up considerably. My steps were lighter as I walked the long farm track back to the road where I had left my car. It was raining and I kept my head down. As I neared the road a voice made me look up.

"Start rolling," I heard the command and looked up. A TV camera crew was at the farm entrance. I recognised the pretty reporter although I did not know her name.

"Will you speak to us?" she asked. I mumbled something about not having time.

"Are you the farmer?"

"No."

"Vet?"

"No."

"Who are you then?" she asked slightly indignantly.

"I'm nobody important," I said "I just came to count some sheep."

"Oh all right then," she said turning away from me with a look of disdain.

As I began to strip off my waterproofs the cameraman whizzed back on to me.

"Do you have to do that?" I said, "I haven't combed my hair today."

"Don't worry mate, just background fillers," he said. The young reporter was busy fixing her own hair in a compact mirror.

Just for show I tipped a whole bucket of disinfectant over my head to completely soak my waterproofs. "Got to be done," I said to the cameraman. He looked aghast.

"You have to do that every time?"

"Why do you think I don't comb my hair?" I replied. With that I ripped off my disposable suit costing £2 per time which MAFF would not pay for, left it in the dirty box and drove off in my car.

That night, national evening news featured me walking up the farm lane towards the cameras. They did not show me disinfecting! The vet Tanis Brough saw the report and some time later chided me for not zipping my waterproof jacket up instead allowing it to flap freely as I walked up the track.

"Me" I thought, "can't do right for wrong."

The only thing I noticed on the report that night was the "zoom in" shot which the cameraman did to end the report. The shot was of the beautiful Blencathra 'saddle' which stood several miles distant but directly behind the Jackson's farm. The sheep that died that day could see their home pastures from their slaughter pen. I looked on and did not even see myself on the screen.

9

A Wedding to Remember

Saturday 24 March
Total national cases: 556

Saturday 24 March was a day that I had looked forward to over the last few weeks. The Soul Traders were booked to play at Wreay village hall near Carlisle. It was a wedding reception. Those sort of evenings are usually the most enjoyable to play. People let their hair down, have usually had a skinful by the time the band take the stage and go crazy when we launch into the routine. Also I had been somewhat preoccupied in recent days. This would be a chance to relax a bit and forget the troubles. Thankfully I had not had any valuation call outs all day.

The band drove to Wreay at 4pm to set up the gear and sound-check on stage. We always like to do this early at weddings so that we can go straight on stage without the obligatory warm up song. It is essential when there are nine band members needing 'miked up'. It also creates a good image with a complete stage set up, and all the instruments shining under the lights when people first walk in. It was a gloomy evening and we even had time for a football kick about on the village green before set up. Within two hours I was on my way home to see my wife and children before changing and going back to play later in the evening.

I pulled up outside my house as the phone rang. It was Ian Walker, managing director of Ulverston Auction Mart.

"Working late this evening Ian. Don't you have a home to go to?" I enquired jokingly.

"Actually I am still in the office," he responded.

"Oh right, well what can I do you for?" What he said knocked the stuffing out of me.

"Foot and mouth has been confirmed in the Duddon valley. I have to go and value at the infected premises tomorrow."

I was totally gutted. I did not know what to say. The Duddon valley is a beautiful long Lake District valley rising out of the Duddon estuary and climbing up through Seathwaite, bearing right and continually rising to the head of Wrynose Pass. The disease had been discovered on a farm at Seathwaite on the Eskdale side of the valley, close to Hardknott Pass.

It was obvious that Ian was as distressed as I was. This was basically the heart of Lakeland. It was also many many miles from the nearest outbreak in north Cumbria.

I continued to sit in my car and we discussed the situation at length. How had the disease jumped all that way? How many more would there be? The infected premises was a large hill farm with hefted sheep that would be in contact with many other hefted flocks on the fell tops. Each question begged another. We also discussed valuation figures. I had some experience now but Ian had none. I actually felt sorry for him. I did not envy the task he was going to have to undertake the following day.

As we finished our conversation I offered to help in any way I could.

"Don't worry," he said, " you haven't heard the last of this." His words were prophetic.

Once in the house I explained the situation to Paula. This was a potential disaster. All the major Lakeland fell flocks could be wiped out. There might be no sheep left in the Lake District. Hundreds of years of sheep breeding could be wiped out. Some breed lines were irreplaceable. How could a valuer even try and quantify that scenario. I lay in the bath for a long time trying to reason the whole situation. I couldn't make sense of it at all. How had the disease jumped so far? All the scientists were talking about wind-borne virus rising high in to the sky from burning pyres. If this were true then all the livestock in the country would be wiped out. I tried to visualise a Lake District devoid of sheep. It was too depressing to contemplate. I had not even begun to consider the fact that my own livelihood would disappear for many years.

Soon I was on my way back to Wreay trying to lift the gloom that had settled around me. This was a wedding day for the young couple. I had to be on top form, the life and soul of the party. Anything less would spoil the evening.

The first set went reasonably well. The audience had not really got in to a party mode but we had played well. As the band sat resting I decided to ring home to see that all was well.

Paula answered the phone and was frantic.

"Thank God it's you," she said, " this phone has been red hot. There are fourteen messages for you. The farmers are going crazy. Some of them are in tears." Remembering that she was seven months pregnant I tried to calm her down.

"Give me the messages now then put the answer phone on and just go to bed. Everything's going to be all right," I said trying to reassure her. I took down the list of messages. There were several from Lakeland farmers. There was also a heap from farmers in the Aspatria area of north Cumbria. I sat down in a quiet corner and began responding to all the calls. The band sensed that I had problems. They left me to it, save for giving me a piece of wedding cake. For the first time in my life I did not eat my favourite fruitcake.

Most of the farmers just wanted a general talk. The jungle drums were in full cry. The pessimists were ringing to pre-book my services should they go down. Some were clearly distressed and close to breaking point. I was flattered and yet totally deflated by these requests.

Further down the list was Richard Mawdsley from the Dash Farm. This lonely farming outpost lies hidden behind the Skiddaw massif. Richard is a real character whose company I often enjoy on Friday afternoons when he normally comes into my office for the crack and a smoke of his pipe. I think he was probably in bed when I called. He went on to tell me that his cattle were being wintered in a shed on a dairy farm near Aspatria. I knew the farm. It was Crossrigg near West Newton. It had recently changed hands and the new owner Nick Fish had moved up from Lancashire. I had not actually met him.

"Don't worry," Richard Mawdsley said, "he knows of you and he's quite happy for you to value his stock. His poor dairy cows have been confirmed positive. There are also three other people's cattle on the farm," he continued. "They are going to use you as well. I should be your agent," he joked. It was a throw-away line designed to disguise the bitterness and pain in losing his treasured cattle.

He went on to explain that I was to speak to FMD command centre at Carlisle to arrange a time with the vet. He also gave me some information about his cows that would enable me to complete a valuation. With that he wished me good night.

Quickly I rang Carlisle and was amazed to find they were still working late in to the evening. They admitted that things were pretty hectic. I agreed to get on to farm mid-morning. As I put the phone down I saw the band were ready to strike up. I jumped up on stage and gave it everything I had. The words of the Smokey Robinson song were totally appropriate *Behind a painted smile.* I just wanted to get home as quickly as possible.

10

"MAN, I JUST DON'T KNOW WHAT I'M DOING HERE"

Sunday 25 March
Total national cases: 618

I awoke with a start. The bedside phone was ringing. Clumsily I picked up and answered. It could not have been much after 7am. It was MAFF, Carlisle. I groaned having only had a few hours sleep after last night's gig. They said that I was invited to undertake a valuation of sheep near Dalston. Could I get there right away? I explained that I was already booked to go to Aspatria. The line went dead for a moment, then I was instructed to proceed with all haste to Dalston, thereafter to Aspatria. The vet would be arriving late anyway.

In a matter of minutes I was on the road leaving my pregnant wife to cope with a 20-month daughter and the dreadful morning sickness that plagued her throughout her second pregnancy. I feel guilty now that I hardly spared a thought for her situation at the time. She never ever complained. She talked to farmers at length or passed on messages. She never asked to discuss the situation preferring to leave me alone when I sat brooding and miserable. She was a rock throughout the crisis at a time in her life when it should have been the other way around.

Soon I was on the farm at Dalston. There was no one to meet me so I left my car behind an army Land Rover and walked a few hundred yards into the farmyard. It was a hive of activity. The duty vet was a gentleman of broad Irish twang. The happy lilt in his voice hardly betrayed the situation. It was certainly no bad thing. At one end of the yard a valuer from a rival firm was batching and inspecting the farmer's own cattle for slaughter. Within ear-shot of the farmer I asked the valuer what valuation he had made of the last batch of cattle. He told me and I feigned incredulity before turning to the farmer.

"He's doing a grand job for you," I said trying to make the valuer look good in front of his client. This was a stupid mistake because soon after I found out that the rival firm had turned the situation against me and were actively telling farmers that my valuations were well below their own. In reality they had no idea what we were giving but it was disappointing that they should stoop to lowly tactics at this time.

The farmer's son showed me the sheep, which were being wintered, on the farm for a Caldbeck hill farmer called Mr Hope. Being the gentlemen that he was, Mr Hope had instructed me on the phone that morning to use my best judgement and complete the valuation. I need not ring him. Whatever value I put on them would be quite sufficient. The sheep were lovely Swaledale gimmer shearlings. I completed the valuation and rang him any way. He was delighted and thanked me profusely. It was one of the few occasions during the crisis that I actually felt appreciated.

As I drove through Wigton on my way to Aspatria I realised that it was almost lunchtime. I had had nothing to eat and so pulled on to a garage forecourt. Then I realised that I was horribly 'dirty'. I pondered on whether it was safe to go into the garage. Could I deposit live virus in the shop? I did not know. I decided to go in and buy a sandwich. I was the only customer in the shop. Afterwards I did not know if I had done right or wrong. In the end I was glad that I did buy some food for it was several hours before I ate again.

Shortly after, I pulled in at Crossrigg farm near West Newton. I got suited up and walked into the farm to meet the farmer, Nick Fish. He was distressed and had clearly been quite upset. It was very difficult to know what to say in that situation. I decided to let him talk. He explained that he, his wife and young children had moved on to the farm only eighteen months previously. He had brought with him from his family farm in Lancashire some of his favourite dairy cow families. This began to choke him. With difficulty he went on to say that he had supplemented the cows with several locally purchased pedigree cows. A few days ago he noticed that some of the cows were off-colour. Within hours several were showing clinical signs of FMD. Among the worst affected was his favourite old cow. With that he spent a minute or two staring down at the ground, taking deep breaths in a supreme effort not to break down. There was nothing I could do.

Nick went on to tell me that he had been rather upset much earlier in the morning when a car had pulled up outside his farm. Two young valuers from a rival auction firm nonchalantly jumped out of the car and announced that they had come to do his valuation. Nick told them that he did not want them because I was already booked to do the job. They persisted before Nick made it quite clear that they were not welcome.

"How did they know a valuation was due?" he asked me.

"I have not got a clue," I responded "but I will find out."

A car pulled up and we realised that it was the duty vet. A tall, slim, well-tanned man got out of the car. I estimated that he was not far from retiring age. He spoke like a character from the TV soap, Dallas.

"Hiya yawl! J E Hall's the name; just flown in from Carolina." Nick and I stood with our mouths wide open. The vet who turned out to be a very likeable man explained that he was a horse doctor from Carolina who had only just flown in to Manchester airport in the early hours.

"I gotten up to Carlisle," he said " they gave me a pack of papers, keys to this 'ole hire car, a map reference and here I am!" He seemed genuinely excited by the whole prospect.

We could not take offence at this man's nature for it was obvious that he was a total natural even when he likened his position to his father before him. "Ma daddy came over here in 1944 to fight," he told us. "He did his bit and now I want to do mine." He flashed a wide smile. "Now, seems I gotta serve some kinda notices on yawl but I ain't 'xactly sure what."

"Do you mean they haven't given you any instructions?" I asked.

"Nope," he replied with a shake of his head, "I got some sorta manual here though." He looked ruefully at the MAFF FMD pack provided to all vets.

"Come on," I said "we had better sit down."

We went into the kitchen where I helped the vet issue the official 'A' notice and other paperwork. It was an infected premises and there were some sections that I had not seen completed before so he had to ring through to MAFF Carlisle for guidance. Eventually after quite some time we were ready to begin the inspection and valuation.

We started with Richard Mawdsley's hill cows. These were wintering in the sheds at Crossrigg before going back to the fells above Dash farm. The cattle were unique in the fact that they were hefted to the fell. They had, over the generations, been bred to be hardy enough to calve and thrive on the high fells in all but the harshest of winter months. Now just before calving they were getting a little TLC at Crossrigg. They were fully acclimatised to those hard fell conditions. No other cattle could possibly be bought in as replacements. In those conditions they would surely fail and die. These were genuinely hefted cattle and in that sense irreplaceable. They were not ill.

I went on to value three other lots of stock including some very good young dairy heifers and some feeding bulls for other farmers who were using Nick Fish's cattle sheds.

Soon we moved into Nick's own dairy herd. Quietly we moved through the cattle identifying each animal in turn. They were docile but still sensed the unusual presence of both myself and J E Hall who followed us around at ten paces. As we did so, I gave him a running commentary about what I was seeing and valuing. He was shivering in the cool spring air. I showed him the first animal that I saw with clear clinical signs of the disease.

"Man I just never saw that before," he scratched his chin. I could not believe that a seconded vet from abroad was not even given training or at least shown photographs of infected animals.

On and on we went. Occasionally we came across an animal that had already been valued but had walked on in front of us. Nick knew every one. He would tell me about each animal especially those of his own breeding. At times he had to compose himself to get the information out. As we went on, it became harder and harder for him. I really felt for him but maintained a dead pan professional attitude. I did not know what else to do.

Then we came across his favourite old cow. She was lying down and I could not see her properly. I had to make her stand up. As she arose she groaned plaintively. The virus had severely lamed her and her mouth was bleeding and sore with long plumes of mucus streaming from her nose. She turned around to look at Nick and gave a gentle moo of recognition. It was too much for him. He just collapsed over the cubicle rail and broke his heart. I stood helplessly and watched.

"Take some time Nick," I said and beckoned J E Hall away. He came with me shaking his head with disbelief.

"Man," he said, "I just don't know what I'm doing here." At that moment I realised that neither did I.

In a while I went back to Nick who had pulled himself upright. He tried to apologise but it was not necessary. "I just can't bear to see her like that," he said.

Soon we had completed the inspection and we moved back to the house to sort out the paperwork. I filled out all the forms for J E Hall who by then had also recovered his composure. Even so he could not drink a cup of tea or eat a piece of cake. For a while he had been genuinely shocked by the whole situation. I hoped he would get up to speed quickly for his job had not even started.

The phone rang and it was Nick Fish's mother who was on the holiday of a lifetime, a Caribbean cruise. She had heard the news about what was happening in Cumbria and wanted to know if everything was all right.

"Don't worry Mum everything's fine, just fine." After he put the phone down Nick admitted that he did not want to ruin her holiday.

By the time we completed the valuation it was growing dark. I made my goodbyes and was very glad to get away from the farm. The killing crew would be on farm the next day. I hoped that Nick and his family would get through it. I did not know at that stage that the dead bodies would lie right outside the kitchen door for many days before MAFF could find the resources to dispose of them. Each day Nick took it upon himself to physically pour disinfectant on the rotting heap of his treasured cows. It was a futile gesture on his part to try and ensure that any live FMD virus being shed by the carcasses was destroyed. The bodies began to decompose and the situation was so bad that the young children had to be sent away to prevent unnecessary distress. What it did to Nick and his wife, only they truly know.

I later found out that Nick's young son who at the time of slaughter was just beginning to talk, stopped communicating when the cows disappeared. When Nick was finally able to buy dairy cows back on to the farm, only then did the little boy begin to speak again. The very day that the cows came back, he seemed to burst into life. I wonder what distress a toddler could feel inside that made him clam up for so long.

Occasionally thereafter I saw Nick at some FMD public meetings. It was quite obvious that he held a bitter resentment about how his particular case had been dealt with by MAFF. Who could blame him? Like everyone else, much later on he was able to restock his farm. In the early months of 2003, Mitchell's achieved a small goal within the new market by holding a successful first sale of pedigree-bred Holstein dairy cattle. Among the crowd that day was Nick Fish. He purchased several animals and I had the pleasure of helping him load his trailer to take them home. No words were said about those dreadful days at Crossrigg but I thanked him for coming to support our new venture. As he drove away I grinned with a little sense of satisfaction. We had both survived and were recovering. It felt good.

Having driven home from Crossrigg after the FMD valuation, I had a five minute shower and disinfection then took Paula and Olivia to my mother-in-law's house for supper. I did not want to talk about the day and to their credit, they did not ask. I was hopeless company and Paula wisely made our early goodbyes. When we got home there were several messages on the answer phone. The most distressing was from Neil Hodgson.

Neil and Christine Hodgson lived and farmed at Cockly Beck in the Seathwaite valley, high above the Duddon estuary. Their neighbouring farm had been the infected premises that Ian Walker had valued on that very day. Neil told me that MAFF were going to confirm in the morning whether all of the Cockly Beck sheep flock and their beef cattle would have to be slaughtered as dangerous contacts. Ian Walker was to be proved right after all.

Neil asked me if I would do the valuation. Yet again I was honoured and saddened. I accepted and wished them well. I also knew that I would be making the trip down to the farm next morning.

Having completed my message answering which was now becoming stressful and repetitive work each evening. I went to bed immediately and slept like a log. I doubt that poor Nick Fish was able to do the same.

11
The Valley of Death

Monday 26 March
Total National cases: 667

It was lunchtime as I eased my car up and round the tight steep bends of Hardknottt Pass. Normally I am at my happiest driving along the Eskdale valley stopping along the way to see my farmers. The welcome here is always one of the best but on this day I was not enjoying the journey for one second.

Roman legionnaires may have pillaged the land and settlements centuries ago, now the fells were about to be pillaged of sheep. I crept up the hill past the old fort and scarcely gave it a thought.

Soon I was over the top and dropping down the equally steep and twisting Seathwaite side of the pass. Ahead of me stretched the long barren and rock strewn valley leading up to Wrynose Pass. Down in the valley bottom, shrouded in dark wisps of cold late winter rain, lay the destination of my travels, Cockly Beck farm.

The Hodgsons are a young farming couple in their mid-30s with three young children. They had been tenants of the National Trust for seven years and in that time had enhanced their reputation among the Lakeland fell farming fraternity. Their stocksmanship and knowledge of sheep, especially the Herdwick is of the highest standard. They work tremendously hard as a rock solid husband and wife team. They are thoroughly likeable people.

I pulled up outside the farmhouse and it was raining hard. I quickly suited up and dashed into the kitchen where I was greeted by Neil, Christine and the duty vet who was a privateer from the Carlisle area. He was a man who specialised mainly in small animal practice. The Hodgson children had been sent away to Christine's sisters house. Neil told me their eldest boy had done everything he could to persuade them to let him stay. Some of the sheep were his own. At eleven years of age he felt a responsibility and did not want to leave them.

With a cup of coffee for fortification, the vet began to brief me as to what must happen that day. Cockly Beck fell had not been completely gathered due to the weather conditions. The same had happened over the other side of the valley where Ian Walker had been called back for a second day to his client's farm. I could see streams of sheep pouring down from the fell tops above Black Hall. It was the last time those sheep would return to the fold.

It was expected that by the following morning all of the sheep on both sides of the valley could be brought down to the farms for slaughter. Today we were to value all of the cattle and as many sheep as we could get to around the farm. The vet was also waiting for a decision from Page Street as to whether more of the Hodgsons' stock on other farms should also be taken as dangerous contacts as well. Neil told me that some of his best sheep were away wintering on land near Millom, which was several miles away. Thankfully he had not had recent contact with them and he hoped to save them. I shrugged my shoulders. I knew that the stock answer from Page Street would be "Kill them." It was going to be a long and miserable day.

Christine being the totally organised person that she is, had already begun to fill in the valuation forms for the cattle. This saved me some time and effort and allowed me to simply complete the form by filling in my valuation figure against each animal. I think she was glad to do the job because it kept her busy. She ploughed on despite the tears, which were rolling, down her cheeks. She did not make a sound and dealt with her own grief in silence for the fell farmers are a tough breed.

Eventually we were ready to begin the valuation inspections. We moved down to the cattle buildings further down the road. The cattle were very good quality Limousin cattle, which were both a hobby and a commercial venture. They had invested a lot of money in the cattle to continually improve the quality. A good indicator of this was the championship honours, which their suckled calf won at Cockermouth Mart the previous autumn. We all remembered that day as being a good one. Neil seemed a little disappointed in my valuation based on the time and effort they had put into their small herd over the last few years, although we did not disagree.

We moved back up to the sheep yards. Earlier in the day they had gathered as many sheep together as possible in the fell bottom intacks just above the farmyard. These walled enclosures served the job well and quite quickly we brought the sheep down into the holding yards. I instructed them to batch the sheep just as they liked and to tell me anything about the stock that might add value. We all worked together quietly. Neil and

Christine sorted the sheep whilst I operated the shedding gates. In a while they had the sheep batched up. It was only then that I began to realise the scale of the operation. The holding yards were crammed with many hundreds of sheep. They were mostly Herdwick, the indigenous breed of the Lakeland fells. I suddenly remembered the many hundreds of sheep the Hodgsons sold at Cockermouth each year. On the other side of the valley the same process was being undertaken on the infected premises. The valley bottom was awash with in-lamb ewes about to die.

"My God," I thought, "I'm losing a lot of commission off this farm." I looked over to the couple who were openly distressed whilst pointing out special sheep to each other. A huge wave of guilt swept over me. How could I be so selfish at this time? Looking back I know it was the sub-conscious realisation that if many of the large Lakeland fell farms went down then there would be no need for the auction mart. There would be nothing left to sell. I think it struck me for the first time at that point that I was in danger of valuing myself out of a job. There would be nothing left for me at the end. As time went on, this constant fear proved harder and harder to bear.

We moved through the sheep group by group. After a while we came across a particular family of Herdwicks that Neil's father had bred at Bays Brown farm in Langdale. Neil had lost his father at the age of 22. He had kept his father's blood-lines and brought them with him to Cockly Beck. Now a whole family of sheep was to disappear forever. No amount of money could compensate Neil for this loss. We spent many minutes looking at the sheep. Through his tears Neil spoke of his father.

"I just hope that he would be proud of what I've done. I've tried really hard," he said.

"I know he would be proud," I replied. It just did not seem an adequate thing to say but it was true.

Christine produced a video camera and filmed some of the sheep. She made a point of filming the children's special sheep. It was a brave and useful idea. In time when the shock and pain of their losses had subsided it would be good to look back with pride on what the family had achieved. I'm sure there were many such videos of this nature made on Cumbrian farms.

By late afternoon we had valued all of the sheep that had been gathered. This included old established flocks from Cockly Beck, Bays

Brown and Dale Head. There were also many sheep from other farms throughout central Lake District. These were strays that had wandered over to the Cockly Beck hefts from their own patch.

Hefting is a peculiar in-built instinct that fell sheep pass on from generation to generation. In simple terms, the farms located in the valley bottoms all have their own flocks of sheep, which graze the common fell ground above. Over the last several hundred years each individual flock has grown acclimatised to its own patch of the fell. This is the heft. The territorial instinct to graze the heft is in-bred. Each new generation of sheep moving to the fell for the first time, usually as young lambs following their mothers, instinctively moves to the heft. The vast majority of the flock does not stray from the heft. The flock may not allow strangers from other flocks to graze the area. Occasionally there are strays that break the mould and move across the fell. At gathering times those strays are traditionally penned up and shepherds' meets are held to reclaim the strays. The owners take them back to their own farms.

The strays gathered at Cockly Beck would not be going back to their own farms again. In one afternoon hundreds of years of breeding would be completely obliterated. The hefts would be lost for many years if not for good.

The duty vet, who was busy organising slaughter teams and preparing for the kill the following day, announced that Page Street required a valuation of feeding hoggs belonging to Neil further down the valley. Neil had been in contact with them every day. He was a dangerous contact and therefore so were the hoggs. They would be slaughtered in the field.

Page Street was the central head quarters of MAFF in London. It was here that the major decisions were taken as to whether certain farms would be taken out as infected premises or dangerous contacts. Despite the advice or recommendations of the vet's on the ground, the answer was always the same. The animals had to die.

On the way down the valley I was asked to value a field of sheep for another farmer. By now I was getting more and more uncomfortable. MAFF were now taking out field after field of sheep. I began to wonder where the stopping point would be in the valley, which runs for several miles down to the Duddon estuary. At this point, I was accompanied by a local vet whose name was Rick Brown. He was working among his customers just as I was. We both must have shared the same emotions but did not talk of them. Strictly speaking we were both working for

MAFF and yet so clearly wanting to do out best for our friends and customers. It was a hopeless situation.

We completed this set of valuations in the growing gloom. I expected that we would return to Cockly Beck but it was not to be. By now Rick Brown had moved on and I was back with the duty vet. He had new instructions from Page Street to value and destroy a field of Herdwick ewes many miles away in the Whicham valley near Millom. Neil was wintering these sheep on good lowland ground because they had been scanned in lamb and expecting twins. This new instruction was just too much for Neil.

"Please," he argued "don't take the sheep. I have only been to the field once in the last three weeks. I counted them from the gate and put a mineral lick next to the gate. I didn't even go through it. I have a man who looks the sheep every day because they are so far away." Neil looked at the vet who remained impassive.

Neither of us could see why the sheep had to be slaughtered. The risk of dangerous contact was minuscule. If MAFF thought there was a risk, why did they not take every single sheep out in the area? The vet just shrugged his shoulders. "I'm sorry," he said, " I have my orders."

We made the long journey in silence. I knew Neil was wishing he had not been so honest. I would be feeling the same way in his shoes. I realised that the whole subject of dangerous contacts was not clearly defined. The future of all our livestock was hanging in the hands of Page Street. It was an uneasy realisation for me.

We arrived at the field and quickly counted the sheep. They were very good types, which made the whole thing worse for both Neil and I. The vet rang MAFF (Carlisle) to take instructions. He was told to stay at the field and meet the slaughter team who were going to shoot the sheep that evening.

"Sorry guys," he said, "we are here for the duration." I began to get indignant when he told me that the slaughtermen would arrive in one hour's time. It was already after six o'clock at night and getting quite dark. Again we sat in Neil's Land Rover with little to say. Eventually the killing crew arrived. The vet showed them the sheep and we immediately left the scene. By 8.15pm we were back at Cockly Beck. At the kitchen table we completed the paperwork. Neil set about cooking a fry-up, which was thoroughly enjoyed despite the circumstances. I think Neil was glad of the chore to keep him busy. There was no sign of

Christine. By10pm I was ready to leave.

"I will need you back tomorrow please," said the vet as he signed my papers.

"I already have three valuations booked for tomorrow," I said thinking of all the time that had been wasted earlier in the day and knowing I would have to fit them in if I could.

"I take precedent," said the vet, and that was that.

Driving back over the high passes of Wrynose and Kirkstone I found that visibility was almost zero. The snow was blizzarding and I almost did not make it over the top. It was well after midnight when I crawled into bed next to Paula. She was sound asleep. I put my hands around her growing bump and was dead to the world in seconds. The dozen or so messages she had taken for me up until 11.30pm went unanswered. Many were neighbours of the Hodgsons who wanted to know what was happening and to book me should their turn come around.

12
RETURN TO THE VALLEY OF DEATH

Tuesday 27 March
Total National cases: 790

First light saw me make my way over the A66 to a farm at Stoddah near Penrith. The owner of the farm, Peter Stoechen had been in regular contact with me over the last three weeks. He was president of the Deer Farming Association and farmed several different species of deer in his own right. A neighbouring farm had become an infected premises earlier in the month, the farmer having brought lambs home from Longtown mart. There was a regularly used public footpath between the two farms. Soon after the neighbouring farm went down some of the deer became ill. Peter called MAFF and they took blood samples. The test, which was the same one used on sheep, failed to detect foot and mouth virus. MAFF therefore refused to slaughter the animals.

Peter called me regularly to update me and to ask my help should a valuation be required. Throughout this period he remained adamant that the deer had the virus even if the tests were inconclusive. After two or three blood testings and inspections MAFF conceded that some of the deer did not appear to look well. As a precaution, after three weeks contemplation they decided to slaughter the entire stock. I agreed to put a valuation case together as long as MAFF were happy to approve my appointment on the basis that I had no experience of deer farming, breeding or prices. MAFF agreed to this and sent a vet who was a breeder and specialised in deer medicine. He would closely scrutinise my valuation, which was to be based on comparable evidence supplied from other breeders and previous sale records.

Following a quick briefing meeting, Peter, the vet, and I began the inspection. I was fascinated by the enterprise. I became totally engrossed in the whole concept of deer farming. For a short while foot and mouth disease was completely forgotten. I saw red, fallow, thikka, Pere David and all manner of deer species. I learned about breeding for temperament, antler points and the required specification for meat production. I later found out from breeding records that Peter's deer had a very good reputation.

We moved to another shed. Peter asked me to comment on what I saw. When we approached the pen most of the deer ran to the back of the shed. About six deer did not move. They just stood there with their heads down. They were also shivering as if very cold. They looked miserable.

"Those deer are not well," I said. It was not difficult to see. The vet took much interest in them. Only one had shown the classic F&M clinical sign for deer, a rash around the anus. It was certainly clear that some species showed no symptoms whatsoever, while others did in varying degrees. Throughout the campaign MAFF refused to confirm that deer, be they wild or farmed, actually contracted foot and mouth. Many farmers claim to have seen lame or ill wild deer around their farms before they became infected premises. The vet thought it could well be foot and mouth.

Having completed the valuation we moved back to Peter's office to begin putting the case together. I sifted through many documents from other deer farms and estates and also Peter's own sales records. It became clear that Peter was a renowned breeder. He was however being far too modest about his stock and I had to constantly pressure him for information. The expert vet backed up every valuation statement I made. Within two hours I had completed my task. It seemed such a waste of life and yet if the deer were infected they would be spewing out large amounts of virus into the atmosphere.

So specialist was the slaughter procedure that Peter was going to have to use his own restraining equipment and help to kill all of his own deer himself. I thought that it was more than any farmer should have to go through in the name of science.

I did not know it at the time but according to MAFF's revised payment schedule, by the time I had left Peter Stoechen's farm, I had earned my daily fee and would be paid no more for all the work that I was to do later in the day. More of that one later. In reality no amount of money would have been adequate for what I had to endure over the two wretched days in the Duddon valley.

Having completed the deer valuation I was soon on the long road back over the mountains to Cockly Beck. Last night's snow had all but disappeared. I arrived early afternoon to see yet more sheep gathered from the fell awaiting valuation. There were hundreds and hundreds of sheep filling every garth and fold above the farm as well as every collecting pen and yard within it. It was a magnificent and yet heart-rending sight to behold. Quickly we began the task. As we worked the slaughter team began to arrive. I knew the head slaughterman well for we often did business in peacetime. I shook his hand and casually asked him how much stock he had slaughtered over the last few days.

"75,000" he replied and burst into tears. I was shocked. I could not believe that a hard man like Mark Duerden had been reduced to this level. He was clearly at the end of his tether.

"Honestly Adam, someone has to stop this madness," he continued, eyes red with anger and pain. "This isn't right," he said looking over a thousand or so in-lamb ewes waiting to die. "If you know anyone who can stop this, please get onto them. This has got to stop. There's going to be nothing left!"

"Come on Mark," I said lamely "don't do this here."

" I can't bear this much more," he fired back, "all those healthy sheep wasted." With that he turned and walked away. I turned back to the sheep pens. I was shocked by the slaughterman's outburst. It upset me although I refused to let my own guard drop. There was nothing that I could do. We were both small links in a long chain. We could have walked away if we wanted, but that would have been like deserting from duty. None of us could have lived with the guilt. So we all went on and on, day after day.

In a while just behind our backs the killing started. There were shouts of laughter from the killing team. They made fun of one another, chastising each other but at all times treating the animals with courtesy. Not once throughout the campaign did I see a slaughter crew abuse an animal. I could see that all the noise was just a front. They were all just trying to get through the job day after day after day. It was a hopeless and surreal situation. We were all taking part in a mass execution that was destroying our livelihoods and our sanity. It was truly shocking.

Many months later Mark Duerden explained to me that the toll of killing the animals day after day was an immense pressure on all of his team. That dreadful day at Cockly Beck Mark's slaughter team had been working on another farm and had been asked to leave it to go to the Duddon valley. This had upset the team who did not want to leave a job half done. They could not understand why they had been requested to do so and had refused to leave until they were finished. Added to that was the fact that he had many employees in his businesses that were now without work in his closed slaughterhouse. He was proud that he did not make a single member of his staff redundant although at that time he, like many of us, thought that he was going to lose his business at the end of FMD. Thankfully it did not happen. In those dark days it seemed very much a reality.

Christine by now had left the yard although Neil was still with me. I begged him to go back to the house. I could see he was getting mad at the slaughter crew. I tried to make him see that they were not getting any pleasure from their work, in fact just the opposite. What he saw was nothing but a smoke screen.

"It is the only way they can get through this," I said in their defence. Neil understood but it did not help him because there was now a long line of dead sheep running the length of his holding yard almost up to the fell gate. It was a horrific sight to behold; the bodies piled one on top of the other where they fell. The only sound was the chatter of the men and crack of the pistols as one by one the sheep were dispatched. The scene remains vivid in my mind even today.

Thankfully there were large container wagons standing by to remove the dead bodies that night. That was a small blessing on such a thoroughly dismal day. The following day it would be as if nothing had happened except in the minds of every person who took part in the dreadful operation on both sides of the valley that March day.

It was late afternoon and we were back in the farmhouse kitchen completing the valuation forms. There were several forms to do because of the number of stray sheep from other farms that had been gathered down to Cockly Beck. I spent a long time calling all the farmers on the telephone to get their agreement to value the sheep. They were all happy for me to do the job.

The phone rang. It was MAFF wanting to speak to the duty vet. He was drying out from being thoroughly soaked in constant drizzle as he supervised the slaughter and carcass removal.

He came back into the kitchen with more bad news. Neil had more sheep at Colwith on the Langdale side of Wrynose Pass. His nephew farmed there. Neil had not been over to Colwith for several weeks. His nephew however had been to Cockly Beck to pick up a farm implement from the yard. The duty vet had passed the information on to MAFF but even said himself that it would be highly doubtful that Page Street would class this act as a dangerous contact. The look on the vet's face told a different story. The sheep at Colwith must die. I could see the despair on the Hodgsons' faces. How much more would they have to endure. I wondered how anyone could truly justify this as dangerous contact. It was plainly ridiculous.

The vet asked us all to go to Colwith as soon as possible because it was now getting dark. Within half an hour we were there. In the rapidly diminishing light we valued the sheep. The last few inspections were done in complete darkness save one electric light at the end of the shed. Once again it was raining hard and we were all soaked. The sheep were very good registered Herdwick and included some of Neil's favourites. There were also five top quality breeding cattle. With a stroke of the vet's pen the fate of Neil's last remaining cattle were sealed for good. The forms were signed and the next day all of the stock would be killed.

By 9.30pm my job was done. Goodbyes were said and I wished Neil good luck for the future. What else could I say? I hoped that he would get back into the farm again as soon as possible.

It was a lonely drive home but it gave me time to ponder the situation and evaluate my own performance over the last few days. I believed that I had done the best I could for the farmers without resorting to telling a mistruth. Satisfied that I had done as much as possible I decided to draw a line under the last few days and move onto the next challenge. I was determined not to keep reliving the past. If I thought about what was happening I knew I probably would not get out of bed the next day. "One day at a time sweet Jesus," or so the song goes.

As for Neil and Christine Hodgson, blood sample results taken from their stock by the vet, at the time of slaughter failed to reveal one single case of foot and mouth. No amount of money could compensate for their loss. A few months later they gave up their tenancy and left the farm to start afresh in the east of the county. That area's gain was our loss. It saddens me still.

I arrived home well after midnight - it was the second night in succession. Paula was again fast asleep. I had hardly seen her or talked to her over the last few days. It was going to get much worse. Another long list of telephone messages awaited me in the morning. I climbed into bed and tried to forget about the last two days. It was not easy.

13
A Voluntary Cull?

Wednesday 28 March
Total national cases: 667

I was sitting in the office late Wednesday morning finding it very difficult to concentrate on the tasks at hand. It was however necessary to update my growing pile of paperwork and hand over copies of valuation forms so that our administration staff could invoice MAFF for the work that I had undertaken on their behalf.

I received a telephone call from another valuer who asked me my opinion of the new FMD "book price". I knew nothing of it and asked for more details. Apparently whilst I was working down in the valley of death, Nick Brown, Minister for Agriculture had made a statement to the House of Commons. He said this:

"Wherever possible we have reduced the time between when a vet makes one inspection and when he or she can make the next one; where the disease risk is minimal this turn-round time has been reduced to 24 hours. We have simplified the valuation arrangements - whilst at the same time safeguarding farmers' interests - by introducing a generous standard tariff."

The standard tariff or book price turned out to be a set of standard valuation figures for different classes of livestock. An affected farmer could choose the book price without resorting to requesting a professional valuation. We agreed that this must be a ploy to lessen the role of auctioneers and possibly do away with us altogether. We both thought that the majority of farmers would not trust this system. In most cases we were right. MAFF later tried to blame valuers for slowing down the slaughter and disposal process. This was particularly galling to many of us who were not getting home until after midnight, leaving again at 7am and working seven days a week to boot. Not once was I ever late to a valuation appointment although I did once have to ring a vet on her mobile phone one hour after our agreed appointment. She was still in bed having had a 'real night out' the previous evening. It took her almost 90 minutes to get from Carlisle down to the affected farm whilst we all waited around.

We also discussed the fact that dirty valuers could now visit uncon-firmed farms within 24 hours of leaving infected premises. This was a mighty U-turn on original policy of a seven day cooling off period. "What about the virus in the nasal hair?" I thought.

Following the phone call I checked the MAFF website and sure enough there were the details of the book price. I was told that they had been put on the internet a few days previously but nobody bothered to inform the auctioneers. Some of the prices did appear to be generous, while others were too low. I wondered who had advised MAFF in setting the rates. Perhaps they used a computer model like the one, which was supposed to predict the end of the crisis, by coincidence on the proposed day of the general election. In any case I knew that for the quality and type of stock that I was valuing, my own valuations would for the most part be rather higher than the book price.

I need not have worried. The farmers still wanted their auctioneers to inspect the stock. I have no doubt that part of the farmer's will to do this was simply a matter of pride. That is what makes the auction ring spe-cial. Most farmers are proud to stand up and sell their stock. It is a shop window especially for those farmers who sell breeding stock to others. Also for many farmers it was a last chance to show to someone who gen-uinely took an interest, the final results of a lifetime's work before it was lost forever. Sad that a person like me was the last to appreciate the stock.

Next I contacted MAFF at Carlisle and was passed around the houses before finally talking to someone in the animal health department who confirmed that vets and therefore auctioneers could move from dirty to clean farms in 24 hours. Irrespective of that advice I decided that only as a last resort would I do that.

Finally we tried again to find out more information about the so-called 3k or voluntary cull. A command centre had been set up at Penrith auc-tion mart from which the whole cull would be managed. Many of the staff were well known to me which was comforting. There was also a large army contingent as well as a host of local livestock hauliers who were employed to cart away the livestock.

The basis of the cull was to clear out all of the sheep within a three-kilo-metre circle of an infected premises. MAFF believed that this would act as a fire-break and lessen the risk of continued spread of the virus. Farmers would 'volunteer' their sheep by contacting the command centre who would then notify the farmer's chosen valuer of the type of sheep and their location. Although there was no immediate rush to get out into the field we nevertheless tried to complete the task as soon as possible. In time the farmers did not bother to contact the command centre but instead contacted us direct.

The animals valued on the voluntary cull were picked up from their fields and transported alive to landfill sites where they were slaughtered before being buried. In the first instance they were taken to Great Orton airfield near Wigton. When this was full they went to Distington, but more of that later.

Because the valuation was voluntary, no vets or MAFF officials were there to supervise. The valuer simply drove to the location of the sheep and completed his inspection and valuation there and then. Often the farmers would not accompany us either. A few days later after the form was processed at Penrith the sheep were removed by hauliers to go to slaughter. Many farmers found this more distressing than seeing them shot on the farm. It was not a pleasant experience to see young lambs only a few days old being split from their mothers and herded on to separate wagons. I have talked since to some of the hauliers who had to do this. It broke their hearts too.

We tried to find out why the official valuation forms were entitled 'Voluntary Depopulation Scheme'. No one from MAFF ever gave a definitive answer. The closest we got was a suggestion that the whole scheme was to a great extent funded by European money. This title fitted in with a European directive that would make it easier for the Government to claim 'aid' from Europe. Whether this was true or not I do know. That aside, the scheme was up and running. With the amount of 'dirty' valuations taking place around the county there was a growing need for clean valuers. We were getting a few requests from MAFF on this subject. FMD had not reared its ugly head in West Cumbria so I took a decision to go 'clean'. I waited 48 hours before undertaking my first 'voluntary'. It was to be the first of many.

Time and again we were to be questioned by farmers about whether the sheep had to go or whether it was indeed a voluntary valuation. There was no written guidance from MAFF until well into April when the following letter was issued:

"In March the Minister for Agriculture announced that all sheep in the 3km zones around an infected premises in certain areas of Cumbria must be slaughtered. This was following the advice of the Chief Veterinary Officer and MAFF's scientific advisors who believe that sheep within these zones will have been exposed to infection. They also believe that by slaughtering these sheep the impact of the spread of the disease will be reduced.

"Following consultation with members of the NFU a decision was made to remove sheep from farms in the 3km zones to a central place for slaughter. This gave farmers the opportunity to avoid the slaughter of sheep on their own premises and enabled the slaughter of about 20,000 sheep a day without impacting heavily on the available resources. To this end local auction marts contacted farmers in the 3km zones and invited them to be valued, collected and slaughtered.

"Your name has been passed to us by the auction marts. According to their records you were not willing to give up your sheep. This letter is to advise you what arrangements are now being put in place to include your sheep in this cull.

"In the infected area, sheep, goats and pigs on premises within 3km of infected premises will be treated as dangerous contacts. This means that MAFF will make arrangements for your sheep to be slaughtered on the farm. Compensation will be paid for your sheep.

"If you have reason to believe that your flock has not been exposed to infection it may be possible to arrange for them to be subjected to repeated serological surveillance to confirm your beliefs. You will need to contact your local veterinary surgeon and ask him, at your expense to visit your flock and make a submission to the Senior Veterinary Office. He will need to include arguments why your flock or parts of it, should be exempt from the cull. He will need to prove that your stock has been isolated from other stock and that high levels of bio-security have been sustained since the end of February.

"If rather than have your sheep slaughtered on farm you would like them to be taken away for slaughter please phone... and ask for... they will arrange for your sheep to be valued and transported to Great Orton or Carlisle abattoir for slaughter."

The telephone number given on the letter was that of Carlisle auction mart which had become a temporary command post for MAFF.

More importantly, the letter was a clear indication that the 3km cull was in fact a compulsory slaughter. The only voluntary bit was whether you had the sheep killed at home or taken away for slaughter! Also I cannot recall ever passing the name of a farmer to MAFF in order for them to make contact about the voluntary cull.

It worked because so many farmers were intimidated into letting their sheep go on the cull. The reason for the cull was clearly placed in the hands of scientific advice and the chief vet. The outcome of the cull was to remove thousands of healthy sheep from Cumbrian farms. Maybe there is some truth in the rumour that the voluntary depopulation scheme (as it was officially entitled on valuation forms) was sponsored by Europe and part of an agreement already struck by Tony Blair in Brussels some years previously. I do not know. However there are many of us who have an uneasy belief that if all of the sheep in the Cockermouth area had not been taken, then the disease might well have spread further into west Cumbria. Did the 3km actually work for us? We will never truly know. That said, it leaves me bitter and sour that so many healthy animals had to die. For the truth is that it should never have got to this situation in the first place.

14
FRIENDS IN NEED

Friday 30 March
Total national cases: 840

Friday 30 March was a bleak day in Cumbria for there were almost 30 confirmed cases and goodness knows how many dangerous contacts all being taken out. Add to that the growing number of 'voluntary' 3km cull valuations and it is no exaggeration to say the disease and its effects was like a Sydney bush fire raging through the county sealing the fate of all livestock in its path. How could Nick Brown possibly say the spread of disease was under control and following expected patterns? Of course the usual politician-speak was to say that he was taking expert advice. Unfortunately his advice was based on computer generated patterns using data set up to track the spread of human sexually transmitted diseases. Some experts were saying that the computer models were flawed due to inadequate data. To a simple auctioneer it was all too much. I wanted to hear facts and information that were plain and simple. It did not happen.

By now the subject of vaccination was very much a focal point in the press. The EU Standing Veterinary Committee had agreed to a UK vaccination policy but it was said this prohibited the slaughter of cattle after vaccination. The NFU and some scientists were totally opposed to vaccination stating that it would destroy any hope of resuming exports at the end of the epidemic. There were also heavy rumours flying around that vaccinated stock would have to be destroyed anyway. At this time I was almost of the opinion that Cumbria should vaccinate before we were wiped out altogether. If this was the case then it was pointless vaccinating anyway. The disease might as well run its course in the hope that it eventually petered out. I could not however understand why vaccinated and therefore immune stock with a build-up of antibodies should then have to die. This policy continued to puzzle as antibody positive sheep were continually slaughtered after the epidemic was over. I was always told that it was good to have antibodies and strong immunity levels to combat serious diseases.

That aside, the end of the month was upon us. One million animals were earmarked for slaughter. Many were dead but not disposed of. The momentum of the cull was gathering pace. Some farms were devoid of life, empty sheds, silent milking parlours and bare fields. What must it have been like for the farmers and their families to get up each morning, knowing their herds and flocks were all dead and gone? The more unlucky farmers would of course still be seeing their animals lying on pyres waiting to be lit, or lying in stinking piles in farmyards or at the edge of fields. Then there were the farmers who were watching the cull creeping closer to them. Not knowing what they might find in their sheds when they got up next morning or dreading a phone call from a neighbour: "Sorry we've got it," knowing they would be next. Meanwhile the FMD front-line soldiers of which we were a part, kept going and going, not wanting to let anybody down, not wanting to be the weak link in the chain. I swear that we never were.

It was Thursday evening when my good friend Robin Edmondson rang me from Matterdale End. As I answered the phone I was mulling over the events of the last two days. I had valued a lovely pen of registered Herdwick hoggs including some of good tup breeding potential for Derrick and Jean Wilson from Dockray. The Herdwicks were always close to my heart and I spent some time in the pen with both them and the vet. I told him what good sheep they were. He was not much interested but I understood why. Being a local vet, the farm on which these Herdwicks were wintering represented yet another lost customer. The vets were just like the auctioneers, working themselves to exhaustion just to see another customer go down the drain. Another nail in the coffin of their own business. What cruel and perverse jobs we had to do at this time.

Earlier that day I had been part of a strange performance where I had sent a colleague to value on an infected premises. I was in the process of going 'clean' and could not enter the farm. So as my colleague inspected the sheep, some of which were again away-wintering Herdwicks, I gave him advice on the phone as to how to value them. There were several hundred gathered in one big shed. My colleague, the vet, field officer and a soldier vainly tried to count the sheep as they flew around the shed in circles. I could hear the profanities on the phone. Eventually the job was done to the satisfaction of all. My colleague who was undertaking his first dirty valuation admitted he was glad not to have seen any slaughtering that day. "Don't worry," I thought, "you will be used to it by the time you finish."

"Hello Robin, how are you doing?" I tried to sound up beat as I snapped back into reality.

"Oh - not good," he responded in a resigned tone, "we've decided to let the sheep go on the voluntary cull. We don't want to do it but the dairy herd is just too valuable to us. We've got to save the cows!"

He went on to explain that there was an infected premises close by and they knew the virus was all around.

"At least if the sheep go out of the fields there is less chance of bringing the disease in to the cattle sheds," he said.

I could see his logic but I knew the loss of the sheep would be a big blow to the family. Robin loved his sheep.

"I'll be their tomorrow," I said. Finally I explained that I had been dirty 48 hours previously but was now officially clean. Robin thought that was good enough.

My first job that Friday morning was to visit Edwin Hickson at Castle Carrock. We had often sold stock for Edwin within Cockermouth mart even though he was many miles distant near Brampton in the east of the county. Edwin had decided to let all of his sheep go on the voluntary cull to save his 200 cow dairy herd. Like so many others this was a tormenting decision to make. He was however at the epicentre of a massive hotspot of virus. All around him neighbours were dropping like flies. Realistically we all thought it was just a matter of time for him.

We had spoken briefly the previous night and I had arranged to be there early in the morning. From there I would dash back to Robin's farm near Penrith for his voluntary cull valuation. The pace was beginning to hot up.

The next morning I travelled up the East Fellside of the Pennines to Castle Carrock. There I met up with Edwin Hickson and we jumped in to his Land Rover in order to travel around the fields. Edwin was being helped by his young daughter and a friendly neighbour who was a teacher or an engineer. I'm afraid I did not take a lot of notice although the man was most helpful. We proceeded to view several hundred Swaledale ewes. Some were in the process of lambing and many had lambs running at foot. I was pleased with the quality of the stock. I expressed an opinion that the sheep were better types than I had imagined they would be. As I said it I realised that Edwin may have been offended by my statement. He was not. Instead he explained that he had gradually been improving the quality of the flock over several years by buying good replacement stock from noted breeders.

Towards the end of the valuation we moved into a field of ewes with newly born lambs. As we quietly walked through them, the ewes moved away from us warily. Every few paces they turned around to sniff their lambs. It was a reassuring gesture both for the lambs and the mothers who were guarding their offspring. The lambs still had the sticky remnants of birth on their coats. They stumbled clumsily on shaky new-born legs bleating plaintively as they ran with their mothers. I began to explain to Edwin how the hauliers would split the lambs from the ewes and put them on separate wagon to take them to slaughter. I looked at the lambs and could not get the thought of that cruel act out of my head. The ewes would be frantic, the lambs lost and panicking. What distress to cause the creatures! I realised that I was in danger of losing control of my emotions. My eyes began to fill up with tears and my nose was running.

"I'll just go over here and fill in my valuation forms," I said shakily trying not to sob. I moved away from the other people quickly, hoping they had not seen me begin to break down. I stood against a dry stone wall looking out over green fields. For several minutes I took deep breaths trying to compose myself. I wanted to be thoroughly professional in front of my customers but the thought of the lambs being separated from the ewes at that age just broke me up.

Eventually I regained control and was able to return to Edwin and his helpers. We went back to the farm and completed the paperwork. The family held onto the hope that the dairy cattle would be spared. I thought it would be a forlorn hope but did not say so. I was proved wrong for Edwin's cows did survive and remained healthy for the rest of the campaign. It was however like living on a knife-edge for the Hicksons, as neighbour upon neighbour succumbed to the disease.

Long after FMD was over, Edwin and his brother Frank from Cockermouth, were to move to pastures new. A fresh start came their way by moving into the Borders of Scotland. Sadly too far away for us to sell regularly on their behalf, thankfully close enough to not lose touch altogether. For the Hicksons were and still are good supporters of Cockermouth auction.

Soon I was on the road. I drove down the A6 to Penrith. All along that road there were funeral pyres burning. Towering clouds of smoke and ash were pouring into the sky. I imagined it must have been like this in the blitz during wartime. The stench of burning coal and flesh filled my car. The people of Cumbria who have smelt the pyres will never forget that vile, acrid odour.

In a while I was driving through Matterdale above Lake Ullswater, heading for my next voluntary valuation. Robin and Sandra Edmondson have been friends of mine for many years. I am godfather to their youngest daughter. It was her birthday in two days time and I did not even remember. Later at my own son's christening in November, I finally rectified the situation by giving Sian her birthday present. It was only six months late. Shame on me.

When I got to the farm it was raining very hard. Robin and I made a brief inspection of the sheep but I knew them well enough to know their value anyway. We moved back to the farmhouse and proceeded to put together the valuation form. As we did so Sandra appeared. Without looking up I greeted her in a cheerful manner. It was obviously too cheerful because she snapped at me quite violently. I was rather taken aback. Her eyes were on fire with rage. She was clearly very upset at losing the sheep some of which she had bred herself. I did not know what to say, so I just continued with my work. In a moment she left the room. Robin made no excuses, for none were necessary, except to say that the whole episode was affecting her badly. I hoped for her sake that when the day came for the sheep to be taken from the farm that she was not there to witness it. Every person was affected in a different way. I was to see so many different emotions on FMD farms.

I completed the valuation form, which Robin signed. Then I left the house as soon as possible and drove straight to the voluntary command centre at Penrith Auction. The sooner I handed the form in the better. Every day until the sheep were gone would be a torment for the family.

As usual, the command centre was a hive of activity. Outside there were a number of livestock haulage wagons waiting to be dispatched onto farms such as Robin and Sandra's. From there the transporters would be loaded on farm and travel in convoy to the slaughter and burial site at Great Orton near Wigton. This massive extermination centre was continually being developed to house the hundreds of thousands of bodies either slaughtered on farms or sent there direct from the farm to be slaughtered. There can be very few comparable incidents of such organised and repetitive destruction of life. It was by all accounts a complete hell-hole.

One of our main prime sheep buyers at Cockermouth was effectively out of a job during the crisis there being no auctions to attend. He had a family to keep and was forced into applying for a job at Great Orton. His role was to organise the penning and lairing of the animals prior to slaughter. He does not talk of it and I do not wish to ask him.

Who can forget the aerial photographs of Great Orton? It looked like a First World War battlefield of epic proportions. The huge pits dug deep into the landscape, the bodies being tipped in to form a massive heap of rotting flesh buried beneath the topsoil. The myriad of tents hid the lairage and killing pens from prying eyes. Experts have proved that many mistakes were made in the planning and construction of the site. The resultant liquid or leachate seeping from the dead bodies was of such volume that it had to be collected and tankered away to West Cumbria where at some point it was treated and pumped out into the Solway Firth. Through it all, Great Orton served its purpose and achieved the aims of its creators. Without it the whole foot and mouth contingency plan in Cumbria would have fallen to pieces. It would have been catastrophic. Even so, in time it would be proved that Great Orton was not big enough. Further sites to dispose of the bodies would have to be found. That simply proves the enormous scale of the task.

The men who had to work at Great Orton deserved a medal for it must have been a depressing and dreadful environment to work in. What of the people living in the local villages who had to endure the smell and disruption of thousands of vehicles charging through the countryside with a cargo of live and sometimes dead animals? They too were caught up in the crisis. Their daily lives enmeshed with the war against FMD.

Inside the voluntary cull command centre at Penrith, the staff milled around for most of the hours in the day. They were either Penrith auction staff who I knew well or soldiers who were organising the campaign. On the wall there was a huge map of Cumbria with individual pins to represent infected farms. The map was a seething mass of pins. From a distance it looked like a bad case of measles or maybe even foot and mouth blisters. It would have been more appropriate. More than 90% of the stock being slaughtered did not have such clinical signs anyway for they did not have the disease.

I spent several minutes studying the map trying to appreciate the scale of what was happening. Sometimes I got there quite late at night. Often their staff worked 18 hour days too. Everyone has their own story to tell.

Nevertheless they were always courteous and most helpful. The Cockermouth valuers were grateful for this support throughout the campaign.

At home there was the usual pile of messages. I tried to prioritise them but in the end they all had to be answered.

Later that night with Paula and Olivia safely tucked up in bed I watched the film *Saving Private Ryan*. At the end of the film an aged and tearful John Ryan asks his wife to tell him that he has "been a good man and lived a good life." Throughout the film I had been thinking of my role in the FMD crisis up to date and the fact that I was trying to do my best but it was getting much harder to keep a stiff upper lip. Then I thought of Edwin Hickson's young lambs and was shocked to find myself bursting into tears. I cried for several minutes and could not stop. I had not realised just how much emotion had built up within me over the last week. Eventually I was able to settle myself. I felt relieved and yet embarrassed. I could not remember the last time I had cried like that. I was glad my wife and daughter were tucked up in bed. Stronger people than me had shed those same tears. Afterwards the same problems were still there and yet it was if a pressure valve had been released. I felt better and went to bed knowing that the battle would begin again tomorrow. I knew I would be ready. I had to be, like so many others.

15

FOUR VALUATIONS AND A WEDDING

Saturday 31 March
Total national cases: 880

During the last few weeks I had been so preoccupied with FMD that I had rather neglected my duties with our band the Soul Traders. Saturday 31 March should have been one of those hugely enjoyable days spent in anticipation of a fun filled evening entertaining at a wedding. The wedding in question was a young couple, John and Clare, whom I knew well. They had booked the band to perform at the evening reception many months before. Due to my obvious work load we had not had much chance to practice. This was especially worrying in view of the fact that they had asked us to sing a difficult Elton John song for the first dance. Driving to my first valuation of the day, I realised that I had not learned the lyrics and could not even remember how many verses the song had. I did not relish letting the couple down on their important night, especially when I personally knew so many of the people who would be in the audience. In just a few hours I would have to 'wing it'.

The first of my farm visits was to Saltcoats high up on the Solway coast. There were two lots of away-wintered fell sheep here. These included some of the best Herdwick sheep in existence. It really was a crying shame to see the animals knowing that they would soon be destined for the pit at Great Orton. It was heartbreaking for Andrew and Karen Nicholson to even tell me about their sheep in preparation for their valuation. This young farming couple whom I classed as friends were full of life and spirit before foot and mouth. Gradually it was to wear them down. At this time they could console themselves that the disease was far from their home in the Lorton valley. Their consolation would be brief.

The farmers at Saltcoats did not greet me and I did not expect it. They had given me instruction as to where the sheep were and I turned up to count the sheep. I did not even go into the fields, but easily viewed them over the dyke. I think they were glad to see the sheep go although they did not express that view. The Solway farmers all wanted rid of the sheep as soon as possible to try and protect their own cattle. In some cases where the sheep farmers tried to resist the voluntary cull, this led to resentment and bitterness. In one case a Solway farmer kept ringing me to go and value some away-wintered sheep which were on his farm. He certainly wanted rid of them immediately. The owner of the sheep however felt that the animals were far too valuable to let go on the cull.

"Don't go any where near them," he instructed me, "those sheep are stopping until the end."

Unfortunately this left me in somewhat of a predicament. I was a go-between for two men who would hardly speak to each other. The foot and mouth crisis was to make friends and neighbours into enemies before its course was run. Eventually I did go and value the sheep. Like the rest they ended up in the pit at Great Orton.

Soon I was on my way back to the Penrith area, where my next stop was near Skelton. It was yet another dairy farm with away-wintered fell sheep. This time I was valuing Swaledale gimmer hoggs and shearlings for two related families. Val and Richard Edmondson in Borrowdale had hoggs to value and John and Fiona Edmondson up at Low Snab, Newlands had hoggs and shearlings. Some of the sheep were crowned pedigrees. The dairy farmer called Andrew Bargh escorted me to the sheep. He also had some good Texels of his own. Although he had not done business with me before, he asked me to value them for him. They too went on the cull.

Just as I was stripping off my waterproofs after disinfecting, my mobile phone rang. It was Christine Crowe from Woodend farm high up on Birker Moor in the southern Lake District. She was quite hysterical.

"MAFF are coming to take us out," she sobbed. "You have to come right away." I tried to ascertain from her just why MAFF wanted to take this course of action. Christine could not speak. She cried and cried. In the end I was very firm with her.

"Put the phone down now," I ordered "calm down a bit then ring me back in ten minutes."

She did as she was told. I began driving to Penrith and wondered what the hell was happening up on Birker Moor. If Woodend had foot and mouth there would be God-knows how many dangerous contacts. I wondered whether they themselves were dangerous contacts. Perhaps the disease had spread up from the Duddon Valley. "Oh Christ," I thought "all of Eskdale could go." I felt sick to the pit of my stomach.

In a while Christine rang back. By now she was in control. My second theory was correct. Another case had apparently been discovered lower down the Duddon valley from Cockly Beck. The sheep from this farm ran up the sides of the valley and onto Birker Moor. As a result two of my favourite customers were going to be taken out. Poor old John Harrison at Crosbythwaite was going to suffer the same fate as the Crowes. My valuation book was full for the day. There was no way I could get down there. Tactfully I tried to explain that neither I, nor any of my colleagues could represent them that day. They would have to use somebody else.

Christine took it well. I felt absolutely gutted and totally guilty. Thankfully they were in good hands as my old sparring partner Ian Walker from Ulverston looked after the Crowes and did a very good job for them.

It bothered me for several days that I had let my friends down. Deep down inside I knew I could not have done anything more to help. I heard later that the family had a dreadful time during the slaughter. I know it affected them all badly. Many months later in the following spring I was eventually able to visit the farm that Dennis and Christine were restocking. Even so the legacy of that painful day was all too evident. I still wish I could have done more.

On my way to the next valuation I stopped at the hotel where the band were setting up for the wedding reception. We enjoyed a brief half an hour rehearsal including the infamous Elton song. I got through it but my mind was on other things. I knew it was going to be a long and difficult night.

As I departed I had a brief chat with Jamie our bass player. A road engineer by trade, he was now subcontracted by MAFF to travel onto infected premises to plan the siting and construction of temporary slurry stores. Scientific advice suggested that FMD virus could live in animal slurry for several months. Therefore slurry collected and stored before foot and mouth would have to be transferred off the farmyard and into temporary stores located in fields. This would allow the farmyards, buildings and stores to be cleaned and disinfected. Eventually the stored slurry could be spread onto the land. I could not for the life of me understand why the slurry could not just be spread onto land immediately. I was told that the virus was killed by ultra-violet light or sunshine and could not live out of the body of a living being for more than a few hours. Apparently the virus can exist outside the body because it is not actually 'alive' but is activated when it finds a 'host' body. Surely the risk from slurry after being spread onto land was minimal? Obviously not and Jamie was now in the foot and mouth employee's club. Our paths never met. He was visiting the farms whilst the dead bodies were still in the yards or after they had gone. Either way it was not pleasant for him. Even he had some distressing experiences having to visit distraught farmers to discuss a meaningless task when a lifetime's work was lying dead in front of them. Everyone had their own job to do and their own tales to tell. Jamie and I tried not to speak too much about it.

My next call was up onto the hills above Watermillock. Lake Ullswater lay just behind us. Yet again I was on a farm to value away-wintered sheep. The farmer and I enjoyed a brisk walk around the fields to value the in-lamb ewes. We enjoyed a brief talk about golf and decided that when this was all over we might enjoy a round together at Keswick where he was a member.

Finally on my way home I stopped off at Penruddock on the A66. My job was to value yet more Swaledale sheep. Yet again the shepherd was letting his sheep go to try and save his neighbour's dairy herd. The disease was all around and most sheep farmers were sacrificing their flocks on the cull. Philip Teasdale said he could not live with himself if the Davidson's cows at Spedding Farm went down with the disease and there was a chance that his sheep might be in some way responsible for the spread of disease. Thankfully that herd was to survive but there were no sheep left in the area at all.

By late afternoon I had handed my valuation forms in at Penrith command centre. My colleague Alisdare Bruce had also been working in the same area but our paths had not crossed. He had been seconded in by Penrith Farmers' & Kidd's at Penrith to help them out with their valuations. It was simply indicative of the situation. There were so many farms going down in the Eden area. The region was supposedly awash with virus. Desperately farmers volunteered their sheep to try and halt the spread. We as auctioneers even tried to help each other for once.

I was relieved to get home to see Paula and Olivia and spend a few hours with them. It had been a dreadful week. It did not help that Paula was by now very tired being only six weeks or so from childbirth. I felt guilty that I was going off again to perform at the wedding. Try as I might I could not get any enthusiasm going. All I wanted to do was sit at home and vegetate. I too was quite tired. By 8pm I was on my way to the hotel.

"Good evening Ladies and Gentlemen," the band were on stage, the instruments gleaming in the stage lights. There was already a really good buzz within the room. The invited guests were up for it I could tell. Quickly I introduced the happy couple and invited them to the dance floor.

"Tonight Matthew," I said, "I'm going to be Elton John." We launched into the first song and never looked back. The evening was a resounding success. The dance floor was packed from start to finish. The bridegroom was a big Elvis fan. He took to the microphone and launched in to *Suspicious Minds*. The guests went wild.

So many people in that room had so little idea of what was going on amongst the farming communities of Cumbria. There were no thoughts of FMD at all. To most people it did not exist. The drink flowed and the room was full of excited people talking, dancing and having a great time. Meanwhile at that very same moment around the county, people like Dennis and Christine Crowe were living in hell trying to come to terms with the shock of feeding their animals for the last time that night, knowing they would all be dead the next morning. I'm glad I never stopped to think of that as I sang and played my guitar. Sometimes you just have to escape reality even if just for a moment.

Some months later I was thinking about Christine one day. On an impulse I rang her. She was genuinely pleased to hear from me. I told her that I wanted to apologise for not being there for them. Not for one second did they hold that against me. I was relieved for it was a weight lifted on my shoulders. They were some of the few farmers that I felt I had let down in the dark days. How pleased I was to see them when they walked into the new auction at Cockermouth for the first time.

16
OUR WORST NIGHTMARE

Sunday 1 April
Total national cases: 907

I awoke on Sunday morning feeling quite tired from the night before. I was however in a good humour because the phone had not rung. This meant that I had received no invitations from MAFF to value stock. As the morning wore on I was lulled into a false sense of security. Paula was pleased because this meant we could go to our friends' christening party. After a short church service we all congregated at Penrith Rugby Club. Believing I was off duty for the day, I thoroughly enjoyed a couple of pints with several old rugby mates. Obviously Paula would not be drinking!

By mid-afternoon we were home and I sent Paula upstairs for a rest. She certainly needed it. In a while the phone rang. It was Richard Weir from Borrowdale.

"Bad job isn't it?" he said.

"What's a bad job?" I asked innocently.

"Have you not heard? Steel's at Annshill have foot and mouth and some of my sheep are there." My heart sank so fast you could hear it hit the floor. Annshill was a dairy farm only one mile north of Cockermouth.

"That's it," I thought, " we're all dead now." I tried not to sound so defeatist. Richard wanted me to travel to Cockermouth immediately to value his stock. I explained that I could not due to the fact that I had had a pint or two. I did however agree to speak to the valuer from another firm who gone to value the cattle at Annshill. I rang the farm and gave the valuer an indication of the prices I had been giving for Herdwick sheep. I then rang Richard Weir to assure him that the job was in hand. For the next few hours the phone hardly stopped ringing. What could I say to the farmers around the Cockermouth area? They all wanted to know about the procedure if they got FMD. The same old questions were asked and answered again and again.

I just prayed that by some miracle the disease would spread no further. Maybe it was an isolated case. Just maybe we would all survive for it was truly our worst nightmare.

At around 9.30pm I took a call from Robin Bell at Moorland Close on the south side of Cockermouth. He sounded low and weary.

"I'm pretty sure we've got it Adam," he said. "The blood tests will tell us in the morning." He went on to explain that they had seen pretty clear clinical signs in some of his Suffolk sheep. We both wondered how the hell it had got there. There were numerous possibilities. Smoke from the pyres, everyone was talking about that one. What about dirty delivery vehicles or milk tankers? What about vets coming to inspect the stock? This was the most annoying thing about FMD. Nobody could ever be sure just how the disease travelled. Everybody had a theory but nobody could ever prove it. Either way, all the valuation work that I had done up to now was just a warm up. Now we were really in the heat of the battle. Cockermouth was front line now with no escape.

I promised Robin we would do what was necessary. That night I discussed the situation with Paula. She wanted to know where we stood if the new auction development could not go ahead. Now this stark possibility was becoming quite real. I realised that without the mart I would be out of a job with little hope of getting another in the field that I enjoyed so much. I tried not to be too pessimistic but I had to prepare Paula for the fact that we may have to sell the house we had busted a gut to buy only the previous year.

"We could always go around the world," I jested. The longer the campaign went on, the more I begin to think seriously about emigrating. Many other people engaged in the battle against foot and mouth probably felt the same way. Things were much different now. All of the valuation work I had undertaken previously had been out of 'our patch'. Now we were truly fighting our own front line battle. We were fighting for our farmers and truly for our own business now. I did not sleep well that night.

17
A FIGHT TO THE DEATH

Monday 2 April
Total national cases: 950

I arrived into the office early and held a conference with my colleagues. It appeared now that Cockermouth was surrounded by FMD. We were fairly sure from watching the Longtown, Carlisle and Penrith areas that the virus was being spread because slaughtered animals were not being disposed of quickly enough. Farmers were now being asked to volunteer their sheep for slaughter in an attempt to stop the spread. Clinical signs of the disease in sheep were in all cases difficult to spot. So difficult in fact that I was never actually shown a diseased sheep at any valuation I undertook. The cattle were of course a different matter.

Calls from local sheep farmers were coming in by the dozen. They all wanted a valuation immediately. Our resources were severely stretched. Up to that point, my colleague Alisdare Bruce and I had undertaken all of the valuation work. I was doing most of the dirty valuations while Alisdare concentrated for the most part on clean valuations. He was in a difficult position in that he and his wife owned sheep and cattle of their own. Therefore if he had contact with infected animals he could not go home. If he did so then MAFF made it quite clear that they would have no choice but to kill all of the Bruce's animals.

Sadly Alisdare did get caught on an infected premises although he obviously did not know at the time. Consequently he had to spend a few days in a hotel until he became clean. Had he gone home MAFF would have killed all of his wife's sheep and cattle immediately. Other valuers who were in the same predicament spent several weeks away from home in an effort to beat the disease. To some young and carefree valuers it would add to the excitement of the adventure. To older valuers whom may have been family men it would be a hardship to bear. I remain thankful that I was not affected in this manner. It was bad enough coming home from valuations late at night and crawling into bed next to my sleeping pregnant wife. At least I was there.

Robin Bell rang through. FMD was confirmed at Moorland Close and he needed us immediately. Now we had a problem; Alisdare and I were clean and we had no other dirty valuer. If either of us went dirty, we would be very undermanned to handle all of the voluntaries that were coming in. Our company secretary John Marrs spoke up.

"I'll go and do the valuation," he said without hesitation. It made sense. John's knowledge of livestock and especially dairy cattle was second to none within our company. His commitment to Cockermouth Mart had been unfaltering for over 30 years. Now in the hour of need he was up for the task. It was a massive gesture.

I rang Robin Bell to explain the situation. He was a little concerned that John had not valued for the FMD cull before. I assured him that Alisdare and I had fully briefed John. Robin agreed that John's stock judgement was unquestionable. I promised Robin that he would not be let down and John ensured that the promise was upheld in full.

With John duly dispatched to Moorland Close, Alisdare and I went off to our voluntary cull valuations. Our senior land agent also began to undertake this work. There was more than enough to keep us all busy.

I spent the rest of the day and many more besides in the Silloth area valuing field after field of away-wintered fell sheep. Nearly every Lakeland hill farm would be affected by the foot and mouth outbreak. Thousand upon thousand of gimmer hoggs, gimmer shearlings and breeding rams were all destined to die. Money could not replace this loss both to the Lake District farmer, and to the environment of Lakeland, be it overgrazed or not.

Meanwhile Alisdare was also in the field, valuing sheep within 3km of Annshill. Unbeknown to me he was having a spectacular argument with MAFF to save a dairy herd that was on an adjacent farm to the infected premises yet separated by the main A595 highway. Alisdare won and the cattle were saved. The Robinson family at Woodhall told me many months later how grateful they were that day for Alisdare's obstinate refusal to let the cattle go. Sadly there was little that could be done to save the sheep. There were many quality commercial flocks lost within that 3k, cull. Even now in 2003 some of those farms are only just beginning to restock with sheep.

I arrived home at 7pm and was disappointed to find that Olivia had already gone to bed. After supper I felt unable to sit down and watch television. I decided to go outside into the heavily overgrown garden that we had inherited when the house was bought the previous year. I began to dig a patch of dense weed and found that I rather enjoyed myself. It was without doubt quite therapeutic so I just kept going. My garden was to be my solace many nights through summer when I returned home from valuation days. I tried not to watch the television pictures from foot and mouth farms. Maybe I was putting my head in the sand, or maybe I was just trying to get by.

It was quite dark when I eventually came into the house. Paula had been watching the news. Tony Blair had postponed the election. "Great," I thought, " he's finally admitting that we have a problem here, even if he can't quite come out and say it." At least Nick Brown was no longer saying he had it under control. Instead, the disease was now following 'expected patterns'. I wish that those people who were obviously in the know had bothered to forewarn the farmers of Cockermouth! Now we were involved in a fight to the death. Like the rest of the county, we would beat the disease or it would beat us. At least we were ready for it.

18

"AND NE'ER THE TWAIN SHALL MEET"

Tuesday 3 April
Total national cases: 994

It was a cold and frosty spring morning as I travelled up to the village of Penruddock situated between Penrith and Keswick. I was to value some Swaledale ewes and breeding rams, again belonging to the Lamb family from Threlkeld. Previously I had already made two valuations on their behalf, both on infected premises. Some of my colleagues had also completed valuations for them. It was a pretty miserable time for that family. Thankfully their own farm did not succumb to the disease.

Whilst looking at the sheep I learned that most of the other sheep in surrounding fields had already been valued for the voluntary cull. In a few days all the fields around Penruddock, Motherby and Greystoke would be totally devoid of sheep. I completed the valuation and made my way back to the office to spend the rest of the morning trying to catch up on message requests for phone calls.

In the afternoon I visited Frank Hickson at Park House on the outskirts of Cockermouth. He was one of the most loyal supporters of Cockermouth mart. With a heavy heart he was sending all of his sheep on the voluntary cull in order to save his beef herd. The Annshill case was little more than a mile away over the River Derwent. In a few strokes of my pen 2,300 head of ewes, lambs and rams were destined for the pit at Great Orton. It was a sad and difficult day. I was losing one of my biggest sheep customers and he was losing far more than I was. Now he and his brother Edwin at Castle Carrock were both waiting uneasily to see if the sacrifice would be worthwhile. Frank was not to be so lucky.

Whilst in the final field of sheep at Park House, my mobile phone rang. It was MAFF (Carlisle).

"We would like you to proceed with all haste to Messrs Stamper's farm at Wellington. All stock must be slaughtered as dangerous contacts."

This was the neighbouring farm to Robin and Anne Bell at Moorland Close. Their stock had been slaughtered the previous day and now the dangerous contacts were being mopped up.

"Hang on a minute," I said to the MAFF official, "is this a dirty or a clean valuation? If it is dirty I cannot do it." The line went blank for a few seconds then the voice returned.

"It is a clean dangerous contact," they assured me. I had not heard of this before and pressed the point home.

"So the vet you are sending is clean too?" I questioned.

"Oh yes," came the reply, "we must have the valuation completed tonight." They went on to tell me that there were also two lots of away-wintered sheep on the farm to be valued as well. I thought it strange that the stock being dangerous contact, was to be slaughtered on the farm. However they had given me a cast iron assurance that the farm was clean. Therefore there could be no clinical signs on view. No doubt this would be confirmed by blood test after the animals were dead. Their proximity to Moorland Close was not in doubt. The diseased sheep there were just over the boundary from the sheep on Wellington. There could be no arguments on that score.

By 5pm I was at Wellington farm. By a strange quirk of fate both Moorland Close and Wellington were the farms from which the land for our new auction mart development was going to be purchased if the planned auction mart survived the foot and mouth disaster. It did not even register in my mind at that time. I was only concerned with getting the job done.

The Stampers and myself waited for some time for the vet to arrive. Eventually at around 6pm he arrived, left his car at the bottom of the farm lane and began to walk up to the farmyard. From a distance I asked him to confirm that he was a clean vet.

"No way," he shouted back, "I'm as dirty as hell." Indeed he had just come from an infected premises. I left him in no doubt that he should return from whence he came until I had spoken to MAFF (Carlisle). He went down the lane rather faster than he had come up it.

I rang them and gave them my opinion as to their handling of this particular case. The fact that I had been lied to was despicable. They had compromised me and possibly all of my colleagues through their desire to get the job done at all costs. There was no apology. Not wanting to let the Stampers down, I gave MAFF a solution.

"I will do the valuation if the vet stays off the premises until I complete my task."

"Not possible," came the reply, "our man has to oversee the valuation to make sure that it is undertaken in a correct manner."

"OK then," I persisted, "how about if I do the valuation and all paperwork then leave the farm and wait at the gate while the vet looks around all the stock and satisfies himself that I have done the job correctly?"

MAFF was hesitant. "Well I'll just leave now then," I said petulantly.

"No, no," they said "just let us speak to the vet on the phone."

"Well he's bloody well not holding mine," I shouted.

They rang him and he agreed to the whole procedure. Again I made them confirm that this was a clean valuation. They did so, and we were ready to start. While the vet sat in his car, Jim, Leigh and Hodgson Stamper and I began to put the dairy herd through the handling race. The vet had insisted that every single beast be separately identified and noted on the valuation. It was an endless task. As every cow came into the holding crush its ear number was checked and information given to me about its breeding, milk output, family history and so on. I asked for any snippet of information that would add value to the animal. Soon it was dark and we continued with the aid of a rigged-up light bulb and torch. It was a pretty thankless task but eventually we were done.

We were all glad to get into the kitchen for a cup of tea. It had gone very cold and our fingers were numb. By now the vet who had been standing about for a few hours was understandably impatient. He had had a long day and wanted to get finished. It was not his fault in any way. He was just doing his job. By 11.30pm the paperwork was done. I walked off the farm and handed the papers to the vet. Then I waited a few minutes while the vet completed his inspection. Soon he came into view and gave me the thumbs up. I was 'OK to go'. We had both done our jobs without being in contact. I was reminded of the poem "and ne'er the twain shall meet." Indeed we did not.

Months later Jim Stamper told me that the vet had done a good job and that he had rather taken to him, especially as a car full of MAFF field officers had pulled into the yard as we were valuing the animals. They had come to take blood samples from the cattle. The vet had not authorised them to enter the farm and they were sent away in even more forthright terms than I had used earlier. This had rather tickled Jim even at that very distressing time. The vet had intimated that the field officers should have been wearing spurs and stetsons!

As I drove home I pondered the whole performance and was increasingly annoyed by the performance of the valuation organisers at Carlisle. They had shown a blatant disregard for my health 'status'. The potential knock-on effect to my colleagues and other farmers could have been disastrous. Maybe it was felt that a clean valuer working along side a dirty vet was not sufficient dangerous contact. In that case, what the hell were we all doing there anyway?

How disappointing then that some time later on there were mutterings about the potential spread of disease from valuers and farmers themselves. We used so much disinfectant that it ruined our clothes, bleached our hair and destroyed our vehicles brake pads. It is as a rival auctioneer was to say: "We live in a blame culture and they are going to try and blame everything on everyone else."

When the Stampers received their valuation payment it was several thousands of pounds short. The reason given was that MAFF would not pay the slaughter premium charge that every farmer was entitled to claim when a beast goes from his holding to slaughter.

This was particularly strange in that the guidance documentation for the valuation procedure states that the valuer should take into account all premium payments for which the animal is eligible. The Stampers like many other farmers in the county have to date not been paid the slaughter premium. Even more frustrating is the fact there are others that have been paid the full amount. At this point in time it looks increasingly likely that farmers will have to take their own legal action in order to recoup their rightful valuation money in full.

19
But is it Enough?

Wednesday 4 April
Total national cases: 1024

The Dubbs farm at Eaglesfield near Cockermouth lies down a long narrow track. It is hidden from view, however the fact that it has a boundary with Moorland Close had not escaped MAFF's vigilance. In their opinion there was dangerous contact and the animals must die. Again I asked for confirmation that the valuation was clean. Again I was told that there were no clinical signs and so it could be deemed a clean valuation. On a bright sunny morning I made my way down to the farm.

Roger and Sarah Steel were yet more good customers of our company and they had strong plans for the future to bring their eldest son into the farming business as he left school. Now the plans were in tatters.

Roger and I travelled to my old home village of Mosser to value some sheep he was wintering on a rented farm. We were only a stone's throw now from the Loweswater valley. I was pleased not to see any of my old neighbours on the road as we drove along. It would have been painful to have to stop and explain. Nor did I want to give the vet who was travelling with us any opportunity to ask questions as to who farmed what livestock and where.

The three of us then spent an entertaining hour trying to round up the ewes, lambs and hoggs that were charging around the open plan fields, in order to count them. Cruelly we made the young female vet chase them as fast as she could. She had not had much experience with sheep and it was obvious.

"Don't let them past you, quick run, run, run. Awwh you let them escape again." She was a game one and she insisted on gathering them again and again. Each time they broke past her and we chided her for not being fast enough. It was a little light relief but we all knew that the worst was yet to come.

Back at the Dubbs, we began the cattle valuation this time under the supervision of a different vet. He was very good to work with. He had a 'you do your job and I'll do mine' attitude. He asked us not to waste time valuing individual animals on the sheets but instead to group them up into suitable valuation lots. This made my job far quicker and easier. The vet left me to do my work and promised to leave me alone until he was ready to sign the completed papers. It was smooth and easy except in the calf pens, for as soon as I had valued a pen of calves and Roger accepted the valuation, a team of slaughtermen began to bullet the young calves. The noise of the gun is not particularly loud but it does make a savage cracking noise. As we moved around the pens, heaps of calves lay behind us kicking their last. Roger visibly winced at the sound. We both tried not to look behind us as the calves dropped one by one to the floor. To ensure that the kill was a successful, one slaughter man had to pith the cattle. This involves inserting a length of sturdy steel wire through the newly made bullet hole and into the animal's brain. The animal may been stunned and paralysed by the bullet but may not clinically brain dead. By 'pithing' or vigorously ramming the steel wire into the brain, the slaughter man can be quite sure that the animal is totally dead.

Seeing this operation no matter how professionally undertaken was not pleasant for either Roger or me. We were both glad to get out of the shed and leave the killing crew to their work.

After a couple of hours I had completed the valuation and the paperwork. I called the vet into the farmer's kitchen where I had been working. Quickly we completed the paperwork and my job was done. As I packed up my belongings I asked Roger if he was genuinely satisfied with the valuation I had made on his dairy stock, beef stock and sheep.

After considering his response he said: "Well it looks good on paper but is it enough?" I looked at him quizzically. "Can you assure me that when I come to restock this farm in the autumn or whenever, that you have given me enough money to buy back the same animals at the same price? If you can tell me that now then I am satisfied." He sat back and looked me in the eye.

I realised with an uncomfortable shock that I could not give him that guarantee. This troubled me all the way back to the office and for several more hours. What if the valuations all we auctioneers were giving was not enough to enable farmers to restock? Nobody could answer the question because nobody could see into the future. I worried over this for quite some time especially as more and more stock was slaughtered within Cumbria and beyond. I have no doubt that every valuer was troubled by these thoughts as the campaign drew on.

On my way back to the office I was to value a single sheep for a lady in a local village who kept it as a pet in her orchard. She had been talking to the local farmers and wanted to be seen to do the right thing by volunteering poor Bessie, just as the local shepherds were volunteering their sheep. It was a nice and rather sad gesture.

Meanwhile my colleagues continued their daily grind to value other dangerous contact farms and voluntary culls as well. Each man was going through exactly the same procedure as me. We hardly ever met in the office to discuss the situation. We were never there at the same time. That said each has their own story to tell. I can only speak for myself.

One day two years later in the new auction, I broached the subject with Roger. I began to talk about his valuation day. Even then he could not talk about it and walked away from me. I will never mention it again. We both look to the future now.

"But is it enough?" Looking back now at the devastation, the loss of life and the human distress caused during the foot and mouth crisis, I don't think it ever will be enough!

20
'Twas the Sound of his Horn'

Thursday 5 April
Total national cases: 1060

I was in John Peel country on a cool overcast spring morning. However it was not the cry of the hounds or the rasp of a hunting horn that 'brought me from my bed', but rather the sound of my own car horn as I persuaded an old Swaledale ewe to cross the Caldbeck common road in front of me. Within a few days there would be little worry of motorists bumping into sheep on that particular common. My job was to value all of the sheep belonging to John Hickson at Beck Grange on the voluntary cull. This was the third Hickson brother that I had been called in to work for within the space of a few days. It was yet another valuation of hefted sheep in large numbers. Again the disease was kicking around in the neighbourhood, but no one could be sure where. There were several different hefts of Swaledale fell sheep to value and some very good blue-faced Leicester sheep too.

Soon the Caldbeck fells would be virtually devoid of sheep. Now it is hard to truly comprehend such a loss of life. They may never return to those fells in such number, for the hill shepherds have been persuaded not to restock in anything like the same number. Indeed it is proposed to restock the fells to only 30% of the original flock. In a few years people will be moaning that the fells are becoming over grown scrubs and the paths will be disappearing. "Where have all the sheep gone that we used to see?" will be the question. Of course the old hefts will have gone and with them part of Lakeland's wonderful farming heritage.

Soon I was on the road down to the Solway Plain to value yet more pure Herdwick hoggs and shearlings for several customers. In particular I was to value 90 young Herdwicks for Jean and Derek Wilson from Dockray. Jean is an enthusiast through and through. They were devastated to lose these sheep. Many were blood-lines that marked a lifetime's work and even more. The sheep were very strong and very good. I feel a little guilty that I did not spend more time admiring them, but I truly did not have the time. A quick count, inspection and valuation and I was on my way.

It was only many months later that I was to find out just how much they both grieved the loss of these sheep. Derek admitted that on the day that I completed the valuation he sat in his pick-up many miles away at his home and cried buckets. How brave of him to admit it. For Jean the loss must have been unbearable. They both wished they could have seen the sheep just one last time. Instead I was the one who had the privilege. It was one that I neither wanted nor had earned. I wish I had thought to take a photograph for them.

Thankfully Jean's enthusiasm for her sheep has not been dented even if her blood-lines have. Over one year later I visited the Wilson's own farm at Dockray near Penrith. As we travelled around the farm she pointed out various sheep asking my opinion of certain individuals. As I commented I continued to listen and learn for Jean and many of her contemporaries have forgotten more about the breed than I could ever hope to learn. Such days are among my most pleasurable. They were few and far between in the year of foot and mouth.

Those sheep on the Solway plain were gone, not forgotten and sadly missed, but as Derek says of Jean: "She was born with it and she will die with it for it is in her blood." No amount of money can buy that knowledge or replace the sheep that they lost. That is the truth of it.

It was late afternoon when I made my last call of the day. This was to see Arthur Ewbank who had previously farmed near Cockermouth but had recently retired to a farm near Wigton. My job was to value the sheep that Arthur had taken with him from the old farm to keep him and his brother occupied in their retirement.

Arthur is well known in horse racing circles formerly as a jockey, then as a trainer and now as a steward at Carlisle racecourse. In the past I have jokingly asked him to give me a tip because I have no knowledge of the 'form' whatsoever. On more than one occasion he has given me a winner. He is too modest a man to remind me, so I always remind him and he laughs.

On that particular day it was the early stages of Aintree weekend. As we sat and drank tea, we watched a race on TV. Arthur gave me a form guide of the horses without referring to the paper or the TV pundits. He knew his stuff and it was fascinating.

Once the race was run, we went to see the sheep and also inspected an old cow and calf that Arthur housed in his barn. It was the only cattle he owned and he was loath to turn them out into the fields with the virus floating about amongst his neighbours. He desperately wanted rid of the animals as soon as possible but MAFF would not take them even on welfare grounds. I promised to write a letter to support him and even offered a valuation figure. Eventually they were taken away as welfare cases. I am sure it was a relief to the Ewbanks.

By 7pm I was home, but yet again I had missed seeing my little girl whilst awake. No sooner had I walked through the front door than I heard a timid knock. It was Mrs Todd who lived in the village. She owned a few sheep which she kept as a hobby and because she was born of a farming family. Now she knew she must let the sheep go especially as so many sheep around the village had already been taken. I agreed to walk down to her fields. She even had some grazing the grass around the village hall. There was no grass left for the sheep and she had not been allowed to move them at all, so she was having to buy food for them and feed them almost by hand. I made the valuation for her and she insisted I take a pound coin to buy Olivia an ice cream from the village shop. It was a nice gesture.

In a few days the sheep had been taken away. Most of the fields were empty. Those that were not soon would be. My little girl asked me one evening why she could not see the sheep in the fields in front of our house.

"Where have all the sheep gone daddy?"

I choked on my reply: "They have all gone away but they will come back one day," I promised her. Indeed it was to be a joyous morning many months later, to be awoken by the sound of sheep in the field behind our house. They belonged to Mark Potter, the breeder of the record priced Herdwick tup. It was like Christmas. "Look what's in the field," I said to Olivia.

"Ooh," she exclaimed, "the sheep have come back." For very different reasons both father and daughter were delighted.

21
I'LL TAKE THE LOW ROAD

Friday 6 April
Total national cases: 1137

Friday morning was supposed to be a rare chance to catch up with office matters and some of the more 'normal' auction mart manager's jobs. Unfortunately it was not to be, for a local farmer who did business with several auction marts in Cumbria contacted me. Keith Harryman was a Lakeland farmer from the Newlands valley who in addition to his own hill farm rented various parcels of ground throughout the north of the county. That morning he asked me to go and do a voluntary cull valuation on approximately 100 ewes that were in the process of lambing. They were located on a huge rented grass park of around 70 acres a few miles south of Cockermouth. The land had been rented for the winter. Because of the close proximity of the disease he understandably had no desire to come anywhere near the sheep but he wanted to try and help other local farmers by getting the sheep off the premises as soon as possible. The problem was that he could not be sure of exactly how many sheep there were to value. They had brought the sheep to the fields in several journeys from home. As local custom dictates they would normally count, agree and pay for the number of live sheep, which they would then remove from the holding at the end of the winter grazing term.

"Sorry," said the farmer "you'll just have to count them yourself."

"I don't have a sheep dog," I said wryly.

Thankfully I did have a very supportive colleague in our land agent Rupert Joule who agreed to come with me to help me count the sheep. We arrived and walked into the park. The sheep were evenly spread out the length and breadth of the park. They certainly could not all be seen. Way in the distance there was some discernible movement in large patches of sieves. The sheep were in there somewhere, but the tall, rough grass hid them from view.

We decided to split the field into sections in order to try and count the sheep. We did not want them to panic and bolt. That would have made counting them impossible. I took the top third of the park and Rupert took the second third. We agreed to meet at the bottom next to the rough ground to see if we could flush the sheep out of the tall sieves.

I walked quietly and easily through the sheep. They were heavy in lamb and some had lambs at foot. Then I came across a ewe in distress. She had tried to push her lamb out for several hours but had been unsuccessful. She was clearly exhausted to the point of collapse. The lamb whose head had been delivered but nothing else was quite dead. I caught hold of her and attempted to pull the lamb out but I could not get it. Luckily Rupert had seen the problem and made his way over to assist. I held the ewe fast and Rupert managed to get a hand into the ewe to deliver the lamb. The dead lamb flopped to the ground. It was a huge single lamb. At least there were no others to get out. The ewe made a vain attempt to get to her feet but she could not manage, she was spent.

Rupert and I spent a while deciding what we should do. All of the sheep would be picked up and taken to Great Orton within a couple of days anyway. We made the ewe comfortable against the dike cast in the hope that she would not suffer any further until she was picked up. We left the lamb with her. What else could we do? No vet would have thanked us for the call out. It certainly was not the farmer's fault. He had not been near the sheep for several days. His own neighbours would have crucified him if they thought he had been travelling into an infected area. The sheep had been left to fend for themselves. The owner of the park was a businessman who may well have been out of the county. In any case it would have been unfair to expect him to tend the sheep. It was a horrible situation.

We returned to our original job. As Rupert and I moved down the field together we came across the carcasses of several more lambs and two dead sheep as well. It was grim. There were however several sheep that had lambed successfully and continued to suckle perfectly healthy lambs. Within the hour we had achieved what we felt was a fairly accurate count. I rushed back to the office and faxed the valuation sheet to the voluntary command centre at Penrith. The form would itself be handed in later on. For now I just wanted to get the valuation into the system in order to save any further suffering on the animals' part.

By late morning I was on my way to Eastriggs near Annan. This was to be my first valuation over the border. The sheep however were familiar to me. Two very well known Lakeland fell farms traditionally sent hoggs to winter on this farm each year. The female Herdwicks I saw were some of the best from Buttermere and Coniston. The Buttermere sheep belonged to Willie Richardson at Gatesgarth farm and were heafed to the Redpike and Fleetwith Pike mountain ranges. The Tilberthwaite sheep were owned by the Wilkinson family and were heafed to the Coniston fells. The forebears of the hoggs had been bred for generations to endure the hard winter conditions on these famous Lakeland fells. The pedigrees of some of the sheep could be traced back over 100 years at least.

The dairy farmer at Eastriggs was a true gentleman by the name of Mr Glendenning. He wanted the sheep to go as soon as possible in order to protect his own pride and joy, his dairy herd. He was however very sorry for the two farmers because he knew just what a loss the Herdwick sheep would be. He had put no pressure on the shepherds. Together we inspected the sheep which were of very high quality. It was, we agreed, a great shame that they must go. The valuation sheet was duly completed and I was soon on my way over to Brampton in the far north east of the county.

It was raining very hard as I pulled up to the end of the farm lane at Kinghill. The owner was a farmer's son from Cockermouth called Graham Hewitson. He had recently married and had bought the Brampton farm with his bride Zena to begin dairying in their own right. It was a very attractive farm. I watched Graham coming down the farm lane towards me. Understandably he did not want me to drive onto the farm. I had to remember that I was visiting from an infected area even though by MAFF standards I was quite clean myself.

Graham was wintering several hundred Herdwick and Swaledale hoggs for his father-in-law, Gordon Tyson who operated a big Lakeland hill farm at Troutbeck near Ambleside. Yet again Graham had not put any pressure on his wife's father. The decision to let the sheep go on the voluntary cull was purely the family's own. In turn they did not want to lose the sheep at all but felt a sense of duty to Graham to volunteer the sheep so that his own farm might be saved. All around Brampton the disease was raging. Graham however had battened down the hatches and was dogging it out.

We inspected the sheep in the pouring rain. They were good commercial hoggs that had wintered and done very well at Brampton. They would never see home again. Graham and I chatted a while longer, I think he was glad to talk. During that time for many farmers, the only means of communication was by telephone. There were no auctions to visit. Most farmers who escaped the disease hardly left their farms, as they felt like outcasts or lepers. Seeing me was probably the highlight of Graham's day. That shows just how dreadful a time we were all having! What a shame that I was not able to spend a leisurely hour or two having a walk around the farm with Graham. It would have been an absolute pleasure at any other time. Now I just wanted to get the hell out of there.

My last call of the day was to the south side of Brampton where I met up with Edwin Hickson yet again. I had seen so much of the Hicksons I was beginning to think that I was part of the family. At least I was in a rather more composed state of mind than the last time I had valued for him at home.

We inspected a batch of in-lamb ewes that had wintered on his rented ground on the outskirts of Brampton. The rain continued to teem down. It was as miserable as poor Edwin's mood. He had lost his sheep and was resigned to losing his dairy herd.

"It's going to get us sooner or later," he warned me, "be ready for a phone call" he said. Thankfully the phone call never came.

As evening fell I made my way back down the motorway. I had covered many miles and was tired and miserable. Pyres continued to burn and smoulder. All of my colleagues would be on their way home just like me. I had hardly given them a second thought but we were all living the same desperate hell. It was a savage existence. I looked forward very much to a decent meal at home with my long suffering wife. Maybe we would get the chance to have a talk this evening if I could get through all my telephone messages before she tired and went to bed. The one thing I really did not want to discuss was foot and mouth.

22
To Volunteer or not to Volunteer?

Monday 9 April
Total national cases: 1176

Over the weekend I undertook a couple of voluntary cull or 3km valuations in the Skelton area close to Penrith. By now these jobs were becoming routine. I am sad to think that I gradually became blasé about the number of Lakeland fell sheep that were being taken from away-wintering farms. With hindsight maybe I was blocking the reality out. In many cases I just wanted to get the job done and move on to the next farm. Most of all, I worked all day just looking forward to driving home in the evening.

On Saturday night I was contacted by Mark Potter who was fighting to save his very best Herdwick gimmer hoggs. They were away-wintering on a farm near Appleby. Now the disease had reached those parts. Many farms on the east fellside of the Pennine ranges were being taken out. For every infected farm that MAFF listed on the website, at least another four neighbours were being taken out as dangerous contacts. The Government refused to acknowledge these farms in their official figures. The valuers of Cumbria knew the truth very well.

Now the Pennine range, the backbone of England, was under attack. Many of the farms that make the fellside what it is were having their backs broken. We all carried on regardless.

Mark Potter whom I had spoken to many times during the crisis appreciated the concerns of the farmers near Appleby.

"It's no good Adam lad," he sighed "I know I'll never get them home now."

"People have to know what's going on Mark," I said. "This is not right. Something more has to be done to save the sheep."

"If only we could," he said.

I told him we needed publicity. I had been contacted by Channel Four News who wanted to film a valuation actually taking place. I asked Mark if he would let them interview him. He considered it but decided against it. I understood, why should he bare his soul on national TV? What difference would it make? Ben Gill the NFU president had broken down on national TV after a meeting with the Government. It had not done any good. Those of us connected to the crisis on the ground knew just why he felt so utterly helpless and demoralised. The people who he was trying to connect with were so remote; they hadn't got a clue what had been going on. Mr Brown continued to tell us that they were in control. Mr Gill's emotional outburst proved how wide of the mark those statements really were.

"I wish Blair would get himself onto a farm," I said bitterly and not for the first time, "then he would understand." None of the politicians had the guts to do it until well after the killing had stopped. There was not much of the Churchill spirit in our ministers at the time.

I contacted Channel Four News and offered to meet them on a voluntary cull valuation as they had previously requested. I wanted them to understand the effects of losing so many of our fell sheep. They decided not to bother. I suppose it was not an exciting enough story. There had to be bodies and smoke and tears while I wanted to show them live healthy sheep.

That night actually on Channel Four News, Nick Brown was heard to say that EU approval had been gained to vaccinate sheep hefted to particular areas. I wondered whether our Minister for Agriculture even knew what a hefted Lakeland sheep looked like. The last time I saw him interviewed on TV the female news presenter had pushed Mr Brown on the published number of foot and mouth affected farms. Time and again he repeated that every single infected premises was named on the MAFF website and gave the current total as if it was only a trivial number showing that the problem was well under control. He had often repeated it. His definition of control differed somewhat from the rest of us.

"Ask him about the dangerous contacts," I screamed at the TV presenter, "go on ask him!" But it was no use. The presenter was obviously not well enough briefed and she let the matter drop. Had she asked him the question I wonder whether he would have admitted how many other farms had been taken out across the country. For that would have been a truer representation of the scale of the disaster.

So upset was I that the minister had been let off the hook that I must admit I had a good rant for about five minutes before I calmed down. My long-suffering wife just shook her head. "What good will it do? she enquired. Sadly she was right for the answer to her question was "not one iota." The minister was 'spinning' and we were the ones that could not get off the merry-go-round.

Early on Monday I travelled to Flusco near the old Troutbeck mart on the A66. Here I met Mark Potter and we went to value some in-lamb ewes that would have to go on the voluntary cull.

"Answer me this Adam lad," he quizzed, "just because these sheep are within three kilometres of an infected premises, do I really have to 'volunteer' them?"

"I think you do," I replied.

"Then why is it called voluntary then?" It was the same old question that kept coming back again and again. The fact that the EU was supposed to be funding the majority of the contiguous cull led me to believe that our Government must have done a deal with the EU to reduce the number of sheep in this country. It all began to look very suspicious. Nevertheless I did not subscribe to the many conspiracy theories that were being bandied about. I reckoned that men far more learned than me would get to the bottom of the voluntary valuation concept. My job was to go to the farms where farmers wished me to value their stock either for immediate slaughter or to be taken away. Recriminations would start later. In fact in 2003 for the first time, some damning evidence has been produced particularly by a university research group which challenges the whole legality of the contiguous cull. At the time of writing this issue is gathering momentum. Sadly it won't take away the dreadful memories of valuing thousands of healthy animals shortly before their death.

Having left a fairly miserable Mark Potter I travelled down to Appleby to value his special hoggs. They were on a farm alongside some sheep owned by Stan Jackson from Rosthwaite in the Borrowdale valley. They both had good sheep. I stood at the top of the bank looking down on them for a few minutes. It was a mild spring morning; the daffodils were in full bloom. Those lambs should have been going home to be dipped, dosed and sent to the high fells for summer. It was not to be. I drove away after completing my valuation.

On my way back to the office I stopped off at Newton Reigny near Penrith to value yet more Herdwick hoggs. These were smaller and plainer than those I had seen earlier in the day. Had I been selling them in the auction I would have joked that they had been born late, meaning that they were younger.

Of course the fell hoggs that I was valuing by the thousand were never ever sold by auction. Their value was in the heafing. The only time they are ever for sale is when a fell farm is taken over by a new farmer. The value of the heaf is added to the general market value that they might be worth in the auction. It is of course in the interests of the incoming farmer to pay the extra for sheep that are bred to his fell and acclimatised to it. Putting a true value to a hefted flock that was going to be wiped out was an all but impossible task. It hurts and disappoints me to say that the values of the sheep culled from Lakeland farms does not reflect the true loss to those shepherds. With hindsight I do not believe that we gave enough money for them. I would not know where to begin to put a true price on these special blood-lines.

The rest of the day was spent in the office. It was difficult to concentrate for long. All of the valuers were tired and drawn. It was not just the physical and mental demands of our work but also the growing realisation that the new mart development, now on hold, may not happen. My wife was becoming increasingly fraught that the new baby would arrive and I would lose my job. I decided to discuss the matter with one of our directors. I asked him if he would guarantee our jobs at least until the epidemic was over even if it took until Christmas. He of course could not make that guarantee. I had a three month notice period on my contract and that is what it would be.

"It won't be long until June," I thought, "the baby will be here and I'll have to sell the house." I drove home miserably wondering whether to tell my wife of the conversation. I even toyed with the idea of handing in my notice and working freelance to build up as much money as possible until the end of the crisis. This might, I reasoned, save my house until I could find a proper job. Thankfully my pride and belief in the new mart proposal would not let me do it. I had stuck it out for so long, I was not going to give in now. I vowed to fight on until the bitter end. All of my colleagues did likewise and much later we were to be rewarded.

23
No Visitors, Thank You

Tuesday 10 April
Total national cases: 1209

If spring was just around the corner there was little to show for it as I made my way across Cumbria. My first port of call was to see a farmer who I did not know. He had some sheep belonging to the Hewitson family of Shatton Lodge near Cockermouth that he was wintering. I had visited their brother at Brampton the previous week. In a normal year the sheep would have returned home long before now. Due to FMD they were stuck fast. Now they were to be destroyed on the voluntary cull. The owner of the farm had his own cattle and wanted to get rid of the sheep as soon as possible. I was greeted with courtesy but told to go and see the sheep myself. The farmer had not been anywhere near them. Nor had the owner of the sheep. It was a pattern I had seen before. The sheep had been left to fend for themselves.

I 'suited and booted' then walked into the cow pasture to view the sheep. It was difficult to get an accurate count especially when so many of the sheep were in the process of lambing. As I walked among the ewes I was a little disturbed to see several lambs lying dead and quite a few lame sheep. I put this down to the fact that the landowner had said that he had not tended the sheep recently. I knew that the disease was close by and for a second I looked at the sheep and wondered whether they had succumbed to the disease. The weather was bitterly cold that week and young texel cross lambs would suffer on any farm in those conditions especially without management.

I completed the task and walked back to the car. I was met by the farmer and assured him that I would send the valuation form into the cull command centre immediately. I then mixed up a strong batch of disinfectant and thoroughly scrubbed up. I finished by pouring the mixture over my hooded head. The farmer laughed accusing me of going over the top. My instinct told me to do it. I had been disturbed by the state of the sheep. It was a precautionary measure. I also pressure washed the car from top to bottom using the farmer's equipment. There was disinfectant in the mixture.

My next visit was a short journey to the village of Edderside. Here I was met by the Scott family who like so many others had a myriad of wintering sheep on the farms. I had gimmer hoggs and shearlings to value from several hill and marginal farms. I was made most welcome despite the fact that the villagers had all but barricaded themselves in. Every access road into Edderside had a temporary barrier across. A sign asked visitors not to enter the village unless really necessary. It was a case of 'no visitors thank you'. I almost felt guilty at moving the barrier. I did not really want to be there anyway.

Mr Scott senior drove me around the farm in his Land Rover. We looked at some very nice Swaledale gimmer shearlings belonging to the Lawson brothers at Cathow Farm near Ennerdale. We also saw some good hoggs from Ted Allan at High Nook, Loweswater. Finally we saw some more of the Hewitson's mule hoggs which were on another farm close by.

Mr Scott was visibly upset by what was happening. As we pulled up at the entrance to one field he could stand it no more. He sobbed for some time.

"I've seen some bad times in my farming life," he said, "but I've never known anything like this."

There was nothing I could say. I sat in uncomfortable silence. Not out of embarrassment but more from a growing realisation that so many people were suffering from what was happening.

Eventually my job was done. I scrubbed up then moved on down to the coast road. The sun had come out. It was early afternoon. I bought a sandwich in Allonby then drove down towards the beach. I sat in the car looking out across the Solway Firth to Scotland. Criffel looked magnificent as always. I could not face going back to the office for a while so I just sat and stared, trying to make sense of what was going on.

My mobile phone rang. It was Peter Greenhill our company chairman. He had been fighting his own battle trying to get to talk to politicians and scientists. He had managed to secure the ear of one of the leading Government politicians involved in FMD. Peter was very much in favour of a vaccination programme to stop the disease outright. He wanted to know what farmers in general were thinking about vaccination.

We talked for a while. My personal opinion was that I did not know enough about the pros and cons. It was a minefield of a subject. What we did agree was that if something was not done to radically alter FMD policy then all livestock could be wiped out in Cumbria. There would be nothing left. I could not get this out of my mind.

I took a last look at the seashore then drove away. In a few minutes I was back at my desk catching up on what my colleagues were doing in their own private war.

A few days later the first farm I had visited that day did succumb to the disease and was posted on the MAFF website. Benson Hewitson saw it and contacted me to question me about the state of the sheep. I was forced to admit that they were in bad condition with many lost lambs. I had put that down to the fact that the farmer had refused to tend the lambing sheep, which he had admitted. Who could blame him? The most distressing thing was that I had gone on to other farms afterwards. That is why instinctively I had scrubbed down so thoroughly that my wellingtons and my eyebrows got bleached!

Many valuers had been caught in similar circumstances. It is easy with hindsight to say I should have contacted MAFF if I had suspected anything. I did not suspect anything at the time for I had enough of my own worries trying to get through the valuations that I had been requested to do. The farmer's excuse was easily plausible. Even so it left me with a very uncomfortable feeling for a while afterwards. None of us truly knew where the disease was as we travelled around doing our jobs. As I have said before it was like guerrilla warfare and we could rarely see the enemy. It was not my job to diagnose FMD in those situations, nor would I even try to.

24
Bringing the Bodies to West Cumbria

Thursday 12 April
Total national cases: 1263

Over the last 48 hours I had travelled over much of north Cumbria valuing away-wintered sheep for the voluntary cull. Little did I know that the small part I was playing was contributing to a massive backlog of animals on Cumbrian farms that were waiting for slaughter or live collection. In fact almost one million cattle, sheep and pigs had been or were being valued for the cull. The so-called 48-hour target was far from being achieved. Those persons in a position of power must have known this. Yet again no one could or would provide sufficient resources to dispose of the animals. Meanwhile those of us on the ground continued daily to do our best as quickly and as professionally as we possibly could. There was no thought of days off or the number of hours we were working. We all had a job to do for our farmers and our county.

On this particular day I found myself fairly close to Cockermouth valuing sheep for Brian Whitfield. He had some sheep wintering on a dairy farm near Deanscales. Brian knew that the sheep would be worrying the farmer David Sanderson who, like so many farmers in a similar position, would prefer them not be there. Reluctantly Brian was letting the sheep go on the voluntary cull. We walked around them. They were nicely bred texel cross lambs.

I had not seen Brian for several weeks and we talked at length about the disease and about the proposed new mart development. I had hardly thought about the new mart plan recently. The scheme was indefinitely on hold. I told Brian that we had worked non-stop over the last few days to try and halt the spread of the disease. The fact that all of the sheep within a three mile radius of Cockermouth were now gone seemed to be paying dividends. No further cases had occurred near Cockermouth and I hoped that the sacrifices made by local sheep farmers would keep West Cumbria clear of disease from now on. We agreed that all the signs were encouraging. If there were no further cases I was sure that we would get a new livestock mart. If however there were more losses in our area, a new mart may not be sustainable. I would be out of a job and local farmers would not have a market. Brian felt that it would be a disaster for all farmers. He wished me luck and I drove back to the office.

I walked into the main office to be met by a lot of glum faces. Trevor Place from Strawberry Howe farm on the outskirts of Cockermouth had just become a confirmed case. We were gutted. After all our efforts we had not beaten foot and mouth. John Marrs yet again volunteered to go and do the valuation leaving the remaining auctioneers clean for voluntary cull valuations. There might be a whole lot more now, as a newly confirmed case would result in a new 3km cull zone. I felt bitterly sorry for Trevor and Mandy, a young farming couple who had just taken on the tenancy of the farm within the last year or so. They were so full of enthusiasm for their new business. Now the dairy herd that had been built up previously by Mandy's parents would be gone. It would be enough to break some farming partnerships. I hoped that this young couple would survive. Thankfully they did, but for now John Marrs had the unenviable task of valuing the whole herd before slaughter.

A phone call was put through to me from Jim Cosker one of our local NFU branch secretaries. I had been very impressed by the efforts of the Cockermouth NFU office throughout the crisis. They kept me informed of all developments, released Government statements and policy amendments. Jim told me that there was to be a public meeting at Distington that very evening. MAFF, the local council and the army wanted to address local people about the possibility of bringing slaughtered foot and mouth infected bodies into the Distington landfill site. I knew there would be massive opposition to such a scheme, especially when considering that there had been no disease whatsoever in West Cumbria beyond Cockermouth. I readily agreed to go.

The school hall at Distington was packed with local people and farmers. Jim and I sat on the front row in front of a table full of local councillors, a MAFF official by the name of David Wallace and our local DEFRA vet John Kelsey, who was well known to me. There were also two representatives of the Environment Agency and an Army officer whose name was Major David Holt. He spoke first.

"If you shout at me," he warned, "I leave. If you heckle me," he continued, "I leave. In fact if you interrupt me at all when I speak, then I leave." A murmur of disapproval travelled around the hall. Major Holt stared long and hard at the audience. It sounded as if he had come for a battle but was going to retreat if he was attacked. He was outwardly aggressive. I felt it to be unnecessary but he was obviously going through his own kind of hell just as we were.

It was long after the end of foot and mouth during an honest conversation with former Brigadier Alex Birtwistle that I came to realise what a massive strain was placed upon the army leaders who had to enter the game so late yet try and make an impact. Major Holt had his job to do and tonight it was going to be done the only way he knew how - his way or not at all.

In matter of fact tones he told the gathered audience that the purpose of the meeting was not to discuss the proposal of using Distington landfill but in fact to inform and explain to everyone that the first load of carcasses had already been delivered to the site fifteen minutes prior to the start of the meeting. There was uproar. People shouted and pleaded against this action. It was a powder keg and Major Holt had lit the fuse.

Local councillors tried to reason with the people. They had obviously been told that it was a *fait accompli*. Reluctantly they were toeing the party line. The MAFF official who spoke with some authority and confidence on disease management explained that every precaution possible would be taken to minimise the risk of disease spreading into West Cumbria. Major Holt added that 'their predictive models' indicated that the disease should already have come this far into West Cumbria. This drew widespread argument around the hall. What models? What predictions? Why were MAFF expecting the disease to already be here? Why was West Cumbria going to be sacrificed as a dumping ground for diseased bodies?

As the meeting went on, the news became more and more grim. Tens of thousands of bodies from all over the North of England were to be brought along the A66 to Distington. They would travel right through the heart of Cumbria. It was obvious to everyone in the room that the plan, which had already been sanctioned at high level, would be a disaster. I felt my hackles rising and decided to speak out. I raised my hand and kept it up until eventually the chairman of the meeting allowed me to say my piece.

"My name is Adam Day," I began trying to keep a level of control in my voice, "I am a local auctioneer who has just spent the last 24 days without a break valuing sheep and cattle about to be destroyed. I have worked alongside some of Major Holt's men recently. We have all tried very hard to stop the disease spreading. The farmers of Cockermouth have sacrificed their sheep in order to try and save West Cumbria. So far we have been successful." I drew a deep breath to deliver my question and punch line.

"Could I ask the gentleman from MAFF to give all the farmers sitting in this room tonight a cast iron guarantee that the safety measures in place at Distington will prevent any chance of the disease spreading to local farms?" I looked the man in the eye.

He stared resolutely to the back of the hall and in a matter of fact tone said: "I cannot give that guarantee." Yet again the room erupted.

"Can I remind you," I shouted over the noise, "can I remind you that you have a duty of care to protect the farmers in this area. If you cannot give such a guarantee then you have failed us all." There were shouts of agreement. I had to sit down because I was becoming too emotional.

Major Holt stood up. To my surprise he thanked me and all the other valuers working with his men. He said he understood what we were going through and we were he thought doing our job very well indeed. There was, he said, no other option other than to use the Distington site. There were other sites that would also be used in the county. Every option had been explored, but there was no other choice. I could tell he was being totally honest. The disposal of bodies had obviously reached melt-down. It was a disaster of epic proportions. So much for Mr Brown and his 'everything is under control' statements.

The meeting began to degenerate. Then Willie Lawson from Stubbsgill who farms the land around the Distington site stood up behind me. He took a few steps towards the top table. I thought he might be about to hit someone but he simply stood before them. There were tears of rage in his eyes. He told them that his sheep grazed alongside the boundary fence within yards of the tipping area. Even if he wanted to move them he was not allowed to due to MAFF's imposed livestock movement restrictions. He told them that MAFF were going to kill his farm and maybe many more friends and neighbours too. There were no answers. The councillors looked at the floor, the MAFF man looked out front, chin held high, Major Holt looked at his watch.

The chairman realising that nothing more could be done brought the meeting to a swift halt. The army left immediately. I saw the MAFF man from a distance. He was smiling, probably with relief, having escaped the ordeal in tact. I felt sick, tired and so very fed up.

Jim and I drove back to Cockermouth. There I phoned my chairman to let him know what was happening. He immediately contacted some people in the local media. He rang me back to say that there was very little could be done. It was the night before the Easter holidays. Most of the press were on low alert or stand down. Nobody wanted to deal with it until Tuesday. I could not help but think that we had been done like a kipper. I felt very bitter driving home that night. Everyone connected with farming in our area was being so badly let down.

I climbed into bed next to Paula knowing that I could not let myself get too down and disheartened. I had to fight on. How many more tragedies would we have to face before we got through this crisis? I was fast approaching the end of the road and beginning to feel like I did not want to carry on much longer. I needed a break but felt guilty for even thinking about it. Even so, sleep came quickly.

25
THE LONG GOOD FRIDAY

Friday 13 April (Good Friday)
Total national cases: 1293

Good Friday has always been a memorable day for me. I can remember several of them as a child at my grandfather's farm, working amongst the new born lambs and rolling pace eggs down the pasture fields. Later as a teenager I remember helping my father lay a paved patio in the scorching heat of a late spring day. During my first proper job I helped the Clark family at Mosser Mains erect hundreds of metres of post and wire fencing. More recently I can remember playing rugby against touring sides and enjoying the festivities afterward. I once spent a drunken Good Friday in Dublin, myself a member of a touring team. In fact I always seem to have had something interesting to do on Good Friday.

I awoke early and remembered that I had a busy working day ahead of me. This Good Friday would be different from any other for I was on the road, valuing sheep for slaughter on the voluntary cull.

My first visit was to a field on the outskirts of my home village Greystoke. Here I met Mike Beaty from Home Farm, Patterdale and inspected yet more Herdwick and Swaledale fell hoggs that were wintering on his own land at Greystoke. It was an all too common pattern and I wondered how many thousands of young sheep from Lakeland farms had or were about to lose their lives. I doubted that we would ever know.

I said my goodbyes and drove to West Cumbria to follow the familiar pattern once more. It was just another working day and it did not occur to me that it was a religious holiday. Perhaps in the back of my mind there was a hankering to be at home with my baby daughter and pregnant wife, but I had an essential job to do.

It was a grey overcast day as I pulled into the lane at East Farm, Crosscannoby. The Carruthers family is stretched across the county. There are several brothers farming with their families in their own right. Now I was at Norman Carruther's farm in order to value away-wintered Swaledale hoggs for his brothers who farm near Bampton, south of Penrith.

As I walked down to the fields with Norman's son Alan, I was struck by how close to the Solway Firth East Farm actually lies. We were but a few hundred yards from the beach. The air was clear and strands of sunlight danced across the open water. Criffel stood across the water in her rounded magnificence. So often I had seen the mountain on my valuation travels over the last few weeks.

My attention soon turned to the sheep and what sheep they were! These Swaledale gimmer hoggs were among the biggest and best I had yet seen.

"What monsters!" I exclaimed.

"Aye not bad sheep," said Alan in a deadpan voice. Cumbrian farmers are always so modest when discussing their own or indeed their family's sheep. I placed a good valuation on them and completed the paperwork there and then.

Walking back to the farm I spied another field full of Swaledale hoggs.

"Whose are they?" I enquired. Alan told me that they belonged to another breeder who did not want me to value them, preferring more of an 'expert' in the Swaledale field. I did not mind but could not help but notice that the sheep I had valued were at least as good if not better than the ones I was walking past. I smiled to myself and thought that it was pretty obvious even to a 'non-expert' like myself.

Soon I was on my way again to my friend and mentor David Robinson's farm at Dovenby Craggs. This was the man who backed his judgement in me as an auctioneer by persuading me to accept a job at Mitchell's Auction Company Limited. As company chairman he persisted in telling me that there would be a new auction at Cockermouth and I was good enough to be part of the team. As a lowly trainee auctioneer at Penrith auction mart, the man's enthusiasm and passion for the cause was infectious to me. Back then in 1994 I was unable to say no. Actually it was not difficult to accept the job because I had 'worked' for Robbo before, in my short time at Aspatria Rugby Club when he persuaded me to have a go at a higher level of rugby. At the time I was bordering on the second XV at Penrith having struggled to recover from major knee surgery. My friends thought I was crackers and would never so much as play one game for Aspatria 1st XV. Not so Robbo. He believed in me and within one month I had played my first game in the national league.

I drove into the yard and was welcomed into the farm kitchen. Many times had I sat at the long table. Sometimes taking praise and sometimes taking real stick, but that is Robbo, firing from the hip with a total passion for all he does. We talked for some time about the disease and of course the valuations. It was now becoming apparent that valuation levels were rising. Stock being killed now was worth more than the same stock killed in the previous month. I do not know who was setting the trends but I did keep in touch with trusted auctioneering acquaintances. I knew exactly what was being given and of course at all times had to follow the market trend. The valuations given by me and my office colleagues were always fair and reasonable. We made sure we could justify every price we submitted to MAFF.

Robbo asked me why prices were rising. I told him that in many cases the stock we were valuing would never ever be for sale on the open market. These were exceptional times requiring exceptional valuations. I also reminded him of the local farmer who had asked me to guarantee him that his valuation money would definitely restock his farm. The amount of dairy farms and hill sheep farms that had lost all or some stock was rising fast. There might be no animals left with which to restock, especially if vaccination took place and all stock had to be killed as a result of the vaccination plan. All these thoughts were playing on the valuers' minds. There was zero guidance from MAFF on the subject other than some ridiculous book price figures that had been published.

Robbo clearly saw the problem we were facing but informed me that certain valuers were gaining reputations for giving more than others. I too had heard this but refused to be in anyway swayed into upping my figures simply because Mr So and So from down the road was offering more than me. Robbo praised our integrity but worried that we might start to lose valuation work if other valuers were touting for trade. I told him that this was already the case. It gave me greater respect for the farmers who carried on using their local auctioneer instead of importing in a valuer who they thought might be prepared to offer more.

We walked down the cow pastures in front of the house and saw Robbos' own pure Texel breeding sheep. They were fine animals to the last.

"Come on how much?" he enquired. I fired a price back at him straight away. He gave me that wide Robbo grin.

"That's just a commercial price," he said gently.

"Yes but you've given me no pedigrees yet," I smiled back.

"Typical Robbo," I thought, "my own director and determined to have a barter." He gave me more information and I considered the sheep.

"Come on then," I said "where do you value them?" Now the boot was on the other foot.

"Well I just don't want to sell them but I have to don't I?" It was a common line among many farmers. Many times I had been told: "If the buggers insist on taking them then they can bloody well pay for the privilege." I could sympathise with that line of thought but it always had to be within the bounds of a reasonable market price.

Robbo suggested a figure. I knew it would be high and of course it was. Over the next few minutes we bartered back and forth. I reminded him that I was actually working for MAFF. "Don't I bloody know it," he said. Eventually we settled on a figure that was fair and reasonable. We both signed the valuation form. All was well and I had enjoyed our innocent barter.

"You know I really don't want to see them go," he said afterwards. I knew he meant it but how could he keep them with so many neighbours around him desperately wanting to save their cattle and so many fields gradually being emptied of sheep on the voluntary cull.

We walked further down the pasture and into a field of away-wintering fell hoggs from Richard Weir at Church Farm in Borrowdale. There were 399 of them and the grass was all but gone. They were starting to lose condition but of course they could not be moved into a fresh field. I looked carefully through them.

"These sheep will have to go quickly," said Robbo. I agreed. There was also another field of hoggs from another farm. The owner had employed a valuer from another company who had visited Dovenby Craggs a few days previously to me. Robbo told me that the valuer had turned up at the farm entrance, viewed the sheep from a distance, not bothered to count or inspect, then said: "That'll do me for today," as he drove off. We both thought that it was not a very professional attitude.

"He must have been in a hurry," I said trying to defend the man who I knew quite well. It was a pretty feeble excuse.

Soon I was back into my office where I met David Charters another of my colleagues who had agreed to 'man' the office at weekends in case any valuation requests came in. He gave me several messages and we chatted over a cup of coffee. We had hardly talked over the last few months. It was nearly 3 o'clock and being Good Friday I told him to knock off early and go home. He did so and over the next hour I completed some valuation forms and filed copies then drove to my last valuation of the day.

As I drove into the yard of Benson and Alison Hewitson at High Stanger I was dog tired. I had already valued several lots of away-wintered sheep for them. They met me and we had a brief look at all the sheep that we had to value. I hardly got out of the Land Rover. I knew the type of sheep well enough having already valued a few lots of away-wintered sheep for them. They are fine stock handlers and always turn their stock out to best advantage. It is an art at which they excel no matter what they sell in the auction mart. We went back to the house and had some tea whilst I wrote up the valuation. I really wanted to get home and soon made my goodbyes.

I felt an innate sense of relief as I flew down the A66 to Penrith. As I approached the auction mart site I rang in to the voluntary cull HQ in the Furniture Hall. By the time I pulled up to the site entrance, Mary, one of the Penrith market staff now working for MAFF met me at the gate and collected a full envelope of completed forms. They had been gathered by me over the last few days and were now being handed in. The big mistake I made, although I did not know it at the time, was that in completing the forms I had put Good Friday's date on all of them. To anyone reading the forms, it looked as if I had done most of the valuations on one day. In fact some of them had been completed on Wednesday and Thursday.

By 6.30pm I was on my way home. Thankfully my little girl was wide awake and we enjoyed a good play together. I let her stay up later than normal just to spend some time with her. She knew nothing of what was going on other than Daddy was not at home very much. Later when she went to bed I sat with Paula and tried to watch TV. It was impossible. I could not concentrate and fidgeted hopelessly. Paula knew what was wrong and did not question me. I just could not face telling her what was happening or how I felt. Looking back I know that I was keeping the shutters down in order to stay in control. I knew I was fast losing it. I also knew that if I did not get a day off pretty soon, I might not be able to carry on. That frightened me more than anything else did. As always I was glad to get into bed and turn the light out. There no one could see me, at least for a few hours.

26
EASTER BODIES, NOT BUNNIES

Saturday 14 April (Easter Saturday)
Total National Cases: 1308

Easter Saturday was just another day of the same routine. So many voluntary cull valuation requests were building up in the file, we could not cope. We were even getting requests from other auctioneers to help them out with their backlog. Meanwhile the number of animals awaiting slaughter kept mounting up, as did some of those already lying dead in heaps on infected premises. I badly wanted to see the request file diminishing but more and more kept coming. By now there were four valuers from Mitchell's doing 'clean' valuations for the voluntary cull and one valuer on the 'dirty' farms. We hoped that this would not have to change. If however the disease did take off in West Cumbria we knew that at least one clean valuer would have to go dirty. I knew it would probably have to be me.

I drove back to West Cumbria first thing in the morning to a farm within a few hundred yards of where I had been the day before. David Anderson made me most welcome at Crosby Hall. He was cheery and up beat even though the disease was rapidly approaching his village. He told me that he was most anxious to get rid of the sheep that he was wintering for others on the farm. His main priority like so many others was to save his herd of quality dairy cattle.

In fact David Anderson had phoned me several times about the sheep to see if the owner had made his mind up to 'let them go' on the cull. The owner of the sheep was David Bland from West Head near Thirlmere. He was wrestling with his conscience as to wether to cull the sheep or let them stay on the farm in order to try and save them, knowing full well that if they contracted foot and mouth then David Anderson and many of his neighbours would be culled out immediately.

David Bland bitterly wanted to save all of his sheep but especially a run of 30 or so Herdwick ram hoggs. These sheep were his farm's total supply of ram hoggs born the previous year. If they died then so would some of David's most noted ram breeding lines. It was a familiar pattern I had seen in other Herdwick sheep both male and female that were destined to die. Such was the loss of this type of sheep that I had already had some breeders refuse to let them go on the cull causing huge resentment from the owner of the land who wanted to save his own stock.

In this case both parties were gentlemen to a tee. David Anderson wanted the sheep to go but would not in anyway try to pressurise David Bland into letting them go. David Bland on the other hand fully appreciated how the other man felt and did not want his sheep to be responsible in the event that foot and mouth appeared in the village. On that basis I had been called in but I knew fine well how it was hurting the Bland family. If they could have had one last look at those hoggs, I knew they would have jumped at the chance. Sadly it could not happen.

Many times since the end of the FMD crisis I have regretted that I did not take a camera with me. However at the time the only priority was to do my job quickly and efficiently. Besides that, taking photographs of animals that would have secured my future employment had they lived would have been quite difficult at the time when I was desperately trying to expunge any thoughts about losing my livelihood at the end of my foot and mouth valuations.

David Anderson and I viewed and counted all of the sheep. Nothing more could be done and I bade him farewell. The sheep were picked up and transported away for slaughter. Soon after, the disease infected several farms in Crosby. David Anderson fought hard to save the lives of his healthy dairy cattle but it was to no avail. Eventually all his animals were killed.

Back on the road I was heading for Aspatria when my mobile phone rang. It was Radio Cumbria wanting a response to the Distington fiasco. Would I give a comment they asked?

"What is the point now?" I asked. "There will already be thousands of bodies dumped in a heap there. It's just too late." I declined to comment any further but the real truth was that I felt so very low driving along. I really had had enough at this time. I felt utterly miserable. I just could not face talking about it on live radio. I wanted to be anywhere else but here.

Soon I reached the village of Baggrow where the Harrison family were hard at work on the roadside mending some fences. They were in good spirits and it rather cheered me up. We enjoyed a laugh about things in general, which was not hard to do in their company. I told them I would rather be working with them than doing my own job.

"Stick in lad," they said, "you boys are doing a grand job." Those few small words meant a lot at a time when there was little encouragement, praise or support to be had.

I moved on down the road a little and valued some away-wintering Swaledale gimmer hoggs for Bob Cubby of Seatoller Farm near Borrowdale. Seatoller is officially the wettest place in Great Britain. The sun certainly had not been shining on Bob who by now had lost all of his hoggs, shearlings and rams wintering on various farms spread all over north Cumbria. Seatoller had effectively lost two full years' worth of female replacement sheep and most of the breeding rams that had been purchased or bred to continue the breeding cycle of the farm. I had valued all of them. All that Bob would be left with was a lot of old ewes and some memories. I really felt for him. Sadly it was all too much for Bob and in failing health he decided the following year to retire from the farm. I was honoured when he asked me to act as his valuer on the official sheep take-over day. Bob moved away from Cumbria and in doing so one of the great characters in Cumbrian farming was lost to the community.

I drove slowly back to the office and met my colleague David once again. There was plenty of paperwork and several days' correspondence to catch up on. I was not really in the mood but knew it had to be done. Besides that I was officially on call and had to be ready to jump should the worst happen.

Two of my colleagues were having a well-deserved day off, and two others were out valuing for the voluntary cull. These were mostly sheep in and around the east side of Cockermouth that were within three kilometres of Strawberry Howe. The valuation request file continued to bulge.

By 4pm I decided I was going home. I had also decided that barring emergencies I was going to take one if not two days break. I rang Paula and she too was relieved. I felt a burden lifting off my shoulders at least for a little while. I knew that I was spent and needed to recharge.

That night I opened a bottle of wine and prepared to watch TV. Paula went off to bed for an early night. I did not blame her for she was by now eight months pregnant although she had not yet packed her bag for the hospital.

The phone rang and I was astonished to find that it was Oliver Maurice, chief executive of the National Trust. He thanked me for the work I had done on behalf of the National Trust tenants and in particular at Cockly Beck. I was honoured that the man had taken the time and trouble on Easter Saturday to do this especially if he was ringing all the valuers who had been involved which I presumed he must be. We chatted for a while and being me I suggested that people like Neil and Christine Hodgson who were now trying to come to terms with their life in the valley of death would have to be looked after, encouraged and supported. The future of the National Trust farms and of course those hard, high Lake District fells was in the balance. The farmers working those hard holdings were I felt a special breed but even more than that would be needed to bring the valleys and the communities back to life. Oliver Maurice seemed to listen and I was pleased to get something off my chest that had been bothering me. We said our goodbyes and I returned to my Chablis.

Sunday was an enjoyable family day although there were a few phone calls to deal with. In the evening I talked to my colleague Alisdare Bruce who had spent a wretched day at a farm near Workington arguing with MAFF officials and the army who insisted that this particular farm should be culled. Despite the protestation from Alisdare that this must be wrong because there was no disease anywhere near that area, the cull went ahead. Only later when the animals were going cold did MAFF realise that a wrong map reference had been given. The farm that should have been culled was over 40 miles away near Brampton. This case made national newspaper headlines. Sadly like so many other farmers the trauma of the loss was too much for the young farming couple. Soon after, the Nuttalls left the farm in search of work away from farming. It was a travesty.

Alisdare also informed me that there had by now been confirmed cases near Whitehaven on the coast of West Cumbria. There were also reports of unconfirmed cases further down the west coast. My heart sank and all the joy of my day off was gone. I tried to fight my rising pessimism but was haunted by a recurring feeling.

"This time," I thought, "we are all going down."

Meanwhile my colleague John Marrs had been undertaking a dangerous contact valuation of pedigree dairy cattle for Frank Chester at Bouch House to the south east of Cockermouth. He is a neighbour to Strawberry Howe. Just over the A66 the same process was going on for Alan and Christine Watson at Byresteads which was also being taken out as a dangerous contact premises. No one could understand why this was the case when the A66 road clearly divided both dangerous contact farms from the infected premises. It was only later that MAFF admitted that they had not used an up to date map with the A66 marked on it. They forgot the road existed and believed the farm boundaries were shared. In the words of the late Dick Emery: "Dad, I think I got it wrong again."

The following day was Easter Monday and we all tried to have a day off. I was prepared to go to the office in case of emergency. Thankfully there were none and by Tuesday I was refreshed and ready to do battle again.

Meanwhile the battle around Cockermouth continued to rage. The Errington family at Annfield were to lose their long established pedigree herd of dairy cows. Their daughter Tracey, with whom I went to school, came home to support the family. She was amazed and appalled by the whole operation as her father and brother David had to take control of the slaughter operation by organising the removal of the slaughtered cows so that the cows that were still alive did not have to trample over the top of their matriarchs. In the end they pulled the bodies out of the way with a tractor and a length of rope.

Two years later, Edward Errington and I had never discussed the situation face to face but the topic did crop up. He went on to tell me of the fight to save his sheep which were grazing in fields all around Cockermouth. Neither Edward nor the sheep were classed as dangerous contacts yet MAFF was insistent that the sheep must die. The argument lasted all afternoon with a team of five MAFF vets and field officers none of whom were prepared to make a lasting decision. In the end the matter was referred to Page Street who dictated that all sheep must die. The Erringtons finally had to give way and sat in the kitchen in stunned silence.

A little while later the vets returned with great news. The sheep had received a stay of execution with Page Street apparently making an unheralded U-turn. Sadly the call had not come through to the vet before all of the young lambs had been killed. The vet thought it was great that the ewes had been saved. There was no thought towards the welfare of those mothers whose lambs had been taken from them. There would be a strong possibility that being full of milk they would be in discomfort and might even get mastitis.

Edward was so upset that he demanded the vets should finish the job for the sake of his ewes. The vets dithered, not having permission from

Page Street. So Edward gave them an ultimatum, go now and finish the job or he would take his own gun and do it for them. He was deadly serious. The vets relented and went away to shoot the remaining sheep.

As Edward recounted the tale it rather choked him and we had to finish the conversation immediately. He left me open mouthed with incredulity at the situation.

During our first pedigree dairy sale in the new mart Edward and Valerie made a very special purchase. A dairy heifer from the famous Hunday herd was offered by the Moffitt family with all proceeds to go to charity. The Erringtons made the final bid for the heifer at £1200. It was a sign that another farming family were on the road to recovery after FMD.

27
WHERE HAVE ALL THE FELL SHEEP GONE?

Tuesday17 April
Total National Cases: 1367

By the time I reached the office some of my colleagues were already in the field of battle. The disease had been confirmed in the Whitehaven area. It seemed that Major Holt's prediction had come true after all. How and why, we will never know. One can only hazard a guess that virus had blown down the coast on the wind, from burning pyres. We had both clean and dirty valuers operating out there. My job was to continue to plough on through as many voluntary cull valuations as possible. There were many requests from within the Cockermouth area but there were also many urgent requests to value thousands of away-wintered fell sheep on lowland farms scattered throughout north Cumbria.

My first call was to Highside farm, Embleton near Cockermouth. This farm, like so many, was within three kilometres of the infected premises to the east of Cockermouth. The high ground marks the true northerly fell boundary to the Lake District. Tom Teasdale welcomed me and we swiftly moved out to value several hundred lambing Swaledale ewes. In fact many had already lambed. It would normally have been a joy to see so many young mule lambs skipping alongside their mothers. Maybe I was hardening to the task but I felt almost detached from the operation. Back in the house we completed the valuation at the kitchen table over a cup of tea. Tom asked me to reassure him that my valuation was competitive and fair. I assured him that it was. In fact it was a very good valuation for that time but I liked the sheep and knew the sort of lambs that they bred for I sold many of them in Cockermouth mart.

Tom is a hard and shrewd man but like so many of my customers the reality of the situation was too much. As we discussed what would happen when the sheep were picked up from the farm to go to slaughter I could see he was becoming visibly upset. I did not want to get embroiled in the emotional side of things and decided to make a swift exit. I was glad I did having just got my self back on track over the last couple of days.

Later Tom told me that when he was eight years old in the early 1950s, FMD had struck the Cockermouth area with Annfield and Scales Farm, Embleton, going down. Tom's father was a dangerous contact but in those days this meant daily visits from the vet to check for clinical signs, rather than instant death. Young Tom had been given a daily task by his father to gather the sheep each day for the vet to look at. He could remember the stock at Annfield and Scales being slaughtered and buried in a pit filled with quick lime. It is strange to think that those two farms were to lose all their stock again in an FMD outbreak so many years later.

My next destination was high up on the Solway coast where I knew I had I number of farms to visit in order to value away-wintered fell sheep. Soon I was at High Laws near Silloth. Here I met the farmer Mr Gilroy. Yet again I was greeted with great courtesy even though the man was desperate to get the sheep off the farm in order to protect his dairy herd.

It was raining hard as we slithered down the steep bank behind his farm buildings above the cow pasture. Below me I could see many breeding rams that I knew were wintering here from several Lakeland hill farms. There were in fact rams from seven separate holdings all being given the best possible chance to recover from the stresses of last autumn's breeding season. There were Swaledales, Texels, Leicesters and several Herdwick rams in the field. Among them was one of the most successful Herdwick breeding rams of all time. He had sired many thousands of pounds worth of Herdwick breeding ram in his own right. His lineage could be traced back to the 1930s. The ancestor of this tup was Gable Blue Boy who in that decade was unbeaten in any show ring until the end of his life. Bred at Gatesgarth Farm, Buttermere and born to live on the high fells so beloved of the fell walker, the bloodline of that famous tup was now almost at an end. Gatesgarth like so many other Lakeland hill farms had lost most of its hoggs, shearlings and now its breeding rams.

As I looked at the old tup descended from Blue Boy I knew that he would end his days in ignominy on the Solway Plain. It seemed such a dreadful waste as we stood in the cold, miserable rain. When Willie Richardson, the owner of Gatesgarth, had begun to tell me of the tup's heritage, the heritage of Gatesgarth, it had all become too much for him. He dropped the phone in abject despair. His girlfriend Judith whose father Bob Cubby had also lost so much recently had to finish the conversation for him. Such heartache! Was it all so necessary? The tup was irreplaceable, one of a kind. He would never have been for sale on the

Left to right, Peter Greenhill, Mitchell's Chairman, Brigadier Birtwistle and Adam Day at the official opening of the Lakeland Livestock Centre.

Sheep and cattle being dumped at the landfill site at Distington, Cumbria. Photos. courtesy of the Whitehaven News.

*Above, selling off the pens in the old mart (August 2001) - the last sale ever...
and below, the first animals to be sold in the new Lakeland Livestock Centre,
owned by Mr. Harry Harper.*

open market. I made my valuation accordingly.

It seemed to take several hours to complete the paperwork that cold and miserable afternoon. There were so many good rams to value. To me it felt like the Lake District was losing far more than a field full of breeding sheep. I left the farm with heavy heart.

In the gloom of early evening I made several other visits to farms in the area to value away-wintered sheep. Finally with my day's work done I headed for home yet again. I wondered whether to ring Willie Richardson but could find no good reason to do so. What could I say that would mitigate his losses on this and every other day he was losing sheep? I knew that given the choice he would have kept the sheep every time rather than take a good valuation figure as compensation. For in truth the money was no compensation for such fell farmers.

I well remember Willie bringing a favourite ram to our annual prize show and sale in October. The sheep was old and had lost a few teeth. Nevertheless he was of a noted bloodline. I was amazed when the bidding passed the 1,000 guinea mark. With a flourish of triumph I took a last look around the ring and banged the hammer down at the magnificent price of 1,100 guineas.

"No," cried Willie, "I'm not selling him." I nearly fell over backwards. The sheep walked out of the ring unsold. I had never seen anything like it. Afterwards I questioned Willie on his refusal.

"Well it's like this," explained Willie, "when I brought him here I knew then that I didn't really want to sell him. When he was in the ring, I thought I could never ever replace him. He is the last of a line. I couldn't sell him could I?" He looked at me and I shrugged my shoulders. It seemed a hell of a price, but money cannot replace blood. During FMD I learned that this was very true.

Some days after my visit to Mr Gilroy's, I decided to look at the MAFF website to see who had gone down with the disease. Normally I tried to forget about it when I got home but on this night I must have been at a loose end. I was shocked to see that Mr Gilroy's farm that I had visited only a few days before had gone down with the disease. I knew when I went there that the virus was in the vicinity. Even so I felt very sorry for him and considered ringing him up. I could not bring myself to do it.

To make matters worse I had even done a TV interview with Border News at the farm with the camera looking into the field where the tups were. Mr Gilroy had stood behind the sheep to give the camera a good angle. Myself and Pauline Blair, a Herdwick breeder in her own right, were trying to raise public awareness of the fact that so many important sheep from the Lakeland fells were being lost. Those very sheep had been taken to slaughter but just a few days later the dairy cows had gone down with the disease.

I felt very sorry for the farmer who had walked around the sheep with me in the pouring rain when I valued them. I began to wonder if the sheep might have been ill even when I was there. There were some lame tups among them. I felt that horrible chill feeling down my spine again. What if I had been infected and gone on to other farms? I knew of other valuers who had faced the same problem. How did any of us know when we went to do a voluntary valuation whether the virus had already beaten us into the sheep fields? This was not the first occasion when a farm had gone down after I had been on it. How could we ever know if the disease was already there?

For yet another night I went to bed in a restless worry. "God let this end soon," I thought. No one seemed to be listening.

28
COCKERMOUTH'S EMPTY FIELDS

Friday 20 April
Total national cases: 1412

Over the next few days I continued my quest to value as many sheep in and around the Cockermouth area as possible. I was only one valuer who saw thousands of sheep. I cannot praise the farmers highly enough for this sacrifice. They were prepared to lose all their sheep if their was any chance that it might stop the disease spreading. We were being told that the contiguous cull was the only way to beat FMD. In the back of our minds we questioned it and yet the thought of doing nothing and watching the disease spread all over West Cumbria and the Lake District was too much to bear. So we carried on day after day responding to our customers requests. By now it had been confirmed in the village of Lorton, three miles south of Cockermouth.

We all worried that it would continue to spread just a few miles further south towards the Buttermere valley. If it did and all those traditional fell flocks were lost, then I knew for sure that my working life as an auctioneer was over. If my colleagues felt the same way then we did not discuss it. We simply got on with the task in hand. Day by day, field after field of sheep around Cockermouth were valued, loaded onto wagons and sent to slaughter at Great Orton or Distington. In a few short days there were virtually no sheep visible from the A66 three miles either side of Cockermouth.

I made visits to long-standing Mitchell's customers including Jos Teasdale at Jenkin farm near Embleton. It was a very similar story to his brother Thomas just down the road. Even Joss' dry sense of humour struggled to come through in this situation. I saw many good sheep in his fields.

I also visited the Christopherson family at Brandlingill who had volunteered their sheep in order to try and save their pride and joy, the rare herd of Ayrshire dairy cattle. They succeeded and the cattle stayed healthy. It was a pleasure to help them begin to re-stock their sheep flock some months later.

Whilst at Brandlingill I had the fortune to meet anattractive Spanish lady vet who had come to 'heenspecta da sheep'. Her command of the English language was not good but that probably did not matter to MAFF as long as she could identify foot and mouth disease. I hoped that she was not one of the keen and enthusiastic types who were determined to find the disease on the first farm to which they were sent. Sadly there were a few such gung-ho types doing the rounds. It would seem that orf is a disease peculiar only to the United Kingdom. It definitely caught out several of our foreign friends from time to time. Many of us wished that FMD was so easy to spot in sheep. For at that time no vet had actually been able to point out to me a genuine case of FMD in any sheep that I was called to value. This made their job all the more difficult.

Now it was Friday morning, a still and calm spring day. I journeyed up to Whitbysteads Hill farm south of Penrith where I met the owner, Tom Lowther. He is an interesting character who began his working life in city journalism before 'retiring' in his 30s back to the family home at Whitbysteads. This had always been a working hill farm in the hands of the shepherd, Syd Scott. Now Tom was working closely with him, learning the skills of a true Lakeland shepherd. Sadly those skills would be needed for only a few hours longer.

Tom really did not want to part with the sheep but had been put under pressure by neighbouring farmers and MAFF to relinquish the sheep and let them go on the cull. Reluctantly he called me in to undertake the valuation. He was seething mad that MAFF had tried to influence him in the matter.

"They have no right to do this," he repeated several times as we drove around looking at the sheep. Soon the job was done. Tom insisted that I hand the valuation form in to command centre at Penrith as soon as possible. I assured him that I would then went on my way.

Back at the office I made sure I photocopied all of the valuations for the file and bundled them up to hand in at Penrith on my way home from work in the evening. Again my mistake was to date most of the valuations with Friday's date, even though some had been done a few days earlier.

Tom Lowther's sheep were taken on the voluntary cull and as a matter of principle he later appealed the valuation. This did not offend me for I knew that his real objection was that the loss of his sheep was in his opinion unnecessary at that time. He had wrongly been put under pressure to let the sheep go. Much later Tom was to vent his frustrations about the handling of the whole crisis, in a series of public meetings. He even stood for parliament as an independent candidate. I admired him for having the guts to put down his deposit.

When restocking commenced I worked hard to try and find replacement sheep for him. In the autumn of 2002 he visited our new market to buy Herdwick ewes for his farm. Could it be said that every cloud has a silver lining? I hope so.

29
ANOTHER GOOD DAY AT THE OFFICE

Saturday 21 April
Total National Cases: 1429

By now the media were again full of talk about vaccination. The 'should we - shouldn't we' debate was raging. Even among Mitchell's board of directors there were totally contrasting opinions. Nick Brown, Minister of Agriculture, was interviewed on *Newsnight* and tried to persuade us that jabbing the sheep in Cumbria might be a good thing. On the other hand the NFU and other bodies were stating that injected animals may have to slaughtered anyway, and that £30m worth of food exports would be jeopardised.

Furthermore Nestle's, who owned the dairy factory near Carlisle were stating that they would not accept milk from farms if they injected their stock. This was disgraceful. There was no proof whatsoever that this milk could be harmful to the milk buying public.

I could not get my head around the fact that vaccination in humans was supposed to encourage immunity. Why was this not the same for animals? Why would they have to be slaughtered when they had been immunised? It did not make any sense. I pondered these facts as I pulled into the farmyard at Winscales near Egremont early on Saturday morning.

Graham Hogg greeted me. He had recently purchased the farm as an addition to the family fell farm on Corney Fell, near Bootle, in the south of the county. Graham's case was a particularly unfortunate one. He had quite legitimately and under licence picked up some away-wintered hoggs from a farm near St Bees and taken them back to the fell farm for summer. Sadly the farm from which he had removed the sheep had been diagnosed with foot and mouth only the day after his sheep had been taken back to Bootle. This had potentially disastrous implications for the fell farmers of South Lakeland. Since the outbreaks in the Duddon valley in March, the disease had apparently been contained. Now there was every chance that it might be back.

Graham was almost in a state of shock. He was visibly trembling as we sat at the kitchen table.

"I've done nothing wrong," he kept saying. The female vet who had been appointed to the case thankfully had a wonderful bedside manner. She assured him that between us the problem would be sorted quickly.

"I'm Vanessa by the way," she smiled, shaking my hand confidently.

We began to discuss the situation. The sheep at Corney would of course have to die and it had now been confirmed that all of the sheep at Winscales would have to go as well. This was because Graham himself having picked up the fell sheep was a dangerous contact. I joked that he had always been a dangerous contact when he had played professional Rugby League for Workington Town.

Then Vanessa produced a newly created MAFF valuation guide sheet, which gave vets a rough indication as to what various classes of livestock might be worth.

"If your valuation is substantially different," she paused, "then I may have to take further advice." She smiled sweetly and I smiled back.

"Well I have sold Graham's stock for several years and I know exactly what it's worth," I replied with a courteous smile. She never flinched nor broke eye contact.

"Of course you have," she said. I liked her style and knew we would get along famously. Having finished our coffee we moved outside to begin the valuation work.

We walked around the farm picking off the fields one by one. We kept a light atmosphere as we worked and cracked about farming and rugby. Vanessa was a Yorkshire farmer's daughter and took our gentle mickey taking in good nature especially when she became stuck fast while straddling a barbed wire fence.

"You push and I'll pull," I said to Graham.

"I can manage thank you," she replied with a grimace.

"Is that an official MAFF slogan?" I asked.

By early afternoon we were on our way down to the fell farm to meet Graham's mother and father. These were sorry times for the Hoggs who had farmed at Foldgate for many years. Prior to FMD they were considering retiring. Later they would decide to do just that with the heart of the farm having been ripped out by the loss of most of the sheep.

Again as we moved around the farm in my car, the atmosphere was fairly light hearted. Graham was bearing up well. We pulled up to a piece of ground behind some cottages. I looked at the sheep and found that they were Swaledale ewes with double lambs suckling them. They had been put into these fields to give the ewes an extra bite of spring grass. It helped for they were doing the lambs very well. The lambs skipped about, jumping on and off their mothers as they chewed their cud. It would normally have been one of those special spring moments. Now it was far from it.

Just then behind me I heard Graham whisper, "Oh no here they come."

I turned around to see a man and woman marching up the road towards us. They were in their early 40s and the man sported an impressive set of dreadlocks, which I rather admired. The man marched straight up to me and thrust his face in front of mine.

"Another good day at the office," he said to me aggressively. I did not take a backward step but was tensed in case he tried to assault me. I felt that he might be that way inclined. I smiled at him.

"What do you mean?" I enquired.

"Another good day for you lot," he repeated.

"Who do you think I am?" I asked.

"Bloody MAFF vet!" he spat at me.

"Why?"

"Because you wearing one of those white suits," he growled. It was laughable really.

"I am not a vet, I am just here to try and help this farmer so please let me get on with my work," I said. Sadly they were not going to allow me to do so. The woman piped up.

"What is going to happen to those sheep?" she asked.

"They are going to be slaughtered there," I replied in a matter of fact tone.

"Well," the woman continued "I'm going to make a complaint because those sheep are starving." I looked at the sheep that were happily chewing their cud. I decided to keep calm and try and reason with the ill-informed people. It was a hopeless task. They would not listen. Finally Vanessa who had kept quiet in the background could stand no more.

"I'm the bloody MAFF vet here," she said, "you want to make a complaint make it too me!" The woman kept on sniping about the whole foot and mouth situation and farming in general.

Vanessa tried to explain: "Don't you realise that we are doing this to try and stop the disease getting onto the fells? We want to make sure all of the sheep in this county are not killed."

"That wouldn't matter," said the woman, "everyone knows the fells don't need sheep on them any way." I was incredulous.

"Just how would you keep the grass down and the paths open without the sheep?" I asked. "It is the sheep that make this land what it is."

"You could spray the grass from a helicopter to keep it down," retorted the woman in all seriousness. I had a job not to burst out laughing. The woman was actually being serious.

Then the man changed the point of attack. Graham had moved away to the field gate so as not to get involved. I could see his eyes reddening with tears of rage. Amazingly the man walked up to Graham.

"Oh well you'll be laughing all the way to the bank," he said.

"Yes," joined in the woman, "everyone knows that these sheep are worth £3 each and you get paid £90." I could not resist a response.

"Actually," I said, "you are well wrong on both counts!"

The situation was degenerating fast. Graham was approaching the end of his tether.

"If you even think I want the money or need the money," he said through gritted teeth, "then you know nothing!" He stared at the man who visibly backed off.

"These sheep have been bred on this farm by my father for generations. They are our sheep and nobody else's. Now we are losing them and you dare to accuse me of being happy about it. You know nothing," he repeated. The man looked shocked at the response for he realised Graham's thoughts were from the heart.

At that point I realised that I had to move. Vanessa was now close to tears. I thought she might take umbrage with the woman in front of her who was still baiting her. I forcefully grabbed Vanessa and pushed her into the car.

"Graham," I said, "my job is done and we are leaving." I also helped him into the car. We drove off swiftly leaving the odd couple in the middle of the road. When the air had cleared in the car and tempers had been composed, I joked that it was the first time that I had been set upon by animal rights activists, although I was not sure whether they were on the side of the sheep, the farmer or the environment. I concluded that they did not really know themselves.

Graham went on to tell me that they were a city couple who had purchased the nearby cottage. They had very fixed views about animal welfare and farmer's methods. They had insisted in the previous season that they should be allowed to keep and rear two badly deformed lambs that had been born in Graham's field. Spina bifida lambs are normally put out of their misery at birth. Instead these lambs were forced to endure a life of pain and handicap in the name of liberty. I'm sure it galled Graham to see those poor lambs in that state.

Back at the farm all valuations and inspections had been completed. Mrs Hogg had very kindly cooked a wonderful lunch for us. Thankfully we were able to put aside the unnecessary trauma of the past hour. The meal was enjoyable and we talked of everything we could think of except foot and mouth and sheep.

Unfortunately not all of the sheep that had to be valued had been successfully gathered from the fell. This meant that an accurate count could not be gained in order to complete the valuation.

Vanessa decided that we should agree the valuation levels based on the sample of sheep we had seen. A final gather would take place early on Sunday morning before the slaughter. Vanessa would then contact me on Monday so that we could meet up and complete the necessary paperwork. Having agreed this plan I then drove Vanessa back up to Winscales so that she could go home.

On the way we discussed what effect this whole disaster was having on us as individuals. There were a few tears in the car but it helped to clear the air. I realised then that the cool professionalism being shown by the vets was as much a front as the wall that valuers such as I were trying to hide behind. The daily grind was also getting to the vets. Maybe to a greater degree than the valuers, for vets are trained to save lives, not end them. We were all tangled up in a horrible mess that showed no signs of improving.

I considered offering to go back on Sunday to assist in the gathering and counting, but I knew it was not really my job. I decided to spend the day with my family although I felt a tinge of guilt knowing that Vanessa's real hard work would take place the following day.

Later when we met up to complete the valuation forms she told me of the horror she had had to endure when the sheep were slaughtered at Fold Gate. Some of the fell sheep were actually lambing in the slaughter pens. Vanessa had to deliver some lambs on the spot and then inject lethal amounts of anaesthetic directly into the hearts of the lambs as they drew their first breath. Vanessa told me it was a difficult task to perform knowing that the sheep were healthy in every way. The lambs never had a chance to draw a breath. Those lambs left in their mother's womb would die as well, starved of oxygen as their mothers died by the bullet.

Throughout the spring many vets had to perform this task on new born and slightly older lambs. I was to witness it myself a short time later. I asked Vanessa why this 'putting to sleep' method had to be done.

"Easy," she replied "because a bullet would blow their heads off completely."

I later found out that blood tests proved that none of Graham's sheep had FMD. Another huge waste of life. Another fell flock savagely dealt with. Meanwhile people like Vanessa and I just got on with our jobs as best we could. We could not question what was happening. We just had to perform. We were told that there was no other way.

I have heard it said that there will be a ruck of post traumatic stress claims issued to the Government in time. From what I had seen and been part of in the early months of foot and mouth, it would not surprise me. Soldiers are trained to go to war but no one received any training or counselling for this different type of battle. No one died and yet the legacy of killing and disposing of animals lives on in everyone who was involved in the fight. I saw this myself when listening to Brigadier Birtwistle who spoke at a farmers' meeting a few months after foot and mouth was over. He talked about the logistics of the carcass disposal operation at Great Orton. Then he stopped for almost a minute, staring at the ground. Having composed himself he continued

"I am sorry gentlemen," he said apologetically, "it's just that I can still see all those thousands of bodies lying in the pit. It will never leave me..."

30
A MISERABLE EVENING IN LORTON

Monday 23 April
Total National Cases: 1451

By now the vaccination debate was becoming decidedly heated. The more I heard, the less I understood. I read an article in a newspaper written by an eminent scientist stating that the slaughter policy was doomed in a widespread outbreak. This seemed to make sense to me. We always seemed to be trying to catch up with the disease. The scientist concluded that countries operating a vaccination policy controlled the disease in less than six weeks no matter how big the outbreak. Other groups such as the National Trust, Friends of the Earth and the Soil Association now appeared to support the cause. On the other hand, the National Farmers Union stayed resolutely opposed to any foot and mouth vaccination programme.

Later in the day Nick Brown announced that the slaughter policy was actually working and that the case for vaccination was receding. MPs were told that 66% of blood tests on slaughtered animals were found to be negative. I was surprised that it was as low as that. Most of the stock I was looking at was perfectly healthy but die they must; such was the pressure on the farmers. In time the true figure of healthy animals that were slaughtered was found to be well over 90%. It is a staggering and distressing statistic.

The Government's chief advisor, Professor Anderson issued computer models predicting that the epidemic curve would fall to zero by 7 June. I thought that this would make Tony Blair pretty happy seeing as that very day had been set for the General Election.

"Oh well," I thought glibly, "only another six weeks killing and this will all be over." In truth I did not believe it for one minute.

Further advice was issued to the farmers from Government. Despite the fact that this was turn out time for cattle that were in-wintered, farmers were told to keep cattle indoors to prevent the further risk of disease spread if it was over the fence among a neighbour's stock. Also it was announced that the contiguous cull (dangerous contact) of cattle was to cease forthwith. However the contiguous cull of sheep within 3km of infected farms was to continue. Cynical observers believed that this policy was helping Government to reduce the national sheep flock and to reduce the need to compensate slaughtered cattle which were of higher value than sheep. In reality it was obvious that it had been logistically impossible to implement fully the contiguous cull. If the 24/48 target was policy then they failed badly. This of course did not help the sheep farmers of Cockermouth or their auctioneers.

Monday afternoon saw me working again in the Embleton area. My first visit was to William and Margaret Hall's farm at Low Netherscales. They had decided to volunteer their sheep as so many of their neighbours were doing. They also had a lot of sheep near Lorton and were worried about travelling the few short miles to that village now that the disease had found its way there. Besides that, to even drive along that road required them to pass an infected farm. They were hemmed in.

I spent a few minutes talking to Margaret. Many years before she had been my form teacher at secondary school. She used to frighten me, but now I addressed her as a friend. She enquired about the new auction. I tried to sound positive but my words were hollow. "Keep fighting," she said, "we must have our new auction mart. We need you." It felt nice to be needed. Margaret cheered me up no end.

Soon William and I made the short journey down to Lorton. The views of the fells were magnificent. Those of us who live and work up and down the valleys grow all too complacent. From William's high ground I could see down the valley to Loweswater and the Buttermere fells. I prayed that foot and mouth would not find a way onto the fells and wipe out the many hefted flocks that make our mountains what they are.

As I inspected the sheep, I kept William informed of my values. He rarely spoke and I was unsure of his thoughts and questioned him.

"No problem Adam. Whatever you put down on the paper will be just fine by me. I trust your judgement." I was working for one of the finest gentlemen I know and it gladdened me.

My job was completed and I drove back to the office only to be called by Andrew Nicholson. He farms with his wife Karen on land just above William Hall's at Lorton. They had been watching me valuing from their own yard. The fact that William had volunteered the sheep had made them feel a little bit guilty. There were four farms in close proximity one of which was a dairy unit. They all felt that they should let the sheep go now in order to try and save the cattle. This was particularly hard for the

Nicholsons for they stood to lose some very valuable Herdwick sheep. I had already valued so many top class sheep that they were wintering on other farms in the north of the county.

Andrew is only just over 30 and yet such is his reputation in the Herdwick fraternity that he is now a fully-fledged council member. This is a high honour for one so young. Herdwicks are in the blood of Andrew and Karen for they were both born of fell farming stock. Andrew's grandfather Gordon Stagg was the first man in history to sell a Herdwick ram for £100. The Nicholsons had already won the supreme championship award at Mitchell's annual ram sale at Cockermouth mart. I had the pleasure of selling the sheep on that occasion. They had only recently moved to High Swinside above the Lorton valley. It had marked a wonderful start to their farming life together; now it was pretty much in tatters.

Andrew wanted to know if I could come back to the valley and value their sheep for the voluntary cull. His two neighbours also wanted me to do the same for them. I agreed to go straight away even though there were only a couple of hours' daylight left. I drove the narrow roads back up to High Lorton.

I sat in the kitchen of High Swinside with Andrew and Karen and we drank coffee as we discussed the breeding lines and exceptional sheep that he was surrendering. Karen was very emotional, not just about the Herdwicks but also a very fine Swaledale flock, which they were breeding up and improving. We looked at a lot of their photographs of the sheep. There were walls full of pictures all around the house so proud were they of their flock. Happy smiles, holding prize-winning sheep in Cockermouth market, good days. Their sheep were their life.

Andrew and I jumped into his Land Rover and we began to move around the valley viewing different fields of sheep. Amongst the Herdwicks he could pick out sheep after sheep and name its bloodline, its past performance both as a breeder and in the show ring. He also could name the dams and grand-dams of most sheep and even some of the prices that they had fetched at auction. I looked perplexed as he spoke about one particular tup that was the great-grandfather of the sheep we were inspecting.

"You remember it," he said trying to prompt me, "it stood third in the show at your mart. You sold it for 700 guineas, 1998 it was." I nodded my head without conviction. I marvelled at his computer like knowledge of his sheep. It was as if he had forgotten why we were looking at the sheep, his enthusiasm shone through. The brighter he was, the darker I became as the mist of misery began to descend upon me. It seemed such a pointless waste. I did not say it, I just noted down my valuations. On any other day it would have been such a great pleasure to amble through the fields enjoying Andrew's company and knowledge. Learning about his breed lines and enjoying the views of Grasmoor and Red Pike, so close by. Now I hardly noticed the scenery.

We returned home and completed the paperwork. Andrew told me he would do anything to try and keep the sheep, especially those all-important Herdwicks. He reminded me that I had already valued every last gimmer shearling and several hoggs that formed the basis of his flock replacements. Now all of his remaining older sheep were going to die but for a few that were living on other farms around the Lake District. Foot and mouth had savaged the Nicholsons without having one animal succumb to the disease proper.

"They have to go," he said miserably, "I could not bear it if Bill's cows went down because of my sheep." It was that oh-so common tale.

My next call was to Andrew's neighbour Bill Shields. He is one of a rare breed of perennially cheerful people. No matter how he is feeling he will share a joke or more probably dish out some abuse, all in jest of course. He wanted me to value his sheep in order to save his pedigree dairy animals.

His type of farm is a dying type. A marginal hill and valley farm with a small mixed dairy and beef herd grazing the lower pastures and sheep grazing right on to the lower reaches of the high fells. One of the biggest disappointments about the changing face in Lakeland agriculture is the slow disappearance of the mixed marginal farm. Only 20 years ago there were many such holdings milking only a few dairy cows often by pipe line in the byre itself. Now the big dairy producers have fast superseded them, with high cow numbers and minimal costs. It is a shame in many respects but understandable in the current economic climate. Of course things are rather different for many of our European partners where such small mixed units are even now grant funded and positively encouraged to continue what they do.

We enjoyed a few minutes of banter, then we inspected the sheep. I placed a valuation upon them and he feigned complete horror,

"You are robbing me. How can you stand there and put such a bad price on my sheep?"

"Cos that's what they are worth you bugger," I retorted, "now sign the form and let me get on with my job."

"All right give us your pen then," he said with a smile.

My next visit was to see Sheila Mills to value her small flock of Swaledale sheep. Every year since I began to work at Cockermouth I had sold a handful of mule gimmers for Mrs Mills at our annual September sale. They were never very big lambs but they were always nicely bred and rather bonny. Having now seen the flock I understood why. Mrs Mills had some nice Swaledale ewes. They were only a hobby flock and yet there was as much pride maintained in these sheep as in any larger flock. Sheila was bitterly disappointed to be losing her sheep. As I left her having completed the valuation she told me that she could not see herself starting up again.

"These sheep are like family," she said. I knew she meant it. The waiting time until the MAFF transport arrived to pick the sheep up would be difficult for her.

I slammed the car door shut with more than an element of frustration. Darkness had descended into the Lorton Valley. It had been a long day and I was cold, tired and hungry. I realised I was missing my family. I tried to ring Paula but my mobile phone had no signal. As I wound my weary way over Whinlatter Pass towards Keswick I felt isolated and alone. I could not wait to get through the front door of my house to greet my wife, look at my sleeping baby girl, have a bath, a meal and bed.

"God please let this end soon," it had now become a plea more than a prayer. I could not truthfully see an end to it all. The disease was always one step ahead or rather MAFF was one step behind. All the time it was grinding me down, day by day. How much longer would we have to go on? No one had the answer.

31
ALL AROUND THE SOLWAY FIRTH

Tuesday 24 April
Total National Cases: 1463

It was a telephone call I hoped I would not get. David Bland called me from West Head farm near Thirlmere. Only a few years earlier he had expanded his family operation by purchasing a farm on the Solway Plain near Aspatria. His new farm was stocked with a good quality flock of Swaledale sheep together with every single breeding ram that he had left following the loss of his Herdwick tup hoggs a few days earlier at Crosby. Now they all had to die as dangerous contacts within 3km of an infected premises of which there were several in the area. This meant that West Head, one of the most noted Herdwick breeding farms with heafed flocks running high on the Helvellyn range, would have virtually none of the old blood-lines left. Generations of breeding were being lost. The Bland family would literally have to start again from scratch.

I agreed to go to the farm straight away that morning where I met the duty vet who was a retired private practitioner from the east of England. Like so many others he was just doing his bit. Gavin Bland who was David's youngest son took me round all of the stock on a quad bike. This was much the preferable way for me to travel. Gavin is a world champion fell runner but I could not have run across the first field and kept up with him.

So we moved through field after field of Swaledale ewes all heavy in lamb. Some had actually lambed and were protecting their new-borns sniffing them reassuringly as we moved by. In the past I would have sold many of the lambs not needed for breeding and also a lot of draft ewes for which David had no further use. They would be eagerly snapped up in Cockermouth auction by regular customers. As usual I felt quite miserable knowing that there would be nothing left.

Soon we came to the field of tups. There were Swaledales, Herdwicks and other crossing breeds. Gavin knew every individual sheep and could give me the breeding and blood-lines without a moment's hesitation. Why shouldn't he for it was a lifetime's work for his family. He was proud and rightly so. He expected that they should be highly valued. He was right and I did so, for many of the sheep were irreplaceable.

How Gavin kept going I do not know, but he did. Even when the killing started he stood right by the pens. The vet was injecting all the young lambs that had been taken from the ewes. A single jab right through the wall of the heart. In seconds the lambs went to sleep in the vet's hand, then they were placed in a big heap to await collection and disposal. I tried to persuade Gavin to come away from the killing pens but he refused.

"These are our sheep," he said, "I might as well lend a hand." I knew what he meant. It was a sense of loyalty to his stock. I had seen it so many times before. It was almost if he was ashamed to walk away.

Gavin was a strong man that day. He felt the burden of his family's loss sitting on his shoulders but he did not show it. All he said was that he would rather it was him doing the job than his father or brother Peter. I am sure they would all have said that. His grief would come out in time although we will never talk of it. During that dreadful day he never once flinched. I felt bitterly sorry for him.

I left the scene having completed my valuation. As I drove away there was a long heap of bodies stretching back into the field. The relentless crack of the humane killers continued to ring out across the Solway Plain. I glanced over at Criffel standing tall on the other side of the Solway Firth. Now I had to make my way around the Firth and over the border into Scotland again. I put The Bland family out of mind and moved on to my next assignment.

Just over two weeks earlier I had travelled over the border to value two flocks of away-wintered Herdwick hoggs. Now I was on my way back again to value the same sheep. Originally I had been contacted by the voluntary cull HQ at Penrith Auction to say that both the farmers in question had requested that I travel to Bridge End farm near Annan. Having done as asked I had recently been contacted by SERAD, the Scottish Executive who informed me that my valuation was not recognised by them because the voluntary cull was apparently only applicable for English-based sheep.

SERAD desperately wanted to see the back of the sheep and poor Mr Glendinning at Bridge End must have been at his wits end, the sheep having remained on his farm since my trip on the 6 April. So I was 'invited' back to retrace my steps and redo the same valuation on the same sheep at the same farm.

In fact my first valuation of the morning was a new one. I made my way further north to Ecclefechan to value yet more Herdwicks on away ground. The same farmers owned them, Glen Wilkinson at Tilberthwaite and Willie Richardson at Gatesgarth.

At the entrance to the farm track the SERAD field officer met me. There were also a pile of carcass disposal trucks and slaughter men. The field officer explained that his job was to oversee the valuation and much of the operational process to kill and dispose of the bodies. The SERAD vet had sole responsibility for the welfare of the sheep. I could not help but be impressed by the set up. The Scottish Office had really got its act together - the organisation and planning was top drawer. Meanwhile in England the poor vets were still doing most of the organising from top to bottom. It was only later that DEFRA pulled itself together by appointing field officers although the performance of some of them left a lot to be desired. For instance I worked with one who did not like sheep or the sight of blood. I wondered why the hell she did the job. It must have been good money!

Meanwhile the Scottish field officer who was very proficient made sure I was booted and suited and drove me down to the farm where I was met by the vet.

"What the hell do you think you are doing?" he snarled at me. I looked at him quizzically.

"There's shit on you boots. You don't think you are coming onto this farm like that do you?" I kept calm.

"Actually it's mud from the roadside verge where I had to park to let the slaughter lorries past," I replied.

"Well get it washed off then," he said in exasperated tones.

"Oh OK then," I said meekly and then rather childishly adding 'wanker' under my breath. The field officer smiled.

The sheep were in the collecting yard and were very strong. I had them valued in a jiffy. The vet was not at all concerned. He just wanted them dead as soon as possible. I wanted to leave immediately so there were no pleasantries. The forms were signed and I was on my way after having my car fully sprayed and disinfected. The field officer followed me the ten or so miles down to Bridge End like a chaperone.

The sheep were in exactly the same fields as the last time and I led the field officer to them. I complained that this was a waste of time but it was to no avail. Scottish rules were Scottish rules and that was that. The paperwork was duly completed and I was on my way back to the office.

On the journey home I responded to a phone message on my answer phone. It was my friend Robin Edmondson from Walloway Farm at Penruddock. I had valued his sheep on the voluntary cull, sacrificed to save the family dairy herd. That had been a difficult day as they were close friends of mine. This was worse because the herd had now been found to have clinical signs of the disease. By the time I responded to the message my colleague Alisdare Bruce was already on his way to the farm.

I felt terribly guilty that I had not been able to take the call and accept the job. There was no point in going down there as a clean valuer and besides they were in the very capable hands of my colleague Alisdare. Even so, I felt that it should have been me there, accepting the responsibility of the job.

I spoke to Robin who was calm as Robin always is. I have never seen him lose his temper or show any sign of anger. He is either of a truly mellow disposition or a brilliant actor. He was however very concerned about how the cattle had contracted the disease.

"I think its MAFF's fault," he said bitterly, "they rang me just after they took the sheep to say that they had sent a dirty wagon to pick them up that had come straight from an infected premises. They have been on the farm regularly inspecting the cattle. It's as if they expect foot and mouth to be here and now it is." I detected a quiver in his voice.

"They've done this to us," he repeated. In fact this sort of tale was quite common. I honestly do not think it was deliberate but these incidents kept happening though poor organisation and lack of resources. MAFF vets were now being ordered to go from dirty to clean farms in less than 24 hours. Valuers had to remain clean for at least 72 hours. If there was any perceived risk to this strategy then it was being ignored.

In fact this type of incident proved to be all too common throughout the crisis. Much later I learned of a dairy farmer close to Cockermouth whose farm had been put on a 'D' notice in September. The reason given at the time was that the milk tanker picking up the day's collection had come directly from an infected premises near Kirkby Stephen in the east of the county. Thankfully there were no major repercussions except a lot of heartache and worry for our local farmer and his family. Even so, I would like to know which clown thought up the transport strategy for sending milk tankers all around the county on the same day at this time. Nice work!

I could do nothing more to help my friends the Edmondsons and I just hoped that Sandra could get through it. I know how badly she suffered through the loss of the sheep. Robin later told me that he really worried about his wife at the time.

Later Robin and Sandra's ten-year-old daughter Olivia wrote a letter to her school friends to explain why she could not go to school. She also described the feelings within the family at losing all of their stock, every last animal on the farm.

Olivia's school teachers were so moved by her words that they sent the letter to the local press who printed it in the letters pages. When I read it on the Saturday of publication I too was moved. I commented to Paula that Mr Blair should be here to see and understand what distress was being caused amongst the farming families of Cumbria. The letter read:

You don't want to get foot and mouth because when you get it you are mad or upset and I have gone through it and it is devastating news. When I found out a school I cried like what you will do as well if you get it. If you go through it, you just wish you could say, 'Don't kill my cows, sheep and pigs.'

When we got it I was mad, very mad. When I got home at night people came to shoot them. We have a shed down the field. When they came we had to put the music up loud but I could still hear the gunshots and I cried. It was heart breaking for us when the cows and sheep went.

I hate the milk from the shops. I miss my sheep and cows but we are going to re-stock again. But we are going to make sure that we will not go through it again. Good luck everyone on the farms. If you get it please be strong. You will get through it, it does get better after a while but it takes time, just be brave.   *Olivia Edmondson, aged 10.*

That night I wanted to phone Robin but I couldn't face it. What could I say? Very sorry and all that? I decided to leave it for a few days.

Many months later when FMD was long gone and the slow process of rebuilding the shattered livestock farms began, I took great pleasure in travelling around Cumbria to unaffected areas accompanied by Robin who was buying back sheep to restock the farm. Robin and so many other farmers must have felt a huge sense of relief and excitement at this.

I knew a farmer who purchased a dairy herd to replace the one he had lost. The herd was delivered on Christmas Eve. He got up on Christmas morning to milk his new cows. Although they could not truly replace what he had lost, it was nevertheless the best Christmas present he had ever had. I still recall his beaming face when he told me the story. Of course that was much later on, for now we remained firmly in the grip of the disease with little light at the end of the tunnel.

32
How Voluntary is it?

Wednesday 25 April onward
Total number of cases: 1477

Over the course of the next three days I continued to travel in and around the Cockermouth area picking off fields of sheep for the voluntary cull. By now there was a real question as to whether the cull was in fact voluntary or compulsory. A close look at the official valuation papers showed that it was entitled the 'Voluntary Depopulation Scheme'. I had already contacted MAFF about this previously and was told that it had to be called by that name because Europe was funding a substantial part of the scheme. It appeared at the time that in many cases it was not a voluntary scheme for the farmers at all. They were often being told that their sheep had to be culled. Herein lies the difficulty. I felt then and still do that had so many farmers not let their sheep die in and around the Cockermouth area then the disease would surely have spread further. Yet in some areas farmers were being press-ganged into 'volunteering' not so much on veterinary grounds but more to dispose of as many sheep as possible. Of course I do not know the truth behind the scheme, I only seek to beg the question - what was it truly all about?

In time others would challenge the legality of the contiguous cull. In reality we will never know whether it was effective or not. What is true, is that we should never had found ourselves in the position whereby it had to be introduced in the first place.

It was at this time that Phoenix the calf literally rose from the dead. We were all sickened by the sight of this wretched little calf caked in mud from top to tail having been found in a pile of dead cattle a few days after they had been slaughtered. Shameful though this neglect was, it had a positive note to it, for the Government was forced into action by the sheer disgust and rage that was provoked throughout the country. At least the general public was asking questions about what was going on in rural areas. This certainly played a part in ending the contiguous cull for cattle. Could there have been a hint of election play making following the saviour of little Phoenix? In truth it hardly mattered to those of us remaining on the front line. There were still so many Cumbrian farms being taken out on a daily basis.

Some time later in the summer, I came across another Phoenix. I was visiting a farm that had lost its entire sheep flock as dangerous contacts. There had been no other cases in that area since then. I was standing in the farmyard passing the time of day when I heard a lamb bleating. I looked at the farmer who just shrugged his shoulders. He went on to explain that one week after all of his sheep had gone, a ewe wandered into the yard with a little lamb trailing behind. Somehow the sheep had managed to evade being gathered for slaughter. She had either hidden away or wandered on to neighbouring ground. Either way she had spared her life and the life of her lamb. Now she had come home; the farmer had tears in his eyes.

"I know I should probably have shot her myself," he said shaking his head, "I just couldn't do it. She's the only sheep I have left." So the farmer had let her live, maybe it was a ray of hope for him, a little something to keep him going. I don't know because I am not a psychologist, but I could see that that old ewe and her lamb were worth more than money to that farmer. So she remained alive and healthy tucked up in the back garden of the farmhouse. If I committed a crime as an accessory after the fact then throw me into gaol, for I decided that day not to tell a single person about the sheep. I have not until now.

That week I visited a local farmer who had some fell sheep wintering on his farm close to Cockermouth. The farmer's own sheep had already been culled. He apologised for the fact that another auctioneer had done the valuation for him. Apparently he had been recommended to use that auctioneer by MAFF because the valuer was 'already in the area'. It was coincidence I'm sure that the valuer in question had a growing reputation for being able to give just a touch more than the rest of us. In any case the farmer had been delighted by the valuation. The sheep were a sideline and his dairy herd remained intact.

In the warm spring sunshine we leaned back against his farmyard wall and put the world to rights. He asked me at length about the new auction. It was the common tale.

"You have to build it or farming's knackered in this area," he lamented. He was struggling to sell some prime cattle due to movement restrictions. Sadly the cattle were to reach 30 months of age and were no longer allowed into the food chain. Overnight they halved in value and had to be burned on the over 30-month scheme. It was not the farmer's fault in any way but there was no compensation to be had. The losses were all his. It was yet another example of an innocent farmer being brow beaten by an unfair system.

Later that afternoon I found myself on a farm at Isel, just above the river Derwent a few miles east of Cockermouth. This is beautiful rolling countryside where men pay a fortune to fish and shoot. The only shooting to go on that afternoon was to destroy a wonderful batch of Swaledale gimmer hoggs owned by the Emmott family. They were top class sheep and had been sired by a tup that in his day had been the best in the breed. Long in the tooth he may have been but his daughters were still tremendous sheep.

As I arrived at the fields I was met by a gamut of slaughtermen, field officers and dog handlers. It was reminiscent of the Scottish operations. I made a mental note that at last MAFF in England were starting to get their act together.

The vet in charge was a striking girl called Lysan who hailed from the Low Countries. She was a dead ringer for a good family friend of ours. I was convinced that one of them must have been given away at birth. In passing I discussed some of the cases I had been involved in recently. In particular we discussed the sad fate of the Herdwicks belonging to Andrew and Karen Nicholson at Lorton. I explained to the vet what a Herdwick was and just how important these sheep were to the Lake District. I must have struck a chord because she genuinely felt that something should be done to save the sheep in extreme circumstances. She was young and keen and decided she would go back to base and make some enquiries. I thought that was the last I would hear of it but I was wrong.

I made separate valuations for two fell farmers, all Swaledale sheep and drove back to the office. The evenings were now getting lighter and summer was on the way. I had read that sunlight kills foot and mouth disease - I hoped it was true. I, like many others, was getting really fed up with the job I was being asked to do.

The following day I received a surprise phone call from Lysan the vet. She had taken the case of the Herdwick sheep to the top in MAFF Carlisle. She had persuaded the top brass to consider these particular sheep and it appeared that if the vet was allowed to monitor the health of the sheep on a daily basis then they would receive a stay of execution. Whilst I thought this was tremendous news, I asked the vet to make sure she was not putting Andrew and Karen in a difficult position. They were worried about upsetting their neighbours who had dairy cows on the next farms. There was so often an undercurrent of guilt associated with these situations. The vet promised to discuss the whole matter with the Nicholsons. Nevertheless I felt that progress was being made within the inner sanctums of MAFF at this stage. Perhaps there were genuine concerns about the future of fell sheep in the Lake District. There had been so very little hope over recent weeks so this felt like a small victory. I decided to back up Lysan's actions by writing my own letter to the chief veterinary officer at Carlisle. It read as follows:

"The above mentioned farming partnership have been asked to volunteer all of their sheep in the Vale of Lorton. Many of the sheep represent some of the most outstanding Herdwick blood-lines currently alive within the Lake District. I have been charged with the unfortunate task of valuing the above mentioned sheep prior to slaughter but no amount of compensation can replace the loss of these outstanding sheep.

"As a measure of the loss felt by many Herdwick breeders, attempts have been made to collect semen and embryos from special sheep that have already been slaughtered... The TVI appointed to this farm... is of the opinion that a suitable plan can be put in place to quarantine the sheep and save a few of the most important...

"I fully understand the incredibly difficult position you are in at the moment... however if time and resources can in any way be used to spare some of these blood-lines... then I urge you try. In doing so you will be helping the many Lakeland farmers who rely on breeders like the Nicholsons."

It was now Friday afternoon and Paul Nicholson contacted me from Lorton Park. He was no relation to Andrew. This estate was very close to the other farms I had recently visited in that area. Paul is a highly regarded barrister whose passionate hobby is to breed Herdwick sheep that run freely over the pastures of Lorton Park. Paul had been well advised by retired farmer and Herdwick expert Harry Hardisty. Paul had heard that most of the sheep in the area were going on the voluntary cull and he felt duty bound to let his own go. This put me in a difficult position because I had indeed undertaken many valuations in the area but of course Andrew Nicholson's Herdwicks were maybe going to be spared.

I confirmed that the valuations had been done but the sheep had not yet been slaughtered. Paul Nicholson decided immediately that his own sheep would have to go. I walked straight out to my car. Within fifteen minutes we were walking through the wonderful parkland admiring the sheep and the scenery. For not the first time during the crisis I was surprised by the overall quality of the sheep. Of course the verdant parkland had done them well, but Paul had also been using well-bred tups. One of them, a hired in tup from the Hartley family from Turner Hall way down in the south of the county, was an exceptional type. I made my valuation and said my goodbyes. It was now early evening and for the second time that week I made my way over Whinlatter Pass on my way home.

I recalled a conversation with an old college friend of mine several years earlier. He had landed a plum job in the city on leaving college. His salary was immense, as was his two-hour journey to work at 6 o'clock every morning.

"I couldn't do it," I said "not for all the tea in China."

"The Lake District's all right," he replied "but it is for holidays really, not for working in."

As I popped over the top of Whinlatter I wondered at that time whether my old friend Clinchy really had made a good point. The joy and privilege I had always felt at working in the Lake District had been but a memory recently. I longed for the day when the enjoyment would come back to me. For now my work was a sentence to endure. My only consolation was the fact that tomorrow I was due to play in a game of rugby. I really could not wait.

33

A GAME OF RUGBY

Saturday 28 April
Total national cases: 1503

This was a day that I had long looked forward to. I had been invited to take part in a game of rugby at Penrith Rugby Club. The occasion was to mark the 40th birthday of an old team-mate of mine. I was to play for the Old Boys side against the current first team. I last played for the first team the previous year at the age of 35. I had actually got myself very fit at that point only to suffer a severe back injury. I had not run a step for six months and had of course put on much weight.

Now more than six months later and as a result of the foot and mouth crisis I had lost much of the weight again and was in fairly good condition at least physically. I knew I would not disgrace myself against the first team. Stupidly I felt I had a point to prove and now the day was here and I was determined to enjoy it.

My morning was spent at Alan and Anne Richardson's farm at Brathay Hill near Bassenthwaite. They were life long customers of Cockermouth Auction. Alan is one of those people who is skilled in the art of the wind up, however he does it in such a way that one could never take offence. Better still he can give it and take it.

This morning was a sad day for over the years they had put much effort into the breeding of their Suffolk and blue-faced Leicester sheep. Now they had to let them go in order to try and protect their dairy herd.

I wandered into the kitchen where they had just finished breakfast. We enjoyed a cup of coffee and some idle banter. It was certainly more subdued than normal. I put it down to the upsetting nature of my visit, however it was not that at all.

At last Alan spoke up: "Listen Adam I have to ask you something," he began, "we would never go past you at all but we have been told that you do not give the best prices as far as valuers go at the moment. We just want to be sure we are getting as much as anyone else."

The ugly spectre of farmers comparing valuers in terms of how much they were prepared to give was raising its head more and more. I appreciated Alan's honesty and assured him that I would give as much as I possibly could within the bounds of professionalism. I told him that he could appeal against my valuation if he felt it necessary although to my knowledge no one had seen fit to do so up to that point. Alan seemed very relieved to get his question out of the way. I was not offended and was glad that he had come right out and discussed it man to man.

We moved out to the car and began to travel around the farm inspecting and valuing the sheep. Later we returned to the kitchen to discuss and complete the valuation. We began with his pure Suffolk ewes. Alan had a good reputation for breeding pure Suffolk ram lambs. He often won prizes in our autumn show and sale.

I asked Alan to value the sheep for me. He told me what he thought they were worth and put a price on them. I shook my head.

"No Alan," I said. His face dropped. "Actually for sheep like this we've been giving rather more. You are just too modest," I said. His smile returned.

"Oh dear, I've asked you too little," he said.

"It's all right it won't happen again," I smiled, "because I'm not going to ask you!"

Soon our work was done and I promised to hand the completed valuation in at Penrith immediately. This was comforting to the Richardsons because now that they knew that the sheep were going, they wanted it to happen as soon as possible.

In just over a year's time the Richardsons would retire from the farm. They were true to their word and asked me to sell the dairy herd privately off the farm. They did not want the cows to be split up on to a multitude of farms through an auction sale. The cows were batched up and sold in number to local farmers. It was of course another customer less in the auction.

I said my goodbyes and drove down the road to Penrith. On my way to the rugby club I dropped off several valuation forms at the voluntary cull command centre. Driving along I tried not to think about the huge number of sheep that had disappeared from our business area. At some stage I knew I would be asked by the board of directors to make an assessment of how much stock would be left to sell if we built a new auction. What a position I would be placed in.

"No sorry gentlemen there just is not enough stock left to make it viable so give me my P45 now and I'll just go quietly along to the dole office. And by the way could Mitchell's Lakeland Properties kindly sell my house now that I cannot afford the mortgage. Oh yes and we have a new baby on the way, would anyone take it off our hands too?"

I realised at that point how bitter and frightened I was about the whole situation. Thankfully when I walked into the dressing room at the rugby club my troubles were forgotten as the old boys banter began. It was just like the old days.

The game began and I found myself on the bench. This made sense I reasoned because most of my team were still playing regularly. I had not been seen for a while. We actually scored first much to the embarrassment of the first team. They raised their game as my old mate Garry tore a hamstring and limped off in agony. I reminded him that his 'hammies' were shot at ten years ago when he was in his prime.

Gradually the four other substitutes were sent into action by the appointed team manager but he seemed to have forgotten about me. The second half was now being contested and I still had not got on. I was getting frustrated but made no complaints. The old boys were beginning to wain and the firsts were building a healthy lead.

At last the call came and I charged on. We were under enormous pressure now as the opposition turned the screw. I desperately wanted to have a charge with the ball but we could not get our hands on it. I turned to defensive mode and made a few tackles. One in particular was a beauty against one of the biggest and best of the first team forwards. A few seconds later I put another in. I was really enjoying it but we could not win any ball. Back behind the sticks again we tried to rally for the final ten minutes but several of the lads were done in.

I decided to stick in with the tackling but as we ran up to half way to begin the game again the team manager called me off. I had only been on ten minutes. I looked around me. Some of the lads were hoping that it was them being asked to retire. I walked off disconsolately. My chance to show what I could still do had gone.

"Oh well," I thought, "at least I can get a few beers down now." I went off to shower.

Back in the clubhouse I enjoyed a couple of quick pints then remembered that I had left my wallet in the car. It was my round next so I went to get it. As I sat in the car I noticed that there were some messages on my answer phone. In fact there were several messages mostly from my colleague John Marrs. I picked up the last couple and he was irate.

"What's the bloody point of having a mobile when you won't switch it on," I heard him say. He went on to explain that the Scottish Executive had found foot and mouth on a farm in Dumfriesshire. I was aware of the farm because there were over 1000 away-wintered hoggs from eight separate Lakeland farms all grazing up there, as they did every year. The Scottish Executive had already tried to insist that the sheep be slaughtered but the Lakeland men had argued like mad against it. The farm's owner had also tried to stop the sheep going. They had looked after sheep from these farms for many years and were proud of them. The previous day I had spoken to the farm owner. All of the Lakeland men had asked me to value should the worst happen. The owner had told me that there was no foot and mouth in the immediate vicinity and the sheep were in no danger. They had even spoken to the chief minister to try and save the sheep but the Scottish Executive were desperate to see the back of the sheep.

On the Saturday morning a vet had 'apparently' found foot and mouth among the farm owner's cattle. Of course it was not a confirmed case but the vets were insistent that the cattle and all of the fell hoggs would now have to die. There was nothing more that could be done.

John Marrs had fielded the call from Scotland asking for me to make my way there immediately. Of course I was off line at that moment as I briefly charged around the rugby pitch. Finally with no other choice John had set off at 4pm on his own to go to Scotland.

Waves of guilt came over me. I should not have played rugby. I should not have had a drink. I considered taking a chance and driving up to Scotland myself. It would have been folly having supped a couple of quick pints on an empty stomach. I couldn't just go back to the clubhouse so I phoned John. He was almost there. He told me which farmers were requiring valuations. I decided to sit in the car and ring them one by one to find out exactly what sheep were up there. It took over an hour but I put together the necessary information and phoned John back. I gave him advice based on what I had gleaned as to how the sheep should be valued. He went back to his job and I still sat in the rugby club car park. I felt as low and deflated as ever. All thoughts of enjoying my night out with the lads had gone. I still felt guilty for taking the time off and leaving John to carry the can.

I started my car and drove home in silence. My wonderful day of rugby and beer had turned sour. At least Paula and Olivia got to see rather more of me than they had expected.

Like it or not the actions of the Scottish Executive had created a 'fire-break' by virtually slaughtering all sheep close to the border with England. This included many thousands of Cheviot hill sheep. All subsequent blood tests were reportedly negative. Sure enough in time Scotland was able to regain its disease free status far sooner than England. Just as annoying was the fact that the rules and regulations under which Scottish markets operated were far less stringent in Scotland than just a few miles south of the border. It was to be as if we were in a different world. It was as one Cumbrian auctioneer said when the markets re-opened: "MAFF must think that the Scottish strain of foot and mouth is far less potent than the English." The rest of us made our own judgements.

34
PLEASE CAN WE HAVE OUR AUCTION BACK?

Sunday 29 April
Total National Cases: 1512

During the previous week I had been conversing with the MAFF field officer who was responsible for the cleansing, disinfection and reopening of Cumbrian auction marts. Of course we had all been shut down on a 'D' notice since early March. No livestock was being traded through auction marts and we had no income other than from FMD valuations. Before the disease appeared we had a nice little Sunday job in the form of a weekly car boot sale. Under a 'D' notice we could not allow the general public access to the mart. It was imperative that we could recommence car boot sales as soon as possible just to get some revenue in.

We could get the 'D' notice lifted if the mart was cleansed and disinfected to a required MAFF standard. Of course since the last livestock sale in February our yard staff had been over the place quite thoroughly. The whole of the mart had been steam cleaned and disinfected. It had not been as clean since the day it was built.

The MAFF representative whose name was Mark had agreed to visit the mart on Sunday morning. We expected that the inspection would be a formality. He arrived, walked down the first aisle of pens and shook his head. He took out a penknife and began to scrape away at the galvanised surface. Some of it came away to reveal small pockets of rust which was understandable in a post some many years old. Then he found some animal hair in a bolthole in one of the gates. We failed the inspection.

He instructed our staff to start all over again now that they knew what he was looking for. He promised to return in three weeks or so to see whether we had made any progress. It was clearly evident that his remit was to make sure that no Cumbrian auction was ready to open in the near future. The fact that some Cumbrian auctions were being publicly blamed by MAFF for spreading the disease meant that we were all tarred with the same brush.

Three weeks later we had had six staff members working on a full-time basis to scrape the auction clean. The field officer duly returned. The penknife came out again and he scraped and prodded around the mart.

"No," he said in a resigned manner, "not good enough. See you in three weeks." We were now getting very irate. This was ridiculous. One of my colleague's wives was now working for MAFF in the same department as the auction inspector. We asked her to come down and verify that what he wanted was in fact correct. She was working on many farms that were now on clean up operations having had foot and mouth. She confirmed that the standards we were being set were applicable across the board in every auction and on every affected farm. Subsequently we found out that one of our own directors had failed his inspection because a piece of baler twine had been found hanging from a rafter in a cattle byre. Apparently that was organic matter and therefore could have been harbouring foot and mouth virus. The whole farm had to be cleansed again.

It reminded me of the film *Cool Hand Luke* about a state penitentiary prisoner who keeps escaping then being caught. Finally in an effort to break him, he is made to dig a deep hole in the middle of the prison compound. He finishes and is told that the hole is too big and that he must dig another one of the right depth next to it. He does so and is told the hole is in the wrong place, do it again. The repetition continues until Luke is exhausted beaten and broken. We too were exhausted but not beaten. However if this pathetic charade continued it would probably have broken us, if only financially!

Many farmers were also getting very irate. The teams of MAFF people that were being employed to help farmers pressure wash and cleanse their buildings were a law unto themselves. It was in some (but not all cases) a licence to print money. It's been said that local gang masters were even employing registered long-term disabled people for cash, paying them £5 per hour and charging MAFF £15 per hour for the same men.

Meanwhile we had to scrub, pressure wash and scrape away at our livestock buildings with no outside assistance from MAFF at all. To make matters worse we spoke to an auctioneering acquaintance in another part of Northern England. He was surprised at the lengths we were being forced to go to. Their local MAFF department watched them give the market a token rinse out, throw some disinfectant down and then removed the 'D' notice.

The pressure on local farms that were disease-free was mounting by the day. As we struggled to cleanse the mart, round and about us local vets were assisting MAFF by taking blood samples from sheep on clean farms. This was known as bleeding and was being performed on a zonal basis as part of the roll-back programme around the county. Once a zone was tested and clear then 'D' notices such as the one served on the auction mart in March could be removed or rolled back. At that point and assuming a clean mart, we could then begin to operate a much needed collection centre for slaughter stock. Such was the demand for the facility, the local NFU branch wrote to MAFF in support as well as local veterinary practices.

The Millcroft veterinary group in Cockermouth issued a very clear indication of the problems. It was a letter to MAFF. Yet again it was another example of local people on the ground with expert knowledge being able to produce a considered solution to a problem. Their letter dated 2 July read as follows:

"There is an immediate need to facilitate controlled movement of stock to slaughter. Current schemes are viable only if the farm has sufficient numbers to justify the economic constraints of haulage to distant abattoirs. The Livestock Welfare Disposal Scheme so often quoted by DEFRA is cumbersome and elusive. Collection centres offer a means of addressing controlled movement to slaughter.

"Mitchell's auction mart located in Cockermouth town centre is in the process of licence application and lies within zone 11. Re-definition of zones would facilitate the licensing of this collection centre and directly improve the welfare prospects of the overstocked western side of Cumbria."

The letter went on to discuss the boundaries of individual zones that they may be altered to allow our reopening. We had no knowledge of the letter until a copy arrived on our doorstep from the vets. The letter backed up what we had been fighting for since March.

The mart cleaning operation had now cost us several thousand pounds. Some of the other Cumbrian markets had employed outside contractors to come in at even greater expense. Eventually the first 'D' notice was lifted in a Cumbrian mart. In late July we also had our restriction removed to allow the public back into the market but not livestock which was still restricted. By this stage it did not really matter. Our car boot sales began again but it was evident that our mart would never reopen again to sell livestock. By August the final deal to sell the site to

Sainsburys would be complete. By the time we handed the mart to them, the money made at the car boot sales did not cover our cleansing costs.

At the end of August we held the very final auction sale within the old market. I auctioned off all the old pens, the rings and anything else that could be taken away and used. The mart was packed out on that day. People came from far and wide just to watch. Many farmers tried to buy something just to take away a piece of memorabilia from the old Cockermouth Mart. I gave a TV interview to Judy Ingham from BBC Look North. She very quickly got a feel of the atmosphere. Her piece that night was positive, the old mart was about to disappear but there was hope for the future as we tried to secure the new mart development. In closing I asked Judy to make sure she came to the opening of the new mart. She did not forget and sure enough she did cover the opening day of the new market.

After the sale of the pens, many of us went across the road to the Tithe Barn pub and enjoyed a social afternoon, which were few and far between at that time. I sat with Bob Benn from Ennerdale, Raymond Matterson from Eskdale and Johnny Bolton from Gosforth. They had come many miles to say goodbye to their old market. We drank to the old mart which was already being torn apart. We also drank to the new mart should it happen. I was beginning to think that it just might.

As a temporary measure until the new mart was completed we operated a small-scale collection centre in a haulage yard in Cleator Moor. We had to spend many thousands of pounds to get the facility up to standard. Our intention was only to provide a service to keep our farmers going until their new market was ready. It was a loss leader from the start.

To rub salt in the wound, there was now a very apparent relaxing of standards on farms being cleansed later in the year. Common sense would say that it was so very unnecessary anyway. The chance of FMD virus being present in out mart was virtually non-existent. We were and still are a genuine farmers' market. All stock that comes through our doors are from local farms.

We live in a blame culture and the whole sorry mess had to blamed on someone, auction marts were pretty good targets. Sadly that included genuine farmers' markets like our own that were supported and relied upon by the farming community for so much more than just the trading of livestock.

Disheartened we may have been but we never gave up. There was still every intention at board level that if at all possible we would build our new mart. That was heartening for the Mitchell's valuers as we ploughed our own furrows around the affected farms of Cumbria. There was a purpose to what we were doing - we had to help our farmers and in doing so help ourselves.

Much later when FMD was long gone and a multitude of Government agencies boasted about how much grant funding was available to regenerate Cumbria, none could see it necessary to support the innocent businesses that lost so much during and after the crisis.

The sheer waste of time, money and effort asked of us to cleanse our old market was in the end a complete disgrace. Much worse were the differing standards of cleansing and operation, which were required in markets depending on their county of location. Cumbria bears the brunt even today with auction marts expected to operate to a standard cleansing and disinfection far in excess of other parts of the country. Why should that be? There was virtually no chance at all that our market could have FMD lurking in it. Only those sitting at MAFF's top table truly know why we were made to pay. Whatever their reason, it was very wrong.

35
LORTON AGAIN

Monday 30 April
Total National Cases: 1522

The number of cases on a per day basis was definitely slowing down. MAFF would of course try to tell us that the mass extinction process was working. Maybe it was true or maybe it was the advent of warmer weather and more hours of daylight. Maybe there had already been a significant loss in the critical mass of available stock left to slaughter. Those of us in the less affected areas of the county hung on and prayed whatever the reason.

It must have been hugely disappointing to our friends in the Ulverston area to see the disease inching closer. Likewise in the south east of the county. Sadly their horror was about to unfold on a massive scale.

Monday saw me making the trip yet again to the Lorton area, south of Cockermouth. I was christened in Lorton church and if money were no object I would surely live in the Lorton or Buttermere valley. It gladdens my heart when I drive through these valleys. What a privilege to call this area my work place. Sadly my colleagues and I had been particularly busy within the valley over recent days as so many sheep were disappearing. One glimmer of light had been the stay of execution of Andrew Nicholson's Herdwicks.

My first visit of the day was to the Graham family at Rogerscale. My formative years were spent growing up at High Mosser, just over the fell from Rogerscale. I had known their son Gordon since school days and knew him to be quietly level headed, sensible and with a sense of humour.

We sat in the parlour with Gordon's mother drinking tea and eating the last of the Christmas cake, which is one of my favourite pleasures. Soon we were in the pick-up travelling around the stock. Gordon had heard how many sheep had been volunteered throughout the area and almost felt duty bound to do the same. The big fear amongst the farmers on the edge of the northern most fells of Lakeland was that the disease would jump into the fell stocks and decimate the irreplaceable sheep. We all shared those concerns. Personally my future as an auctioneer depended on it.

We completed the valuation and Gordon was already planning how he would replace the sheep. He wanted to buy back more Cheviot sheep rather than Swaledale. Many farmers at this time were quite understandably saying that they could not even think of restocking. Some were threatening to retire altogether. I liked Gordon's positive attitude. He was going to buy back a better quality animal that would well suit his marginal farm. I only hoped that the valuation money I had offered would be sufficient. I kept my thoughts to myself and told him that one day I would sell his sheep again. This time in a new mart but deep down I could not even see it myself.

Later in the afternoon I found myself on the other side of Cockermouth at Westray farm near Redmain. The Johnstones had away-wintered hoggs taken in from two Borrowdale farmers. Like so many other fell men Stan Jackson and Joseph Relph had lost sheep all over the county in the voluntary cull and I had already valued many sheep for Stan. The Johnstones wanted to look after their dairy herd. They were pleased that I had come, yet sad for the fell farmers. It was a cold raw afternoon for the end of April. We spent some time discussing the situation in general. We all enjoyed the talk and putting the world to rights. Soon I was on my way back to the office with completed valuation forms in hand.

Months later when FMD was coming to an end Prince Charles made a visit to Borrowdale and in passing sampled some of Mrs Relph's 'herdyburgers'. This is a lamb burger made from home produced Herdwick lamb and is sold in the Relph's farmhouse teashop. HRH was so impressed he promised to return for a holiday and do some walking. He kept his promise and returned to Borrowdale when foot and mouth was over. This was a boost to both the farming and tourism businesses of the area. Of course the tourist-based businesses were being decimated at this time with virtually no Easter trade for the Lake District.

Having sampled the 'herdyburger' during his first visit the Prince then made his way to our own Cockermouth market and we were personally introduced to him. He questioned me about the valuation work and what it was like on the farm. I, in true English form kept a stiff upper lip. What was the point of moaning? We had a job to do. Nevertheless his presence was a boost to us all and his understanding of the situation was very good. He genuinely cared about what was happening. More importantly he took an interest in how the rural communities would pull together and rebuild once the disease was beaten. Meeting the Prince only for a short time rather cheered us up.

I could not help but contrast the Prince's attitude against those of the ministers. Where was their support and concern at our time of need? We all know the answer, for the truth is that they did not care or they would have come to Cumbria and stood by us. How I would have admired any of them had they had the courage to visit us in the field. To my knowledge they never did. They preferred to stay away and rule from afar. It still leaves a bitter taste.

Driving home on the evening of Monday 30 April I realised that I had been valuing animals in the foot and mouth crisis for almost two full months. In that time I, like many others had been in a kind of living hell. I could cope with the day to day routine of visiting farms that were losing stock whether through infection, dangerous contact or the voluntary cull. I had learned new skills in coping with crisis management, counselling enraged or grieving farmers. I had learned to accept the sight of thousands of live healthy animals being slaughtered and kicking their last and of young lambs, their bodies too feeble to take a bullet, being injected though the heart. My own difficulty was the uncertainty of my own future in one month, two or maybe even three. My wife was a matter of days from giving birth and I had not been there. She never moaned or complained. Now it was the month of May. How much longer would we have to go on coping and living the nightmare? It was a question that no one could answer.

That very day was my fathers' birthday. I completely forgot.

36
FIFTEEN DAYS IN MAY

Tuesday 1 May
Total National Cases: 1527

A phone call from Ed Noble at Beckermet Mill, first thing in the morn-ing, jolted me back to some sort of normality. Ed is one of life's jok-ers who can cheer anybody up.

"Are you going to get round to doing my IACS form this year or what?" he asked, " I know you don't like doing it," he continued, "but I'm not going to let you get away with this year just because of foot and mouth."

"Ed," I responded, "after what I've been through recently it will be an absolute pleasure. Can you come in this morning?" He said he could and in the meantime I made a couple of other appointments for regular cus-tomers whose IACS application forms I fill out every year. This is basi-cally the passport for a farmer to claim the appropriate subsidies that are applicable to his farm based on his land usage and livestock numbers on the farm.

As a company we do very many forms at this time of year. They have to be completed by 15 May or farmers get penalised. Although the work can be monotonous, this year would be fun because it marked a return to proper work. I could not wait. Through the next few days I did several IACS forms. It was nice to see normal customers again.

Interspersed between IACS applications were a few voluntary culls on local farms. There were still several hundred away-wintered fell hoggs that should have returned to fell farms weeks ago but were trapped by movement restrictions. It was questionable whether many Lakeland farmers would want to run the risk of the sheep returning to the farm any-way.

The animal welfare scheme (AWS) had been running since the spring. It was badly managed and in many cases impossible to get on. So many of our customers in West Cumbria had stock on hand that needed to be sold or disposed of. These were the most deserving cases but could not get their stock on to the AWS.

Later in the summer the scheme was revised as we all began to worry about the autumn sales period. Who would buy the stock? Could farmers get the stock on to the AWS and if so at what price? I went to several stake-holder meetings to argue the point. In the end the revised AWS came into being. Auction marts were excluded as collection points - more of that later.

What was pleasing at that time, was the fact that the number of valuations was tailing off. There was the odd scare or two locally as suspected cases were reported. Thankfully they were always negative. Gradually through May we began to see a glimmer of hope for ourselves. In the office we began to talk of resurrecting the plan for the new auction.

I looked at the maps of Cumbria and tried to assess what livestock would still be available for sale. My gut feeling was that we were still in the game. Meanwhile we watched in horror as the disease began to run rife down the Eden Valley and through Kirkby Stephen and onward to the high Pennine fells and North Yorkshire. So many very valuable flocks of sheep were being destroyed. I wondered how the local auctioneers were coping. It must have been a terrible nightmare.

Day by day there were still many new entrants on the confirmed case lists. This of course did not include the dangerous contacts that were never named. There were thousands of animals awaiting slaughter and it was believed that 6 million or so were already dead.

On the 9 May Mr Blair announced that the General Election was to be delayed no longer. It would be held on 7 June. It was obvious that FMD would come well down the canvassing agenda in the run up to polling day. To the general public the foot and mouth crisis was all but over. Paula and I shook our heads in disbelief as we watched the TV news. We felt as if we were being hung out to dry. So many times we were being let down.

By Friday 11 May I had completed most of my IACS work, done a few provisional grass lettings should stock eventually be allowed to move from farm to farm, and had started to have meetings with various bodies connected to the new auction plan. We were feeling a bit more positive about our own future but there was still a lot of pressure on us.

A few days later I was contacted by MAFF. I was one of the few 'experienced' valuers of deer. That made me chuckle. I was invited to travel into Dumfriesshire along with a Cumbrian deer breeder. We were to visit a game farm to value 600 semi-wild deer. They were originally farmed deer that had been turned out on to the estate to run wild. The Americans paid a fortune for a couple of days deer hunting. The deer were apparently dangerous contacts to an affected farm. That was all we knew.

When we got there we met the tenant of the estate and his team of trackers. They were sitting in the farmyard twiddling their thumbs. Their guns had been confiscated by MAFF officials who claimed that the locals had 'emotional involvement' with the deer. I found that one particularly hard to fathom since they made their living out of shooting the deer.

The army had been called in that morning to do the deed. The tenant was quite disgusted.

"We could have cleared this estate in two days," he said bitterly. Instead the squaddies had been tearing through the woods on quad bikes trying to chase the deer. It was now mid-afternoon.

"Come and see how successful they've been," said the tenant. We walked around the corner and there in a heap stood the entire day's kill. One roe deer and six wild boar. The boar had been relatively easy to get as they were already in an enclosed pen. The deer had been rather more difficult.

"Every time we get near them they just run off," said one soldier. The rest of us hardly expected them to stand and fight. We had made a pointless journey. We informed the Scottish Executive official that we would return on his say so when the deer were all dead and accounted for.

I made some enquiries and discovered that the army had chased around for a few more days before the slaughter was called off. The deer may well still be alive today. They certainly would not have been had the estate employees been ordered to do the job. Had it not been such an enormous waste of time it would have been laughable.

That night I went home and drank a can of beer. I dared not drink another because Paula was starting to grumble. She had been spring cleaning the house and feeling a few twinges. In farming terms she was beginning to freshen. I had paid so little interest over recent weeks the whole pregnancy had rather passed me by. In some ways it had been an inconvenience although Paula had tried so hard not to let it be so. We both had an early night to see what tomorrow would bring.

37
Soon I'll have to go

Saturday 12 May
Total National cases: 1585

Whilst our own valuation work load was easing, the disease still had a habit of breaking out all over the county. There were still new cases popping up all over the place. There were cases only a few miles north of Cockermouth near Dearham but thereafter it did not spread. Maybe because there were so few sheep left in the area or maybe because the methods and swiftness of slaughter and disposal were now so much better. Maybe it was a bit of both.

Saturday morning was a lovely and warm, early summer day. I spent my time in the garden with Olivia. We ran around with our shirts off playing football and planting shrubs and trees. Since the advent of the lighter nights I had begun to spend a few hours in my garden. Pleased though we were to have been able to buy such a nice house albeit in a decrepit state, our particular road was a summer sea of beautiful colour. Every single garden on the road either side of our house was the pride and joy of its owner. The annual village garden competition and open garden afternoon was the source of fervent activity in those gardens from dusk until dawn. Our garden was a seething mass of vegetation and every one a weed. Each evening as I came home from valuation work I could not bear to sit in the house watching sheep and cattle burning or being buried on the TV news. I still felt claustrophobic and wanted to leave it all behind. So I went out into the jungle and began to dig. Bit by bit the swathes of ground elder and dandelion began to recede.

Neighbours walked by and made noises of encouragement like: "Don't worry, Rome wasn't built in a day." Strangely I enjoyed it . The faster I dug, the more I sweated and FMD disappeared from my mind. Each night in the growing gloom I looked at what I had done and felt that I was achieving something and making a difference. It was only a piece of garden but it was fulfiling a badly missing part of me, the thought that what I was doing had a useful purpose. Plants and shrubs began to appear from neighbour's gardens. They were probably relieved that at last the scrubland that spoiled the whole road was being improved. I planted wherever I thought it might work, with no real idea about what I was doing.

I built a rockery and a gravelled flowerbed. Amazingly the plants began to grow. There were all colours, I did not even know their names and had to ask. I found some old bedding plant troughs and pots and filled them with flowering annuals. It was marvellous. I cut the lawn that had not been cut for years because the old lady who used to live in the house became too frail to do it. Some plants and flowers grew up in their own right. The neighbours recalled that they had been there for years but had been thwarted by the multiplying weeds in the old lady's garden. Then the *piece de resistance* came when our neighbour Eva gave me a strange looking plant almost like a sycamore tree but more bushy. I planted it and it flowered much to the chagrin of my neighbour. She admitted that she had given the plant to me although it had failed to flower in her garden for several seasons. Each morning I looked out at the large catkin like white flowers and felt a strange sense of achievement. I did not know where I was going in life, but my garden kept me on the path of sanity.

When darkness fell I showered and went to bed to sleep like a log. Olivia and I were looking at the plants when Paula called me in.

"What's the matter have you started?" I said.

"No it's bloody MAFF for you - a flaming valuation," she added, "tell them you can't go."

I took the phone call to be told that a confirmed case had been discovered at Threlkeld, between Keswick and Penrith. One of the neighbouring farms would have to be slaughtered as a dangerous contact. It was Harry Wilson at Gate Cragg next to the White Horse pub. It was only ten minutes from home. I agreed to do it and put the phone down. Paula was sitting at the bottom of the stairs resting her hands on her large bump.

"Well?" she enquired. She saw the look on my face, "You bloody idiot," she said, "I think I am starting!"

"Well why the hell didn't you tell me?" I yelled back.

"Because it took 26 hours last time and I didn't want to bother you."

We talked it through and I told her that I was only ten minutes away if contractions really started. I promised to be as quick as I could. I told her to phone her mother if she needed someone there and then. That one went down like a lead balloon.

By now it was early afternoon and the sun was red hot. I suited up at home putting by white protective paper suit over my shorts and tee shirt. It made me sweat like a pig. In a few minutes I was at Gate Cragg with Harry and the vet. I warned them that if I got the phone call that I would be off like a shot. If I missed the birth of my child I would never be forgiven. They all thought it was funny.

"Mind you," said the vet, "our first baby took for ever to be born but she spat the second one out in minutes." That really helped me! We moved quickly around the stock, all Herdwick ewes and hoggs. It was a miserable sad day for Harry. His sheep were more a hobby than anything else nowadays but even so they were irreplaceable Herdwicks.

Back in the kitchen we began to fill in the valuation forms. My phone rang. It was Paula.

"I think something's happening," she stated.

"What do you mean you think?"

"Well something is but I'm not sure what."

"Is it wind?"

"Of course it bloody isn't."

"What do you want me to do?"

"I don't know."

"Shall I come home?"

"I don't know, how long will you be?"

"Five minutes," I said and put the phone down. I turned to the vet.

"Sorry I'll have to go," I apologised.

The vet was great about it. He helped me fill in the necessary forms and agreed to complete the rest by himself. I thanked them and left, ripping off my paper sweat suit as I ran. Soon I was back at my own house where Paula was wandering around the garden in circles rubbing her tummy.

"Hmm," she said as I ran in, "I think, I think, I think it must be a false alarm." It was and there were to be several more over the next few days until the time came. I went back out into the garden to work on my flower beds.

38
A FAIR DAY'S PAY

Wednesday 16 May
Total National Cases: 1601- none reported in the county on this day

I had not been called upon to make any further valuation visits since Saturday. This was a great relief. Two full working days in the office had been useful catch up time. There were also the usual last minute IACS forms to complete and we had enjoyed a fruitful meeting with our bank manager from HSBC. The bank was still highly supportive of the new auction proposal even at this time.

My first call on Wednesday was to Penrith Auction for a meeting of all the livestock auctioneers in Cumbria. Our group was collectively known as CALA, the Cumbria Association of Livestock Auctioneers. Opponents we may have been in the past but during FMD we had tried to help each other where possible, undertaking valuations together or on each other's behalf where needed. Now a serious collective problem was brewing.

During the FMD crisis farmers had the right where reasonable to request the use of the valuer of their choice. In reality it was usually their local auctioneer. This was to change later as some valuers began to get 'reputations' and were called to areas well away from their normal patches. Once the valuation was complete the valuers would submit fee accounts to MAFF who were supposed to pay for the valuation work undertaken on their behalf.

By the end of June it became apparent that MAFF had not paid any of our valuation fees. Even at this stage there were tens of thousands of pounds owed to Mitchell's. Some of the bigger firms in the county were owed far more. We had all contacted MAFF to be told the same story. Apparently our invoices were invalid. There was no dispute that we had undertaken the work on MAFF's behalf but unfortunately there were limits on how much any one valuer could earn in one day. Once the valuer had reached his limit, he would be paid no more on that day. Even if as happened in my case, the valuer undertook several more valuations that day, he would receive no payment. The full story is as follows:

Way back in March when I made my first valuation at Tirril, fee payment was the last thing on my mind. The MAFF vet handed the official pack of valuation papers to me. Contained on one of the pages was a scale of fees on which the valuer would be paid. The formula was based on a sliding scale depending on the monetary value of the livestock in question. This was subject to a maximum fee and a minimum fee so that for example, a valuer required to value a single sheep would not just earn a fee of only a few pence. Conversely, the valuer required to assess a whole herd could potentially make thousands of pounds without some form of cap. The system was in place during the last minor outbreak of foot and mouth in 1980. It had served its purpose then. I remember questioning the vet and as far as he knew, the fee formula as handed to me was correct.

I went back to the office and instructed the accounting staff on how to issue fee accounts to MAFF. In the first month many accounts were issued. In the mean time I checked with other local auctioneers and even had the fee scale faxed through to me from one of them. To my knowledge not a single auctioneer was aware of a daily maximum fee.

One day our accounts department received a telephone call from MAFF payments section. They apologised to us for the fact that the fee formula as stated on the valuation papers was in fact wrong. It had been revised and we must scrap all of our old accounts and submit new ones to MAFF. The new formula was based on a straight-line percentage of the valuation subject to a maximum and minimum 'per valuation'. The rates were slightly different for infected premises and dangerous contacts compared to voluntary cull valuations but the principle was the exactly the same. This was clearly stated by the MAFF representative and in our haste to make sure we received some money, all of the submitted accounts were immediately revised and sent off to MAFF. At no time was there any indication of a maximum fee per day.

Later I contacted other auctioneers who were all having the same problem. We made contact with MAFF's payments section to be told the same story. We were not entitled to those unpaid valuations because the minimum and maximum valuations were subject to a daily cap not an individual valuation cap. Therefore on those days when I had made several calls, very often my first valuation took me to MAFF's daily limit after which they would pay me no more. This was quite different from the information we were given back in March. MAFF said that they had made the arrangements with the Central Association of Agricultural

Valuers but they could not claim to represent the auction firms who were not members of the association.

On the 10 May MAFF wrote the following letter to Mitchell's:

"We have received a number of invoices from you in respect of the work you have undertaken during the current outbreak. We are grateful for the significant effort you have put into assisting the Ministry over the last few weeks, and for the patience you have shown in waiting for payment for your services.

"While I want to make some payment to you quickly we are not in a position to pay against invoices at the moment. As you will be aware, there is a national agreement between MAFF and the CAAV governing the structure of fees. This includes a ceiling per day... but it is clear that some valuers are interpreting this as a maximum per valuation. This could be a very significant extra cost to us.

"It was agreed that the national guidance would be reviewed after six weeks of operation; that is now happening and I hope it will clarify the position. In the meantime, I am arranging for you to receive an 'on account' payment of 40% of the total invoices you have submitted to date... This is on the strict understanding that any resulting over-payment, once we have properly processed the invoices, will be refunded to us. I would be grateful for a letter from you confirming your agreement to this before I authorise payment. I will write again, once the national picture is clearer."

We did not accept the 40% payment and insisted on payment in full. John Marrs our company secretary wrote to MAFF payments section at the end of June confirming the basis on which we and all other auctioneers had been instructed:

"We remind you that at the beginning of this crisis we invoiced as per the letters of instruction given to our valuers at the time of each valuation... upon receipt of these your office returned the original invoices and requested that we re-invoice because the rates had been superseded... at no time did your office indicate a ceiling... per valuer, per day.

"We must inform you that we are not full members of CAAV and so were not aware of the fee structure agreed between MAFF and CAAV. Please find enclose a statement of your account as of today's date together with interest charges accrued."

Sadly in our haste to get the job done valuers had taken MAFF's word on trust. Not one of us had sought confirmation in writing although we had all received the initial scale of fees as stated on the early foot and mouth papers saying it was a minimum/maximum per valuation. Each and very auctioneer had submitted their fee accounts on the same basis.

By now it was late summer. Payments started to trickle in. MAFF did not pay any fees where valuers had gone over the 'daily limit'. We still kept doing the job and not once did we ever refuse to work because we were over the daily limit. MAFF owed us many thousands of pounds in unpaid fees. Other firms in Cumbria were owed several hundred thousand pounds. It was a disgrace and at the CALA meeting we resolved to take legal advice.

I also made contact again with MAFF who agreed to meet me. They sent a representative who began by acknowledging exactly what I was going to say and that he could do absolutely nothing about it. Page Street was handling the matter and they were adamant that the valuers would not be paid beyond a capped figure per day. He smiled at me as he finished his statement.

I did not lose my temper but told him about the days I had worked on MAFF's behalf. Days like those down in the Duddon Valley, leaving home before daylight and getting back the next day only to be back on the same road again before daylight. The MAFF man shrugged his shoulders.

"What can I do about it?" he said rhetorically.

I asked him his opinion on the fact that each and every auctioneer had submitted the same type of account. It was a bit of a coincidence did he not agree? He shrugged his shoulders again. I tried one last tack.

"Would you have done what we had to do?" I enquired, "working 18 hour days back to back knowing that you were not going to get paid? None of us would have done that had we known you were going to do this to us!" He just smiled and shrugged his shoulders.

"I understand," he said.

At that point I knew the meeting was over.

"This is not over," I said to the MAFF man as he left.

"I don't suppose it is," he replied, "but if I can be of any further help…"

Finally we received a letter from DEFRA dated 11 September outlining what was expected of the valuer on valuation day. It also enclosed written details of the basis of fee payment, predictably including a daily cap. At the time of writing the matter of unpaid fees is unresolved. In

2003 a test case is being brought by a Scottish auction company against the Scottish Executive. This mart is owed over £200,000 on exactly the same basis as all of the rest of us. We hope and pray that in all fairness the auction company is successful.

All we ask for is a fair days pay for a fair day's work. With what we all had to endure on the farms of Cumbria and beyond, the outstanding fees are scant reward in reality. Auction marts are now at their weakest in the aftermath of foot and mouth. The farmers have returned to market in droves for they value our worth, but so much stock has been lost as we struggle to survive.

39
THE WHEELS ON THE BUS

Thursday 17 May
Total National Cases: 1604

The disease continued to spread around the county. New areas were affected and pockets of livestock in previously affected areas seemed to get wheedled out as foot and mouth continued to in-fill. There was no discernible pattern. Thankfully West Cumbria remained relatively unaffected although there was some infection too close for comfort a few miles north of Cockermouth.

It was a beautifully warm day and sunlight filled my office as I worked away at my desk on matters pertaining to the new auction development. Then to spoil it all I received a call from MAFF. I was to proceed straight away to a field at Penruddock only a few hundred yards from Walloway where my friends the Edmondsons were just beginning their clean up operation after FMD. Somehow a field of breeding cattle belonging to another farmer had survived after Walloway had gone down. Eventually the Hogg family who were the owners of the cattle had enquired why MAFF had not taken them being so close to an infected premises. Once MAFF knew they were there, the wheels began to roll. By the time I arrived the cattle had been rounded up and penned. There was a multitude of field officers, soldiers and support staff in attendance.

I got booted and suited in the blistering heat. It was the hottest day of the year and we were all sweating profusely. I completed my valuation quickly and even as I signed the forms the official marksman began to shoot the cattle. His job was performed in a totally professional manner and soon the cattle were lying in neat heaps. They never knew a thing.

All was well as I stripped off my protective suit and chatted to the vet. Just then along the road came the school bus. It was brought to a halt by the myriad of official vehicles. The bus crawled past the heap of bodies lying in the sunlight, eyes wide open but seeing nothing, flecks of blood betraying the bullet they had received.

I immediately thought of poor Chris Edmondson who had seen the same sight a few days earlier as his family's own herd was destroyed while the very same bus drove past. I hoped he was not on the bus again.

Even so I could see the faces of the young children pressed against the window. They would be curious and I hoped none of them were upset. It seemed to take an age to let the bus pass by. Soon it was on its way, leaving the miserable scene behind it.

The wheels on the bus go round and round it was my little girl's favourite song. I was only a few miles from home. I decided to get back as soon as possible. Surely Paula could not hang to our unborn baby too much longer, she had been grumbling all week. It was something to look forward to and yet I was strangely detached. I put it down to the fact that it was our second child and the novelty was not as strong. Had I looked inward I might have seen that the reality was a little more disturbing.

40
MASTER LUKE

Saturday 19 May
Total National cases: 1608

Something was definitely stirring. It was the same as last time - the prods in my back throughout the night every time Paula felt a tightening across her stomach. By morning I was well aware that our impending arrival was not too far away. I was now officially off-line and that applied to MAFF also!

Olivia was shipped back to grandma's. She had already spent a couple of nights there earlier in the week as the grumblings inside Paula continued. At that time we had a brief trip to see the midwife who confirmed that all was in order and the baby almost fully engaged. There were a couple of remedies available to us to speed up the course of nature. One was a trip to the local Indian restaurant and the other involved an early night. We both decided we were really quite hungry and set off for Cagney's Tandoori. The net result was bad indigestion for Paula but no sign of baby. By Friday nature had finally taken its course and we were ready for action.

Through the afternoon the contractions got stronger and finally Paula decided it was time to go to hospital. Calmly we drove into Penrith. A quick examination revealed that there was no panic. The midwife thought it could be through the night or the following morning. Given the choice between staying and going home we thought we would go home where there were a few more creature comforts.

We drove to Safeways in Penrith to get some provisions for tea. I left Paula in the car and went shopping. As a force of habit I locked the car with the electronic key fob. After I had gone Paula began to feel stuffy in the hot car. She could not open the window for it too was electronic. Then she realised the door was locked and immediately had a mini panic attack fearing she was trapped in the car. She did not realise that she only had to open the car door to release the door locking system. By the time I sauntered back to the car she was apoplectic, covered in sweat and breathing very heavily. It was so funny that I laughed; wrong move on my part!

The air was blue as we drove home but it was the best thing that could have happened. For as we ate our tea the contractions became a lot stronger, so we loaded the car up again and set off back to Penrith maternity hospital. Soon we were bedded in and Paula lay on the floor as I watched television. I was delighted to see that the film *Die Hard 2* was on TV. I had not seen it before but knew that an action adventure film would pass the evening well as we coped with stage one labour.

Soon Bruce Willis was in top form dashing around a hijacked airport. I became engrossed and hardly noticed Paula beginning to strain a little more. Soon she was telling the midwife that she needed to push, stage two was upon us. With Olivia's birth this lasted about four hours so I knew that I could keep one eye on TV and one on my labouring wife.

By now a plane load of people were about to be crashed onto the airport runway. Bruce dashed out onto the runway in freezing driving snow waving only two blazing torches. Paula was now on her knees on the bed pushing for all she was worth

"Pull up, pull up," screamed Bruce as the plane thundered over him.

"Push down, push down," commanded the midwife as Paula moaned through gritted teeth. The plane crashed and Bruce's efforts were in vain which was just as well because now I could concentrate on Paula. Besides that the midwife had switched the TV off anyway. I thought about arguing but did not want to be accused of being selfish!!

I was just getting settled at Paula's side when the midwife yelled that one more push would do it. I was amazed. This could not be right. Last time it had taken hours of pushing and then a transfer to Carlisle. I decided to go and take a look and as I did so a baby flopped out onto the bed. It was five minutes to midnight.

"What's happened?" shouted Paula as I stared at the little lump. I thought of the *Only Fools and Horses* programme and was determined not to say: "It's a baby!" so I just said nothing.

"You have a little boy," said the midwife, "but he's not so little."

The midwife placed Master Luke James Jackson Day into my arms. I felt somehow detached from the situation. I expected to feel an immediate bond with my son as I had done with Olivia when she was born. The bond did not seem to be there. I held him for some time whilst Paula recovered. She had been a little stunned by the relative speed with which our baby had been born. After a while she asked for him and I handed him over. He was perfect in every way, a bouncing baby boy of 8lb 11oz.

We did not discuss our feelings at this time and it was only in the writing of this chapter that Paula admitted that she too had struggled in the early days to bond with our boy. Maybe this is a common tale, I do not know. Through the early months of our baby's life I did not really get close to him. Of course I fed him when he hit the bottle, changed nappies and bathed him yet I was detached. Gradually in time our bond grew and our family unit became tighter.

Now I feel great pleasure and comfort when my little girl and my little boy sit on my knee watching TV or reading a book. It is like they have always been a part of our lives. Life would be miserable without them. Yet for me it took many months for those intimate feelings to grow after Luke's birth.

I do not sit and think about the situation but I am sure that my detachment was a barrier that I created during foot and mouth. Day after day I witnessed the death of animals, healthy animals mostly, mainly mothers and their very young offspring. Also the pain and suffering of the animals' owners whose mental stresses manifested themselves in many ways. I defy any valuer, vet or slaughter man to state that he or she was not affected by what they had to endure during the crisis. Each and every one of us dealt with the situation in our own way. Mine was to build a wall that stopped me from showing any more emotion. The fact that I had not shared in my wife's pregnancy was also a contributory factor. Her pregnancy was if anything an imposition to me as both she and I struggled to cope with what was happening around us. It was a fraught time that certainly affected our relationship with our new-born, even if at the time we did not realise it.

Drawing a close to this chapter, I now accept that the experience of my son's birth was at the time much affected by what was going on in my day to day work environment. I hope that the net effect on me is minimal. Nowadays I feel very proud of my family and I look forward to my time spent with them. We are indeed lucky to have two fine healthy offspring.

My only regret about Paula's labour with Luke is that I honestly do not know how Bruce Willis beat the baddies. He did beat them didn't he? The righteous always seem to prevail in the end, at least in Hollywood!

41
FURTHER AFIELD

Thursday 31 May
Total National cases: 1669

The few days after my son's birth had been a bit of a whirlwind. Having taken a day and a half in holiday, or was it paternity leave? I was feeling refreshed in myself if not a little jaded physically. The night-time duties were taking their toll but I had no complaints.

FMD continued to rage through East Cumbria within the so-called Penrith spur. We continued to monitor the local radio broadcasts hoping that West Cumbria would not be mentioned. I felt truly sorry for the auctioneers working in the east of the county. Their task must have seemed never ending. Their efforts should be acknowledged and remembered by the farming community for many years to come. For the work they did on behalf of MAFF and their farming communities went far beyond the call of duty. Any farmers who have not rewarded their valuers by supporting the auction to the hilt after foot and mouth should be ashamed of themselves. Without their valuers on the farm during foot and mouth, the farmers would have been stuck with nothing but a book price valuation imposed by MAFF. Yet again the auctioneers were there trying to ensure fair play and a fair price.

The disease or rather the cull was also rife in the Settle area of North Yorkshire forcing the Minister of Agriculture to visit the town. Sadly he would only address a meeting behind closed doors with the NFU and local council. Also a further case had popped up in Devon, the first for many days.

By the last day of May I had not undertaken any valuations for several days. I was not disappointed for we were now heavily focused on bringing the new mart proposal back up to speed having shelved it albeit temporarily at the start of the crisis.

Late on Thursday morning I received a phone call from MAFF to proceed to Hall Farm in the village of Morland a few miles south of Penrith. I had sold much stock for David Gill during my training years at Penrith. Latterly he had worked closely with my friend David Jackson, also an ex-Penrith auctioneer. Jacko was first choice valuer for the job at Hall

Farm but owned his own cattle and sheep. Therefore he could not under-take a confirmed case valuation without having to stay away from his own farm. I was David Gill's second choice and was delighted to be asked even though it was not a job I would look forward to or relish. For the Gills it would be a heartbreaking end to a long family tenancy at Hall Farm. They had farmed there for 47 years and were past retiring age. It was highly unlikely that they would restock after the disaster.

FMD was easily diagnosed among the dairy cows. One beast had been off her food at morning milking, by lunchtime there were 15 or more cows looking very poorly, long trails of mucus dripping from their muz-zles, hopping from foot to foot in discomfort. It was clinically clear cut that they had foot and mouth.

I set off around the fields with David Gill and the vet. Her name was Michelle and I knew that I had worked with her before but had forgotten which valuation it was, there had been so many. Her line of greeting was to say: "Nice to see you again Adam. You haven't improved any with age."

"Charming," I replied trying to think of a suitably rude riposte. None came so I carried on walking. Admittedly I was not at my best - I had conjunctivitis in one eye and had not shaved for a while. Michelle had a point really. Anyway David found it hugely amusing, which lifted our sombre mood, well theirs anyway!

Soon we had inspected all of the stock and I retired to the kitchen table to write up my valuation papers. The slaughter team were already there making preparations. Soon Michelle the vet joined me and we agreed the valuation and she went back down the yard to authorise the start of the cull.

I drank my cup of tea and chatted away to both David and Mrs Gill. Suddenly Mrs Gill began to cry. I was taken aback. I had been so busy writing up my figures and talking aimlessly I had not even noticed Mrs Gill getting upset. I suddenly realised that I had become so blasé about foot and mouth valuations that they had become a routine. It was as if it was just a routine day at the office. I had lost my bedside manner and I felt terrible. I apologised to Mrs Gill and told her that I did not mean to be so flippant about my job it was just that I had done so many it was if I had gone on to automatic pilot.

"I understand," she said, "but I just can't bear to think of our cows..." she paused for breath and composure, "we won't be able to hear the noise will we? I couldn't bear it."

"Oh no," I said "it is done very quickly and quietly." At that point a shot rang out like the crack of a whip followed at regular intervals by others. This was going from bad to worse and it was beginning to affect David now. I looked around the kitchen and spied the television.

"Put the telly on David," I instructed, "we don't need to listen to that." David switched the little portable on and there was a cartoon on.

"Oh good," I thought, "this will be nice and loud." The cartoon was about a man with a large gun chasing what appeared to be an old cow down a dusty road. The man was screaming: "I'm a gonna git yer old cow," as he loosed off several barrels of shot in the general direction of the cow. Mrs Gill looked in horror. I bounced off my chair and turned the TV off. "We needn't watch that rubbish," I said fast wondering what the hell else could go wrong.

Just then Michelle came back and seeing the upset in the house quickly confirmed that it would all be over very shortly. This seemed to help. We had another cup of tea and I was ready to make my goodbyes. I was glad to leave because I realised that I had not been at my best. I certainly had not handled the situation very well and put it down to a combination of the fact that I had lost some concentration over the last few days and was not back up to speed.

The Gills did not restock. They gave notice on their tenancy and quit the farm early in 2002. Despite my performance on valuation day they asked David Jackson and myself to handle their farm sale. Of course there was no livestock to sell, even so it was an absolute pleasure to be holding a real auction sale once again. That pleasure was shared by many of the local farmers who themselves felt that our little farm sale was a long awaited step in the right direction to put distance between themselves and foot and mouth. There were even tears as we walked up and down the rows of lots. Mostly they were tears of joy and relief. Slowly the farming villages were beginning to breathe life. It was a wonderful feeling, which I cannot adequately describe.

Friday was the first day of June. Sitting in my office recounting the previous day's events I was interrupted by the phone. It was MAFF yet again. David Gills neighbour was Edward Hayes at Lowergate. He was another old customer from my Penrith days and his wry wit was always enjoyable. I made my way back up the A66 yet again and drove into Morland early in the afternoon.

Edward greeted me with his usual laconic smile. He told me that the vet had 'been and gone'.

"Don't worry," I said, "he'll be back."

Lowergate was to be taken out as a dangerous contact to Hall Farm. We walked around the yard; none of the cattle had foot and mouth. I valued a wonderful pen of huge prime bullocks. They would have been ready a couple of months previously had it not been for foot and mouth. Since that time Edward had continued to throw feed at them to keep them in tip-top condition. Sometimes pride can be a difficult burden. I wrote my valuation down on my pad. I could sense Edward trying to look at what I had put down. Playfully I put the pad to my chest.

"Go on then," I said, "what do you think?"

"Well 'er a man told me on the phone last night what I should be getting for these good bullocks."

"Oh yes and what did this man say," I questioned. Edward told me and I feigned surprise. Sucking my cheeks in as if in shock I saw the look come over Edwards' face. It said "Oh my God I'm in trouble here." Then I laughed as I showed him my figure. It was within £10 of his price. Edward sighed with relief.

"For a moment I thought I was going to have to sack you," he smiled.

"Well at least you had another good valuer to call on," I replied.

We walked around the farm in the warm summer sunshine. Such a contrast to the bitter springs days in the Duddon Valley even if the objective of my visit was the same.

Soon Jarlath the vet joined us. His western Irish brogue was so strong we had to concentrate really hard to understand him. He began to explain some of the veterinary science behind the FMD cull. I didn't understand a word he said and just nodded dumbly. He seemed to ask me a question so I replied in the affirmative. It must have been the right answer because he nodded back and carried on.

Soon our job was done and I was ready to leave. I wished the Hayes family well and left the farm. Yet again the following year we were to return with David Jackson to hold a farm sale. Edward was another farmer who decided to retire. Sadly at his farm sale I had such a bad throat I could only sell 40 or so lots. David and Alisdare did not mind. They were enjoying themselves immensely.

That night I returned again to the area to sing at the 40th birthday party of a local farmer's wife. She had actually turned 40 during the FMD crisis.

Whilst all the farms around the Armstrongs had succumbed to the disease, Rusty had locked his cows inside through the summer, tended them well and kept them free of disease. It was a miracle. One year later the birthday party was finally held and what a good party it was. My only regret was the state of my voice. After only two songs I sounded like Tom Jones on helium. It was a disgrace but there was no way I could have cried off from that party. No one seemed to mind. Parties had been few and far between for so many months.

42

RUBBERNECKERS AT KESWICK

Saturday 2 June
Total national cases: 1694

I was watching the television on Saturday morning. I think it was a rugby match being beamed live from Australia. The phone rang, it was of course MAFF. I had to proceed to some land near Keswick on the main road to Thirlmere. I was to value some dangerous contact cattle for the Cockbain family at Rakefoot farm. They would actually be glad to see the cattle go because this would create a firebreak between their beloved Swaledale fell sheep and other stock on an infected premises close by.

I arrived and parked at the roadside. Despite the fact that the Lake District was not attracting many tourists or visitors at this time there were plenty of people slowing down to get a good look at what was going on. All the white suits were attracting much attention. Some cars even pulled up at the roadside to get a better view. I believe that the official term for such people is 'rubberneckers'. Perhaps they thought it would be like a road traffic accident with lots of bent metal and a few bodies lying around. I was rather put out by it but as usual said nothing and got on with the job.

Will Cockbain was unflappable in a style that would serve him well during the next year in his time as chairman of Cumbria National Farmers Union. Through the foot and mouth crisis we had talked many times about the bigger picture. Will had major reservations about Government policy and the NFU's own policy. We both felt that there was too little concrete information coming from Government about the crisis. The vaccination debate was the cause of much angst. Will did not want to see their cherished Swaledale flock destroyed either by foot and mouth or after being vaccinated, a policy which the NFU were stating would be implemented in the event of a county wide vaccination policy. I believe Will came close to resigning from the NFU before he could be sure that the correct courses of action were being explored and implemented. It was certainly a time of much stress especially as the Cockbains lost many away-wintered sheep around the county.

Back in the field Will and I walked quietly through the cattle. I gave him a valuation opinion and asked him what he thought. He shrugged his shoulders: "You know the score," he said, "whatever you say will be right by me." As always I was delighted with that sort of attitude. It made me feel like I was doing a worthwhile job.

The valuation was completed and I left Will and the MAFF team to organise the logistics of the kill. The cows and calves were rounded up and disposed of by the bullet with minimum fuss. Will told me afterwards that he was really concerned that the cows would smell blood and panic. Thankfully the whole operation was conducted with thorough professionalism. The rubberneckers probably never knew what was going on at the other side of the hedge.

I walked over to my car to get rid of my disposable white suit and disinfected waterproofs. Amazingly there was a family sitting in a car directly behind my own. They were eating sandwiches.

"Nice day for it," I said pretending to tug my forelock. The driver of the vehicle whom I took to be the head of the family said something that was indistinguishable for his mouth was full of food. I expect he was agreeing with me. I drove home and chuckled rather as I imagined his conversation in the pub.

"We actually came across one of those foot and mouth farms you know. There were lots of people in white suits rounding up some cattle. Then they shot them. We were hungry so we ate our beef sandwiches. What a good day out that was."

That night I travelled with the band to play at Glenridding along the side of Lake Ullswater. I was delighted that quite a lot of local farmers had made the effort to come. My old friend Gordon Teasdale, an almost-retired auctioneer who was a colleague in my Penrith days was also there. He marched up to the stage as I blasted out *Suspicious Minds* and placed a pint of beer in front of me. There was no talk of foot and mouth. Instead everyone enjoyed a good blow out, drinking and dancing the night away. The band enjoyed it so much that we carried on for an hour after the expected 'last song'. It was a little ray of light within the dark tunnel that so many of us had been living and working in.

43

TALK OF THE FUTURE

Wednesday 13 June
Total national Cases: 1741

Work was continuing at full pace on our new mart development, it was exciting and time consuming. It was a passion and of course a welcome distraction from foot and mouth. Around the county the pattern remained the same. The disease drove onward engulfing village after village in East Cumbria. It had gone through Shap and by now it had worked its way down to Orton. Beyond lay the Howgill Fells and of course the uplands of the southern Lake District. No matter where MAFF tried to stop it, FMD was always one step ahead like chasing a feather on a windy day. When you thought it was in your grasp it was away again on the breeze.

It was now blatantly obvious that the disease should have been stamped upon when first diagnosed within the county. Of course hindsight is a wonderful thing but please remember the warnings given to me by the first vet I encountered on an infected premises in March.

"Dead in 24 hours, disposed of in 48 hours," Phil Watson, the vet on my first valuation had been proved right. The experts in the field knew the score. So why did no one at a higher level listen to them? They must have felt as let down as the rest of us. By June 2002 there could be no doubt that the lack of resources offered to save the county in the early days, had contributed heavily to the spread of the disease. I later found out that many vets had strong reservations about the culling policy and in particular contiguous stock. The vets were like the auctioneers, too proud to back out, professional enough to see the job through. A job that was the exact opposite of everything they had been trained to do.

On Thursday 7 June it was General Election day. I voted in the village hall for the local Conservative candidate David Maclean. He had stood up and voiced his opinions with eloquence when it mattered, begging the Government to take action early on during the crisis. He called for the army and much greater resources. He warned them what would happen for he was listening to the opinions of the experts on the ground in Cumbria. I thought that he deserved my vote. It made little difference really because Mr Blair returned to Downing Street for another term. I was learning about the game of politics being played by all parties. The truth is not all-important; it is how to influence the public. Far more sickening was the knowledge that some politicians cared little about what was happening in crisis torn places like Cumbria at this time. How we would have welcomed a brave minister to walk onto a foot and mouth affected farm, to have witnessed the despair, the pain and the sheer wastefulness of what was happening. How we would have admired a man or woman who was brave enough to watch the killing and disposal, to talk to the many people who were working in this environment. It was not to be. They stayed well away from the 'lepers' in the colonies. Fleeting visits through back doors in secret locations, running away from reporters or the public should they spotted in the affected counties.

Soon after that MAFF was to become DEFRA - the Department of Environment, Food and Rural Affairs. Along with it came a new minister in the form of Margaret Beckett. Those of us connected to farming worried about her total inexperience pertaining to any matters which would form part of DEFRA's constitution.

Little wonder that DEFRA's nickname amongst the farming fraternity should become DAFTA. For it seemed that in time an ever-thickening wedge was being driven between the Government's rural ministry and the people it was supposed to guide and help. So often the DEFRA people at ground level could be seen to have a good understanding on what was happening only to be superseded by the higher powers in Page Street. Any business has to be run from the ground floor up. Of course final responsibility finishes at the top, but it is the grunts in the field that truly make the company successful. Until we see far greater regional control again within DEFRA, then it will not be a department that can truly claim to represent and support its people if indeed that is what it wants to do.

I drove to Carlisle in the afternoon at the invitation of Business Link Cumbria. All the auctioneers were there together with some of the top advisors in local government. Their talk was of a sustainable future for Cumbrian farming. A new approach to the red meat sector that is such an integral part of rural Lakeland. The approach was to create a vision that when implemented would secure the future of Cumbrian farming by improving breeding programmes reducing the length of the food chain and improving profitability for Cumbrian farmers. By adopting this plan the auctioneers could carve their niche in the big scheme of things. Maybe by even working together as one within the county.

It was exciting stuff and I believed that it might be a step in the right direction. It could have worked but for the remarkably cool stance of some of the auctioneers who from the start would never consider working with their competitors. They would rather fight to the death than consider another option. For some it would eventually lead to the death of their livestock auctions but that is another story. We must have appeared a pathetic bunch to the business advisors who were trying to provoke some radical thinking. Eventually a major study was undertaken by Cumbria County Council in order to promote a sustainable future for the red meat sector. Sadly it was destined to fail for despite the auctioneers' resistance to a united approach, much of the radical thinking would have removed the competitive auction sales of prime stock altogether. The auction companies would never let this happen and the majority of the farmers would not want it anyway.

Business Link and all of the other advisors were full of enthusiasm. They even came up with an idea as to how the auctioneers could gain some funding from them for IT equipment and marketing initiatives. This would at least help us take the first step to regenerate our own crumbled businesses. All we had to do was create a simple business plan as to why we needed the funding and what we would do with it. In the case of Mitchell's Auction Company we were eligible for several thousand pounds of funding towards computer equipment and the construction of a website. I duly put together a plan with the help our local accountants. They, knowing the funding scheme well, created an appropriate application package and sent it off to Business Link whilst at the same time submitting their fee account for the job.

Some weeks later I received a letter from Business Link telling me that all the funding money had already been awarded and anyway auctioneers did not actually qualify for funding in the first place. Other types of funding would be available to us in the future.

Later there were regeneration funding groups springing up all over the place with public and private money on offer. I believe the final figure was around 170 or so different funding pockets available to those that could apply. Regeneration and rural deprivation were to be the buzz words after FMD. Community self-help was to be the key to unlocking all of the available money. Unfortunately, long established Cumbrian companies like our own were more or less debarred from claiming any form of grant money. Claims from agricultural businesses were for the most part totally brushed aside following foot and mouth.

Even though Mitchell's were prepared to take a step into the unknown by building a brand new mart in order to continue serving the rural communities of Lakeland and even though we knew we could hardly make a living selling what livestock remained for sale after foot and mouth and even though we knew it might take up to five years (if ever) to fully recover from the losses, despite all this, nobody was prepared to give funding to help us.

All the while our farmers were pleading with us to build them a new mart for they knew the consequences for their own businesses if there was no longer a livestock market at Cockermouth. Since we had been shut down by MAFF in February those farmers had been forced to sell prime animals straight to the abattoirs. Prices had fallen dramatically and the farmers had been shown no mercy by the meat buyers. Without the livestock marts there was no real competition for stock. The buyers could name their price.

Regeneration funding appeared to mirror much of the CAP funding programme. Huge amounts of available finance were taken up in the 'administration and management' of the schemes. I began to feel that I was in the wrong job.

Even when Mitchell's came up with auction-based community led schemes which we knew would benefit our customers and help sustain our own business after foot and mouth, we were knocked back.

"Oh yes," we were told, "there is pots of money available for you to create a Health Action Zone and a training centre with computer facilities for the rural community within your auction complex, but unfortunately you are a commercial business. It's easy, all you have to do is make a gift of your premises to a community led committee who will then administer the whole thing. You of course cannot take one penny out of the funding or be seen to make a profit in any way from the facilities you create."

"But that will put our auction company out of business because our shareholders do not see us as a charity even though they are mostly farmers."

"Ah well there you have it. You need to be a charity or similar in order to get the money."

"But our farmers, their families and their neighbours in the rurality will gain great benefit from these facilities especially if they are located at the auction. If the auction is no longer there for them then what do they do?"

"They need to form their own committee, community led you see. You can sit on the committee but you cannot be seen to take any financial gain from the committee."

"Aaaaaaaaaaaaaahhhhhhhhhhhhhh," the cycle continues...

In the year following FMD there was supposed to be £40,000,000 of available regeneration funding for Cumbria following foot and mouth. Where the money will go is anyone's idea. Of course many worthwhile schemes will benefit within the towns and villages of Cumbria. All of them will be community orientated which is of course brilliant, but what about the rest of us, trying to make a living by providing a service to farmers? What about those of us who are struggling against the tide day by day in the aftermath? Even the so-called 'Rural Czar', Lord Haskins is rather scathing of the rather haphazard way in which funding groups have popped up all over Cumbria. With the best intentions in the world could this not have been organised in a more appropriate manner to the benefit of the county of Cumbria? Time will tell.

To compound it all, within a few months of the new mart opening I was contacted by the chief executive of one of the regeneration companies asking whether Mitchell's would consider making a cash donation to the cause. This would, he said, go towards some of the needier cases following on from FMD. With a new mart struggling to re-establish, running at 50% throughput of the old mart and carrying massive extra costs in staffing, cleansing and disinfection, I wondered just how 'needy' a case one had to be. My reply was polite but to the point.

No one expects free hand outs although it would be nice. However there are a wealth of future opportunities, which can be sought and achieved by all of us, connected to Cumbria's traditional industry - farming. We are now trying to extricate some of that funding in an effort to improve our business our facilities and our services. We still have so much to offer the farming community, the meat industry and the general public I only hope that those with their hands on the purse strings (and there are many of those) can see the bigger picture. I truly believe that they can.

44
Two Days out East

Thursday 14 June
Total national cases: 1745

It was mid-morning on Thursday when I took a call from David Jackson. Two of his customers were to be taken out by DEFRA on Orton Scar, the famous limestone plains to the south of Shap. David could not do the valuation because of his own farming commitments. He had recommended me in his place. The incumbents were apparently happy for me to the job.

I had not done a valuation for several days and I certainly was not looking forward to this one in new territory. The journey from Cockermouth seemed to take only a few minutes as I drifted down the A66. Soon I had located the DEFRA fraternity, a veritable platoon of vets, field officers, slaughtermen and support staff. The duty vet was a South African called Andreus. He was a cheerful type and very thorough in his explanation of what he expected to happen. It was refreshing.

There were two flocks of sheep to value up on the scar. The first was a flock of Kendal Rough Fell sheep and the second was a flock of mainly mule ewes with followers.

"So where are the sheep?" I said from our roadside meeting point.

"Up there," he replied pointing up towards Orton Scar. High up on the sky line about three miles away I could make out a few white dots that were obviously the sheep.

"OK, how do I get up there?" I asked.

In his unmistakably droll African tone he replied: "You walk up det 'trek' moy frind."

"I have a better idea," I said, not particularly wanting to yomp across the moor. "How about we borrow a couple of quad bikes from the farm down the road." Andreus liked the idea and he went off to secure the bikes. Soon he was back having persuaded the farmers to allow us to use the bikes.

At this point I was joined by John Errington whose farm was one of the first to go down in the Penrith area because he had bought in some lambs from Longtown Auction the very week that foot and mouth had been discovered. Now he was working for DEFRA as a shepherd/gatherer. His job was to gather all of the sheep on the farm and shepherd them into the killing pens. This saved time for the vets and slaughter men who no longer had to chase the animals around before they killed them.

There was not enough room for Andreus so I took one bike and John the other. We sped quickly up on to the scar and soon identified the sheep for valuation. I whipped around them quickly and made by observations. I was ready to depart when John cut across my bows.

"Hey Adam," he said, "you aren't in a rush are you?"

"Why's that John?"

"Give us a hand down the fell with these sheep," he said, "I'll never get them all on my own with just these two dogs." Of course it did not help that the dogs did not know the terrain either.

I decided I would help out my old acquaintance and together we gathered the sheep and slowly made our way down to the bottom of the scar. It was hard work for there were a few lame sheep among them. These sheep had to be persuaded to walk on. It took nearly an hour to get down. It was wasted time for me but I felt that I was helping the team if nothing else.

Later Andreus was to discover some of the sheep were infected with foot and mouth. That might have accounted for the lame sheep, although if every lame sheep was suspected and therefore destroyed within the county, then a hell of a lot of otherwise healthy sheep would have died without ailment. Sadly that happened far too often during the foot and mouth crisis anyway.

Eventually John and I managed to gently guide all of the sheep including the lame ones down to the bottom of the hill. The sheep were gathered into the killing pens and I met the slaughtermen. They were a team based in Penrith and I knew several of the personally.

"Now then John," I said to the gaffer, "how are you keeping?"

"Crap like every one else," he said. This was not the jovial man that I knew on a drinking night out in Penrith. Gone was the sharp wit and jovial sense of humour. They all looked miserable and down. There was no banter to be heard. They were just like the rest of us; doing a bad job that had to be done by someone.

Andreus the vet approached me. He had word from Page Street that there were some cattle in the fields adjacent to the killing pens. They were in every sense of the word dangerous contacts. They belonged to the owner of one of the sheep flocks. Andreus suggested that we polish off the cattle first. Some temporary cattle pens had been erected at the entrance to the cattle fields adjacent to a small house.

Carefully and with minimum fuss a long line of DEFRA officials, slaughter men and an auctioneer guided the cattle into the pens. It worked very well. The cattle were quickly valued and the slaughtermen tooled up. Just then the owner of the house appeared. He asked for the senior person in charge and Andreus immediately stepped forward. He appeared to be taking some abuse from the man. I could make out much of what the man was saying. He was clearly upset that the killing was to take place in front of his house. It appeared as though he did not think that any animals should be killed at all. With great charm and style Andreus diffused the situation explaining why there was no choice in what had to be done. The man decided he was going to watch the operation like a hawk and stayed throughout, wincing at what he witnessed, for everyone does that the first time they witness a slaughter. In time it hardly registers on the scale of discomfort. Even when the blood flies on to the protective clothing.

Three slaughtermen calmly climbed into the pens. The cattle were very quiet. The bolt action stun guns made little noise as one by one the slaughtermen put the bolt guns to the temples of the beasts. In just a few seconds each animal lay dead on the ground. Not a word had been spoken, not a single second attempt was needed. Immediately an appointed member of the team began to pith the carcasses. This is a humane way of making sure the animal is quite dead. A long steel wire is inserted in the bolthole and vigorously rammed into the brain of the animal. Sometimes the nervous system of the animal is activated by the pithing procedure causing the dead animal to convulse. The first time I saw this I was quite affected by it, believing that the animal might be in pain. I was assured that this was not the case and that the animal was definitely stunned. It was simply a matter of making sure the animal was quite dead. Even after I had seen the operation so many times it still sent shivers down my own spine. In this case it was a thoroughly professional job from start to finish.

I left the cattle pens and walked back to the sheep with Andreus. Here I had a good look at the Rough Fell sheep. David Jackson had briefed me that the sheep were of a high quality and were well respected among Rough fell breeders. In fact I was amazed at the quality and size of the sheep. They were fantastic. Even Andreus agreed that they looked to be very nice sheep.

We completed the paperwork and I was allowed to go on my way. I drove back to Greystoke quite slowly. It had been a long afternoon. My mobile phone rang and I just knew who it would be. Sure enough it was DEFRA. I was on stand by to go back to Orton the following day. One of the farmers who I had valued for that afternoon was to have a meeting with DEFRA the following morning. He was one of the major landowners in the area. In fact he had seventeen contiguous premises to his own. His shepherd had been travelling around the estate during the normal course of his work. He had therefore been in contact with all of the sheep including those I had valued that day. According to the vet, some of them had clinical signs of foot and mouth. The owner had been made aware of what would happen to his neighbours if his home sheep were found to have foot and mouth. The advice given to him was to let DEFRA take out all of his 5,000 or so ewes and lambs in order to try and save the rest of the farming community. There was little choice left for him. I knew I would be returning to Orton the following day. Sure enough the call was to come through during Friday afternoon.

I pulled into Orton village at 4 o'clock on Friday afternoon. I had no idea why it had taken so long to take the decision to proceed. I could only assume that the landowner really did not want to lose the sheep. I met Tanis the vet whom I had worked with before and was to work with again. This was a big job and she was organising the arrival of the slaughtermen and shepherds. Again I knew many of them personally.

Tanis instructed the farm manager and me to inspect all of the sheep as soon as possible. We were to proceed around the whole farm making sure we disinfected the wheels of the vehicle at the gate of every field we entered. It seemed a bit pointless at the time but we did as we were told.

It took an awful long time to see all of the sheep for there were so many. It was early evening when we got back to the farm. There I went through the valuation with the shepherd and the landowner who had just arrived. I was under some pressure from the vet to get on with it so that the slaughter men could make use of the remaining daylight. However the owner of the sheep being a very thorough man wanted to go through the valuation in great detail. Patiently I did so for it was understandable that such a large number of sheep was indeed a great loss to the estate. Eventually all was agreed and the vet was duly informed. With relief she went off to start the killing.

By the time I had enjoyed a parting cup of tea and moved out to my car, several pens of sheep had been killed. It was a pitiful sight. I was glad that I would not have to see the rest of the 5,000 sheep lying in heaps the following day.

I made sure my vehicle was disinfected then drove home in the failing light of the mid-summer evening. As I drove into Greystoke I realised that I was parched and that I had not set foot in the Boot and Shoe, my local pub since the beginning of foot and mouth. I decided that enough was enough and that I should not harbour these feelings of being a leper or an outcast in the community because my job took me to infected farms. Many of the local farms had being taken out anyway.

I pulled up to the pub and got out of my car. As I walked up to the front door I spied two Land Rovers close to my own vehicle. They were obviously working farmers' vehicles although I did not recognise them. What if they had not had foot and mouth? What if they suspected I had been on an infected premises? What if they then succumbed to the disease and blamed me for having the audacity to stand and drink next to them in the pub?

I just could not face it so I turned tail and walked back to my car. At home Paula had gone to bed. I opened a can of beer but hardly wanted to drink it. I stared at the television screen without taking any of the programme in. The whole foot and mouth crisis was making me thoroughly fed up. It was little consolation to think of the auctioneers who were in a far worse state than I was. I went to bed wishing that the whole thing would be over once and for all.

I was not alone in my misery or disquiet. For there were now growing calls for a public enquiry into the whole crisis. The Trading Standards Institute and the RCVS as well as several MPs were united in their demands for an inquiry. By mid-June there were 1,762 confirmed cases plus DEFRA's own estimate of 1,400 dangerous contacts which from our local knowledge would most certainly be about a fifth of the real figure.

45

A First Visit to the Bampton Valley

Monday 16 July
Total national cases: 1858

July arrived and I had not had to undertake a valuation for more than a fortnight. Still foot and mouth rumbled on around the county but also around the country as a whole. Meanwhile we kept watching and waiting. We were looking forward to achieving our goal of the new market yet looking over our shoulder praying that it would not be pulled from our grasp by the cruellest of animal diseases.

Early July saw a massive cull of hill sheep on the Brecon Beacons. A huge blood testing operation was under way. Any sheep found to have anti-bodies to foot and mouth, and therefore presumably exposure to the disease, were slaughtered together with the rest of the flock and any others in close proximity. It was a continuation of the slash and burn policy that we had first seen in the Duddon valley in March. Even if only two or three sheep out of a flock were anti-body positive then they all had to die and their neighbours too. It was reported that such was the extent of the cull that DEFRA could not hope to successfully carry out its 24/48 policy. I heard later from farmers that a single anti-body positive blood test could ensure the extinction of up to 10,000 sheep. It must have been staggering for those upland farmers on the Welsh borders.

At a higher level there was much talk of Britain recovering its disease free status. There is no doubt that the rigorous slaughter policies that were still being adhered to were undertaken partly in an effort to show Europe of our intent to wipe out the disease as soon as possible and at whatever cost in terms of lost livestock. Of course our friends over the Scottish border were well ahead of us as usual. They had wiped out all of the 'high-risk' sheep including thousands of away-wintered Lake District bred fell hoggs and were well on the way to getting that export licence back.

Another new feature of the crisis was the creation of a 'blue box' called the Penrith spur. This was an area of around 100 square miles or so encompassing the hot spot south of Penrith. Within this area no stock could be moved around whatsoever. Vehicles travelling in and out of the hot spot were to have their tyres; wheel arches and under trays sprayed with disinfectant in case there were traces of infection hiding there.

Then DEFRA hit on another good idea. In order to concentrate the minds of farmers who were lax with their on-farm bio-security, they created a special video at a cost of around £750,000 and 90,000 copies were sent out to farmers. My colleague Alisdare got hold of a copy. He threw it in the bin, it was he said 'insulting rubbish'.

Meanwhile it appeared that auctioneers were not the only employees of DEFRA who were finding it difficult to get payment for work already undertaken and successfully completed. With a wry smile I read a local newspaper report in which Cumbria County Council claimed it was owed £1.5 million by DEFRA for clean up work on infected premises. DEFRA did later pay £500,000 on account to the county council.

"If the buggers won't settle their debts with the county," I thought, "then what chance do we stand?"

There appeared to be a common theme around the country. For in Worcester farmers blockaded Government offices demanding payment of more than £11 million which was owed to Farm Assist. This was a Government sponsored group used by farmers to clear carcasses from affected farms. Farm Assist had received no payment for four months requiring desperate action from local farmers. It was clear that whoever was pulling the purse strings were keeping them tightly knotted. Why this should be the case then one can only guess.

Meanwhile in Cumbria case after case appeared on the DEFRA website. Then with great acclaim it was announced that some public footpaths were now open again. The tourist based businesses in the county must have been delighted for they were receiving almost no support or recognition of the fact that foot and mouth was devastating their industry day upon day. On the other hand the farmers were incredulous of the fact that in most areas people would be free to tramp across their farms through their cattle herds and sheep flocks. One day in the north of the county, the next in the west and the following day in south. The farmers however were hardly allowed to move their stock around their own farm even if they were on bare pasture and going hungry.

Monday 16 July was a warm but overcast sort of a day. I was glad to be inside my office that afternoon and even expected that I would get out into the garden that evening to do some digging. The phone rang - it was DEFRA. I was to proceed to the Bampton Valley to the south of Penrith.

The disease seemed to be progressing slowly south through the valley. It had got to the tiny village of Butterwick. Here Nicky Richards had some sheep in a field. His own farm at Woodfoot was further down the valley. We met up and I quickly valued 28 sheep. It was a small job and Nicky would I'm sure have settled for that relatively small loss. He was not convinced at all.

"You know Adam, it's going to get us in the end," he said flatly, "I don't see how they can stop it in this valley now. It's creeping closer and there is nothing we can do about it."

"Just keep hoping," I replied but inside I was as sceptical as he was.

Up and down the valley there were DEFRA officials charging about. It looked as though the time bomb had gone off. Soon the disease would spread through the valley and meet up across the Shap fells with the Orton outbreak. It was looking very ominous for Kentmere and the other valleys above Kendal.

I drove home and soon forgot about the day's efforts. After tea with the kids safely in bed I blitzed the garden again. It was dark by the time I downed tools. I had a cup of tea, showered and went to bed.

46
A REPORT FOR DEFRA

July 2001

Over the recent months I had been talking at regular intervals to a lady farmer from Lorton near Cockermouth. She is an enthusiastic breeder of Herdwick sheep by the name of Pauline Blair. Some months earlier we had given a joint interview to Border TV in front of a field of fell tups that were about to be culled. She felt compelled to stand up and speak out about what the sustained loss of these sheep would do to the Lake District and its people. So concerned was she by the loss of so many fell sheep especially on lowland wintering farms that she took it upon herself to contact the senior vets, directors of MAFF at Carlisle and even our local MP. They must have been impressed by this honest, shrewd and quietly spoken lady for they invited her to go to Carlisle for a series of meetings. Here, she was able to give a Lakeland farmer's overview as to what effect the current policies were having on so many of her fellow farmers. This was exactly the sort of consultation that was needed to create a sensible policy to combat the disease. I was delighted that Pauline was up there to put forward 'our' side.

We talked many times and I would like to think that I helped to give her an insight as to what was happening around the county. Meanwhile Pauline continued her quest so well that MAFF invited her to become part of the team. She in effect became an advisor, and began to work at Carlisle.

She had become involved in the development stages of a plan named 'roll-back'. The plan was to blood test all the sheep in Cumbria and gradually different zones in Cumbria would become de-restricted or 'rolled back' following negative blood tests on sheep in those zones. The implications of the de-restriction were large. Farmers would be able to move livestock around their own farms a little more easily. They could also market prime stock direct to slaughter. In time they would be able to sell some of their stock to other farms for re-stocking purposes. This would be vital to get some money back into the pockets of the farmers who had not got the disease but had not been allowed to sell any of their stock.

Already Pauline was looking ahead. In our last conversation we had discussed a whole range of issues about the fact that there were farmers in certain areas of the county who had much different pressures place upon them.

"What I need to do is clearly and concisely give DEFRA an overview of the whole situation," she said. "How can you expect to go forward when you don't know where you are coming from."

I immediately offered to write a paper in an effort to explain the variety of pressures and problems that were building up on a range of Cumbrian farms. That night when I returned home from the Bampton valley I put pen to paper and wrote the following report.

Animal Welfare and Marketing Issues of Farmers situated in West Cumbria and the Lake District post-FMD

"Over the last few days I have spoken to many of our farmer customers to assess their concerns or difficulties with regard to restocking or selling available livestock throughout the summer and autumn months. It is quite apparent that there are numerous animal welfare and marketing issues that are deeply concerning farmers in West Cumbria and the Lake District. This paper is an attempt to identify the problems that we face and to provide the basis for a workable and safe solution that will ease the pressures facing our farming communities in terms of buying and selling livestock for the rest of the year. It must be recognised that the pressures relating to our customers are very different from other areas of the county where foot and mouth disease has been far more widespread. I would suggest that input from other auction companies would confirm this statement.

The Role of Mitchell's Auction Co Ltd, Cockermouth Mart

"It is now widely accepted that Mitchell's Auction Co. Ltd. is a unique company. As you know we have a large customer database of farmers who regularly use the auction centre at Cockermouth. Our business area extends throughout west and south west Cumbria and includes the north central Lake District. Mitchell's success is built upon demand from other areas of the country for both prime and breeding stock and its central location to facilitate the easy collection of livestock for sale purposes from throughout the Lake District.

"The topography and climate of the Lake District is such that many farmers need to market their stock in small numbers on a regular basis. That is why Cockermouth market is continually busy week upon week. Those farmers in the upland and marginal areas of the Lake District do not have the physical resources on farm to build up prime stock into large numbers before marketing. Therefore there is a great need to sell livestock in small numbers on a regular basis. Unfortunately this system and the remoteness of the area to major conurbations and large abattoirs does not sit well within the dead weight system of buying. Indeed it is quite prohibitive to successful marketing of livestock produced within our region. This then proves the great need for the livestock auction market at Cockermouth. Indeed this very fact was recognised by MAFF whose consent was required and given to facilitate a DTI grant application for Mitchell's new mart project.

"In previous years we have successfully marketed up to 156,000 prime store and breeding sheep together with 12,000 cattle and calves and 2,000 prime pigs on an annual basis.

"More recently our weekly sale of light weight/fell lambs has gained recognition and we are able to supply annually up to 30,000 such lambs mostly into the export market to the benefit of our farmers. The future of this particular market needs careful examination on its own. Mitchell's are attempting to find regular weekly outlets for lightweight lambs into the home markets. Realistically there will insufficient demand to cater for available numbers without the usual export markets. This leads towards the re-establishment of a welfare disposal scheme. This must be seen as a last resort and all attempts must be made to maintain a normal type of trade. Should a welfare scheme become the preferred option of disposal we may also lose established home market demand through lack of supply. Also encouragement must be given for light lambs to be purchased for further feeding and resale as heavier carcasses in the spring of next year. Again demand will depend on finished lamb prices and the ease of purchase and transport from Cumbrian farms.

"Consideration must be given to the fact that lambs will have to be collected to a central point such as Cockermouth mart if they are sold into a welfare scheme. Mitchell's would of course be able to assist DEFRA in the administration of such a scheme. The collection centre scenario is discussed later in this paper.

"The foot and mouth outbreak that continues to pillage our county's livestock farms is producing a range of pressures and problems affecting every single farmer in the county whether he has directly suffered from foot and mouth or not. We are now on a daily basis getting regular inquiries and desperate requests for advice from our farmers many of whom are approaching their wits end. In nearly every case these are farmers who have not actually had foot and mouth on farm.

The effects of FMD on all Farmers in West Cumbria and the Lake District

"Mitchell's business area includes a diverse range of farm locations and types. There are lowland coastal plains, remote Lakeland valleys and hard, high fells and mountains. All types of livestock from these areas have traditionally found a successful market place at Cockermouth Mart.

In foot and mouth terms, Mitchell's customers fall into two distinctive categories:-

■ Farmers who have lost all or some of their livestock through foot and mouth.

■ Those who have not lost any livestock through the disease.

As previously mentioned the pressures on farmers within the categories are distinctly different (ref. other auctions).

"Thankfully outbreaks of foot and mouth have been limited in West Cumbria and the Lake District compared to other areas of the county. That said, large numbers of sheep in the lowland areas of West Cumbria have been slaughtered through voluntary depopulation or infection.

"Farmers in this category urgently need to plan for the future and are reliant upon the following course of events:-

■ Cleansing and disinfection to be completed on affected farms as soon as possible.

■ Lifting of A, D and E Notices depending on the status of the farm (roll-back program)

■ The ability to plan and commence with a re-stocking program. It is essential that this commences in the autumn months to allow stock to be purchased at the most appropriate time. This is discussed in more detail later.

"Farmers who have not lost livestock through foot and mouth disease. This category includes the majority of farmers within Mitchell's business area. Many farmers are now facing horrendous financial and physical pressure on their farms. Indeed the clear message being given to Mitchell's is that many disease-free farms are in a position of far greater hardship than those farmers who have lost all of their livestock through foot and mouth disease. Many of our customers are trying to maintain livestock that should have been sold in the spring months of 2001 but still remain on-farm. Large numbers of prime lambs and prime cattle are now reaching optimum marketable condition. Therefore a large backlog of livestock is continuing to build up which for financial and welfare reasons need to be sold off the farm as soon as possible.

"In turn the backlog of stock is eating into the pasture and mowing land which should be used to make fodder for the oncoming winter season.

"It must be remembered that many beef and sheep farmers in West Cumbria and the Lake District have not sold any livestock whatsoever and therefore had no income since the middle of February. Many will not be in a sound financial position to purchase fodder if they do have a shortfall this winter.

"A further pressure is the fact that market prices now being offered to farmers for prime stock on a dead weight basis are currently so low that in many cases farmers are incurring major losses with little choice but to sell in order to keep the farm running. This is simply compounding the financial difficulties of many farmers.

"Farmers must maintain the regular cycle of purchasing replacement-breeding stock. This is especially important to many fell farmers who will have limited purchasing opportunities in any normal year without even accounting for foot and mouth. I refer particularly to our treasured Herdwicks (I do not say that at all lightly having valued many thousands of away-wintered hoggs, shearlings and rams within the last few months).

"Therefore the necessary course of events for farmers in this category is as follows:-

■ Have the ability to market the backlog of prime and store stock that should have already been sold from the farm immediately. In Mitchell's business area this may include upwards of 2,000 store cattle, 700 prime cattle, 1,000 over 30 month cattle and around 10,000 prime, cast and breeding sheep. This takes into account losses from foot and mouth slaughter, welfare schemes and stock sold direct to slaughter.

■ Be given the opportunity to market prime, store and breeding stock, which will be ready for sale through the summer and autumn months. Again for reference Mitchell's believe there will be the following numbers of livestock requiring sale:-

■ 3,000 store and breeding cattle, 2,000 prime cattle, 1,500 over 30 month cattle including very many cattle that went over age through not being able to be sold from infected areas. Also up to 100,000 breeding and prime sheep available for sale until the end of the year. It must be stated that detailed research has not been undertaken to produce the above mentioned figures. They are however believed to be a fair representation of livestock that will be available for sale on farms in Mitchell's business area.

■ Have the benefit of a roll-back program to de-restrict areas of West Cumbria and the Lake District. This will allow the necessary purchase and/or sale of replacement breeding stock in order to continue the regular cycle of breeding on the farms. It must be implemented as soon as it safe and practically possible to do so. The existing problems can only be compounded as we move towards the autumn months with little or no provision for a marketing scheme to allow the successful trading of livestock.

Summary of the main issues affecting Livestock Farmers in West Cumbria and the Lake District

"The following are a range of comments, which are regularly being reported to Mitchell's by its farmer customers.

Disease affected farms:

■ Unnecessarily slow cleansing and disinfecting operations.

■ An urgent need to begin restocking in the autumn months so allowing the purchase of the right animals within the normal cycle of breeding.

■ A definite DEFRA-guided restocking policy, which will help farmers to plan and implement their restocking operation.

■ Auction company advice as to where animals can be purchased either locally or other areas of the country if necessary.

■ Much guidance needed as to suitable replacement values.

Disease free farms:

■ Little or no income since February leading to severe financial hardship in many cases. This problem will be compounded through the autumn months and into the spring of next year.

■ A backlog of store, prime stock and over 30 month cattle that should have been sold in the spring months of this year and remain trapped on the farm.

■ Massive animal welfare problems building through lack of winter fodder being made due to overstocking.

■ The difficulty in marketing both stores and especially prime stock. Currently, the only sales of livestock allowed are those sales directly from farm to slaughter. In that Mitchell's and all livestock marts play a vital role in organising the sale and disposal of small lots of livestock which reduce the burden of transport costs and timing of sales on farmers as well as aiding the final end-price!

■ Much guidance needed as to possible sales prices and to provide suitable

Contacts for potential purchasers:

■ Guidance needed as to when and where purchases of replacement breeding stock can be found and at what cost.

"To summarise it is quite clear that most farmers in West Cumbria and the Lake District are in a state of turmoil. This especially prevalent for those who have not lost stock through foot and mouth. There is a clear need for sensible and thorough guidance to allow all farmers to plan and implement their restocking and sales program throughout the autumn months. That guidance must come from DEFRA who can be ably assisted by the auction companies.

Issues that must be addressed - Marketing of Prime Stock

All farmers in West Cumbria and the Lake District must be able to market their prime stock to best advantage. The system of dead weight marketing direct to slaughter must now be improved. Farmers need to be able to sell small lots of prime stock as and when they are ready for marketing.

For reasons previously discussed it is impossible for farmers in these areas to hold back livestock that is ready for sale in order to build up larger consignments. Therefore huge transport costs are being incurred for farmers who are forced to pay for their stock to be transported to the major abattoirs in Lancashire, Yorkshire and beyond. In many cases farmers have not even been able to afford to market their stock knowing that large losses were inevitable.

The only workable solution is the provision of a collection centre at Cockermouth being the normal marketing centre for West Cumbria.

Provision of a Collection Centre at Cockermouth

The above paragraph clearly demonstrates that there is an undisputed need to dispose of the back log of prime stock which has yet to be sold and the ongoing build up of prime stock which would normally be marketed from August through to the late months of the year. An organised and well-structured collection centre at Cockermouth will allow farmers to dispose of their prime stock more easily as and when stock is ready for sale. The major transport costs, which are crippling farm businesses at the moment, will be much reduced by a collection centre. Also the flexibility of a collection centre will allow the auction company to place the prime stock to the farmers' best advantage at various abattoirs.

As discussed earlier the collection centre may also be used to facilitate any further welfare schemes which will be used to collect unsaleable light weight and fell lambs during the autumn and winter months.

There will also be a return to the much needed over 30 month collection.

"To that end Mitchell's Auction Co. Ltd. have been working very hard to prepare the existing auction mart as a collection centre. Unfortunately due to the nature, age and size of the building there is a great problem in achieving the necessary standard of cleanliness and disinfection. At the time of writing the main cattle building which is the only part of the market deemed suitable for a collection centre has yet to have its 'D' Notice lifted. Therefore there is no chance whatsoever the collection centre becoming operational until the middle of August. This is now a very difficult problem for the auction company to overcome. It should be noted that at this time of year the auction mart would normally be handling 4,000 to 5,000 prime sheep and over 70 cattle each and every week through the market.

"It cannot be overstated that the collection centre will be a financial lifeline for the company if it is to continue to operate to the benefit of the farming communities of West Cumbria and the Lake District.

"Provision of an on-farm marketing system for store and breeding stock. There are several important reasons why this is necessary in the short term. These can be summarised as follows:-

■ To allow diseased farms to plan and implement a re-stocking program in the autumn months.

■ To allow unaffected farm to sell available store and breeding stock both to restocking farms and to those farms that need to replace breeding stock in the normal natural cycle.

■ Mitchell's Auction Co. Ltd. would like to offer a draft proposal that is workable and safe whilst achieving all the necessary objectives of such a system.

A proposal to facilitate a system of farm to farm transactions for breeding and store stock under strictly controlled conditions

"Mitchell's Auction Co. Ltd. believes that a system could be implemented by DEFRA working in close partnership with Mitchell's to maintain the highest standards of bio-security and safety whilst facilitating a controlled system of farm to farm livestock transactions and animal movements within the business area. The system would operate as follows:-

Mitchell's to build up detailed data bases of:

■ Restocking requirements of diseased affected farmers on a short and long-term basis.

■ None disease affected farms with breeding and store stock available for sale both locally and nationally.

Mitchell's to bring together potential buyers and sellers:

■ By organising individual farm visits allowing inspection of stock and negotiation of sale prices.

■ Mitchell's to assist both parties (if necessary) in the valuation.

■ Mitchell's to collate on behalf of DEFRA complete details of the transaction including livestock numbers, age and type, also confirming the proposed transport route and destination.

■ DEFRA to process a special farm to farm licence which will allow the transaction and subsequent animal movement to proceed.

■ Veterinary inspection and quarantine plans to be issued by DEFRA.

Day of movement

"Mitchell's to help DEFRA vet at inspection by implementing and recording identity marks or tags on the animals, which will allow movement of the animals to proceed to destination farm.

Quarantine period at destination farm.

DEFRA to monitor the quarantine period.

Completion of licence

"At end of quarantine period, DEFRA to complete final part of licence by allowing livestock to be moved on to purchasers holding under normal farming practice.

"It should be noted that this proposal is very much a bare bones concept. We do however believe that with suitable planning and consultation the proposal is workable and secure. This by the fact that the local auction company would work closely with DEFRA to ensure that the highest standards were maintained.

"Mitchell's working on DEFRA's behalf would have the confidence of the farmers in facilitating the movement of their livestock as well as providing a valuation service for them. This would also reduce the need for extra numbers of DEFRA field officers to travel around the farms undertaking the same work which the auction companies could fulfil on DEFRA's behalf.

"Such a system would reduce the need for a comprehensive welfare disposal scheme to mop up unsaleable breeding and store stock. It would therefore be seen as prudent system on DEFRA's behalf.

"We feel confident that this proposal is workable but are conscious that we are so short of time in order to facilitate the proposal. In order for the system of on-farm selling to begin there needs to be a great deal of thought given to the roll back program, its aims, objectives and possible constraints. However we would welcome the opportunity to sit down with you and the DEFRA team in order to try and thoroughly iron out the proposed system.

"It is essential that we get urgent action to address all of the issues mentioned in this paper to produce a safe and workable marketing system for all our farmers this autumn. Failure to do so will have catastrophic effects on the majority of farmers within our wide and varied business area, not to mention the future of West Cumbria's last remaining livestock market."

And there you have it, the product of several hours typing. It was well past midnight when I finished the first draft but I was quite proud of the paper, every sentence was fact and truth. I felt that I had identified the real issues that so many of our customers were complaining about. I had also offered a workable plan that would enable my own company to work closely with DEFRA and in doing so maintain the trust of the local farmers many of whom wanted the local auction to still advise them on marketing and movement policy.

I tidied the document up in the morning and sent it by fax to Pauline. She then made a presentation to DEFRA based on my facts. They had apparently listened and learned. The paper was well received, the problems clearly identified and I never heard another thing. No one wanted to take up my suggestion of a plan to move things forward in West Cumbria. DEFRA did not want any help from an auction company. We were for a long time *persona non-grata*. In truth we could have been a good ally for them. It would have been so much more beneficial to our farmers. Pauline continued with her advisory work and I am full of admiration for her fortitude and patience for though she was careful not to criticise, I knew she was treading a very fine line with DEFRA. Should she overstep the mark I am sure she would have been cast aside. Carefully and quietly she went about her work. She deserves great praise and recognition for what she did. Few people will have any idea of her impact at that time.

My report was filed away and I had forgotten about it until coming across it by chance when researching this part of the book. I do not think anyone else other than those mentioned in this chapter ever saw it. Long-winded it may be, but I hope the reader took the time to digest it. Those were the real problems facing our customers at the time. We were so powerless to do anything to help although we did try.

47

A SOCIAL NIGHT FOR THE FARMERS

Wednesday 18 July
Total National Cases: 1866

We were talking in the office about the fact that we were having so little contact with our regular customers during the FMD crisis. Some farmers did ring up for a chat now and then but most kept themselves very much to themselves. Many in West Cumbria had not strayed off the farm at all, feeling that any contact with the outside world would put the farm in jeopardy. It is also true that some farmers stayed locked away long after foot and mouth had gone. Indeed on the opening day of the Lakeland Livestock Centre in May 2002, I met a farmer who admitted to me that it was the first time he had left the farm since the outbreak began in February 2001.

He said to me: "I realised that if I didn't make an effort to break out to see my new market open, then I never would." Day upon day without a break he had milked his cows morning and night. His wife and family led their lives as normally as the rules would allow. They were not in a foot and mouth-affected area but the worry prayed on his mind. He admitted that he became very depressed. Everything was a concern. Could the feed wagons or the milk tanker inadvertently bring the disease onto his farm? This together with a shed full of prime cattle that he could not get rid of until they were over age and worth only half the price, caused him to retreat into a shell. The opening of the mart meant much more to him than most, for it gave him the chance to break the mould he had set and start again. When he shook my hand his whole body was shaking too, but more importantly, he was smiling.

Our discussions in the office led us to plan a farmers' social evening. There we hoped to update our customers on the new market plans and to give as much information as we could about foot and mouth. The most important thing to discuss would be the traditional autumn sales. How could we help farmers with stock available for sale make a trade when there were no auction sales? On the other hand, how could we help farmers who wanted to buy stock or restock a whole farm? The difficulty was that it might be uncomfortable for some farmers if foot and mouth affected people were sat next to those who were not affected. Even though there was no chance that disease could be passed on, we knew that many un-affected farmers would choose to stay away.

We decided to have two meetings. The first would be in West Cumbria and was advertised as being for those farmers wishing to discuss live-stock sales. The second was to be held close to Cockermouth for those farmers looking to restock. At both meetings the emphasis would be on business and pleasure. We welcomed all for a drink and a crack.

Both meetings were well supported and well received. There were many questions about our work in FMD but mostly the questions were about selling stock and what sort of prices would be made. We had no definite answers at that time.

One farmer mentioned the fact that another firm of auctioneers in Cumbria was currently in Europe looking to import cattle to sell to Cumbrian farmers. There were also reports of imported sheep being available at the appropriate time. My colleague Alisdare had very strong views and voiced them unequivocally.

"Any of you farmers who would consider buying from abroad when there is stock available to sell in this country is a hypocrite. Do not moan to me about foreign meat imports in supermarkets affecting your prices when you would consider doing exactly the same thing to your fellow farmers." There were strong murmurs of agreement.

"There will be plenty of stock to sell," he continued, "if we cannot find it locally then we can look around the country. Only as a last resort need we look abroad."

I agreed with his sentiments and as he forecast in time there would be plenty of stock both within and outside of the county to choose from. Thankfully the import market never truly took off. Many of our customers who had stock to sell were eventually able to do so at decent prices. The difficulty for all auctioneers was trying to please all parties. It was an impossible task, for the un-affected farmers wanted as much of the valuation money as possible put back into their own pockets. The buyers who were restocking wanted to buy as cheaply as possible. There were no auctions in the early days to set the trade and both sides were often disappointed. This together with the sheer volume of enquiries from both sides made the autumn months after foot and mouth just about as miserable a time as during foot and mouth.

I can honestly state that those days of on-farm sales after FMD were more mentally and physically draining than any other time during the year. By Christmas I was just about burnt out. The emotional and physical toll of six months of foot and mouth valuations superseded by trawling around farms with buyers trying to make a deal on the farm took me to an all-time low by the end of the year. Some of my colleagues and several other auctioneers I knew felt the same.

In truth I was so sick and tired that I even applied for another job outside of the whole auction sphere. Thankfully I did not get it and as the new auction rose from the ground in the spring of 2002 so my spirits lifted as well. A new challenge awaited us all. It was simply a matter of putting the last year far behind us. Sadly that was to prove far harder than I thought possible.

Our two farmers' meetings were successful and it was good to see so many old friends. The best thing of all was the common feeling that the new market at Cockermouth must be built. The level of support for the project was fantastic. In time support for the new auction from some farmers would be unequivocal. Others who promised allegiance were not so genuine. When the market was built there were some farmers who promptly forgot their voiced support and chose to sell their stock at other markets or even worse direct to abattoir without giving any auction company a chance.

This would be one of the biggest disappointments after FMD. Especially those farmers who shouted just how important the market at Cockermouth was then expected all the other farmers to support it whilst they went elsewhere. Thankfully those hypocrites were in the vast minority and the new market did get the support that it was promised even despite the restrictions that were imposed on all auctions by the regulatory authorities.

Of course no one has the right to expect that their business should be supported simply because it is there. However those farmers who backed the market through the difficult first few months and stuck with it can feel proud that they were a major factor in the return of a successful livestock market at Cockermouth.

The others who would happily go past our door for the sake of another penny which sometimes they get and sometimes they do not, would do well to remember how they missed the market when it was not there. For if I have learned anything from the unfortunate closure of other markets, these are often the farmers who shout the loudest protests when the market disappears.

48
ANOTHER HERDWICK HORROR

Friday 20 July
Total national cases: 1866

During the previous week I had been contacted by Benny Steele, a regular customer at Cockermouth Mart. He was a fell farmer from Easthwaite in the lower reaches of Nether Wasdale. His farm stretches high onto the screes above Wastwater, the deepest lake in the land. For many years Benny had rented land at Gosforth from a retired farmer called Mr Singleton whom I knew only on nodding terms. Throughout the summer fourteen or so of Ben's very best Herdwick breeding rams had been summering there before the autumn tupping season began. Although foot and mouth disease had made a very brief appearance within Gosforth, its damage had somehow been contained to just a few unfortunate farms. All had been clear since April. DEFRA had left the sheep alone during this time and Benny had thought nothing more of it until he was getting ready to take them home and needed a license to move them. Mr Singleton had always shepherded them on Benny's behalf. Therefore Benny had not been near the sheep all summer.

DEFRA came to blood test the sheep and one ram out of the fourteen was found to be anti-body positive to foot and mouth. Benny rang me to say that DEFRA were to immediately destroy the single sheep and wanted a valuation figure before morning. He told me of the sheep's breeding and type and I gave him an informed opinion thinking little more of it. I received no fee and Benny settled the matter privately with DEFRA.

A week later on this beautiful summer's morning I had been summoned to value the rest of the sheep. Page Street had apparently decided that even though the remaining sheep were blood tested clear of the disease, they were going to be slaughtered anyway. This seemed strange but it was not my job to reason why.

I arrived at Mr Singleton's land, which was adjacent to his bungalow. As a new learner gardener I could not help but admire his front beds awash with colour and not a weed in sight. Quickly though my attention returned to the sheep pens were I could hear raised voices. Booted and suited I walked in. Benny was clearly angry and upset. The vet was

Tanis Brough whom I had worked with on more than one occasion and would do so again. Benny was talking on the mobile phone to his vet. He was instructing Benny to resist the cull at all costs. Benny spied me and thrust the phone at me.

"Here you talk to him," he said. The vet proceeded to tell me that in his opinion the blood tests results on the tups should stand. They were tested clear and DEFRA had no right to insist on their slaughter once the tests were clear. The issue clearly had nothing to do with valuation. Benny wanted and needed to keep the tups alive.

"You don't understand," he said to Tanis, "I can't replace these bloodlines. I won't even have enough tups to serve my ewes. Where the hell will I get any more like these? There's just too many gone all ready." I knew he was right but the situation needed diffusing fast.

I took Tanis to one side to get the full story. She was in a very difficult position and was keeping a cool head. Her clear instructions had been to destroy the sheep without fail. The perceived risk of further infection in the area should the tests be wrong was too great according to the higher powers. A slaughter team was not even going to be dispatched. Tanis had serum in the car and was to put each tup to sleep by lethal injection.

"I have no choice," she said, "the sheep have to die. It is not my decision. If I don't do it someone else will." She looked me in the eye: "You have to help me," she said.

I was now in the mess right up to my neck. "Is there no chance of a reprieve," I asked hopefully. Tanis shook her head, "I cannot leave until the sheep are dead, it's final," she replied.

It was up to me to persuade Benny. By now both him and Mr Singleton were visibly upset by the situation which did seem to be intolerably unfair. I gave it my best shot and quietly asked him to see Tanis' point of view. I told him that she did not want to have to kill the tups but her orders were to do so whatever the objection. If she did not do so she would be in trouble. Benny accepted this and asked me what I thought. I gave him my opinion.

"I think that even if you win today they will come back and finish the job," I said "and if they find one shred of contact with the disease through another blood test, they could start on your farm at home. Let them go and it could save the rest of your farm."

I think Benny realised that I was talking sense. "How do you even begin to value breeding like this?" he asked pointing at the tups. I was just thinking the same myself.

"Don't worry Benny, I've had plenty of practice."

With quiet deliberation we moved through the sheep one by one, making the valuations in turn. Soon we were finished. Tanis produced the valuation forms, which I completed. Then she went off to her car to get the serum.

Benny signed the forms and I persuaded him to go back to Wasdale immediately. He could do no further good by staying. He was worried about Mr Singleton who was distressed by the situation. I promised I would go and have a word with him. Having completed the paperwork I went over to Mr Singleton who was still close to the sheep pens.

"I've never seen anything like this in all my years of farming," he said through a mist of tears. He went on to tell me how proud he was of Benny and his wife Susan. How they had been good tenants and that they did not deserve this treatment.

I steered him away from the sheep and we began to look around his garden which was and is magnificent. He gave me a ripe cabbage to take home. I thanked him. Then he told me that he knew my grandfather because they had both sold their stock at Ulverston auction mart.

"Why did you not use Cockermouth?" I asked.

"I used to as my father did before me," he replied "but I fell out with your lot and never went back." This was a common tale in any auction company when a deal had gone wrong or a farmer felt that the auctioneers had not tried hard enough for them. Farmers are proud men and boycotts can, and do, last generations. I was determined this one would end so I invited Mr Singleton to come to the new mart when it opened. He told me that he had kept his shares in the company for many years. He then said he would come to the market and wished me well as I went on my way.

On the opening day of the Lakeland Livestock Centre one of the first visitors to walk into the building was Mr Singleton. I remembered immediately what we had said on that warm July morning the previous year. I shook him warmly by the hand. Since that day he has not missed a single auction day. One Wednesday I did not see him and it stuck in my conscience, I reminded him of the fact the following week and was rebuked.

"Ah but I was here," he said with a twinkle in his eye, "although I did have to leave early to take the wife shopping."

"Then I must have slept in that morning," I replied and we enjoyed the moment. Those retired farmers are an important part of any auction company for they bring experience and memories of the past. They can tell tales of auctions past and they are the heritage of the auction company. Above all they can remind you that even though we think we are having a hard time, those men farming in the depression of the 20s and 30s were actually far worse off.

"The difference," says Mr Singleton "is that we were poor but knew nought else. The young farmers of today have had it good in the past and find it harder when the good times are not there." To that end he may have a point.

Thankfully customers like Benny and Susan Steele stayed clear of foot and mouth despite losing away-wintering hoggs in the cull. They were to come to the new market at its opening and sell some very good cattle at a deservedly high price. Benny is one of those farmers who has learned the art of 'deadpan'. To see him in the ring with his stock you would be convinced that he is most disgusted with the prices and that he is having a stinker of a trade. On that first day at the new market when Benny was in the ring Mr Singleton was smiling and I swear I saw a faint glimmer cross Benny's face too.

49

BACK TO BAMPTON

Monday 30 July
Total national cases: 1909

July was all but over and poor Nicky Richards was in the wars again down in the Bampton valley. His greatest fear was coming true for the disease was creeping ever closer to home. This time I was called back to value some sheep at Ghyll Head, which was not too far from Woodfoot.

Another blistering hot day if not the hottest yet saw me sweating even more than usual. On the roadside I put my protective white suit on and my wellingtons. A man armed with a clipboard and a bad attitude met me at the field gate.

"Name?" he called as I walked up.

"Adam Day," I replied "and who are you?" I received no reply. "Do you work for DEFRA?" I tried again. Still no reply

He was standing next to the mobile disinfection unit, which was operated by the Snowie Group.

"Ah so your Snowie's man are you?" I said condescendingly. He grunted.

"Sign here," he grunted again.

"Sign what?"

"Look I have to sign everyone in and everyone out; new rules." I signed the form and moved past him.

"You can't go in there," he said.

"Why not?"

"You haven't got waterproofs on."

"I don't have to."

"Yes you do - new rules." This was news to me but I decided to play along. I went back to my car and put a full set of oilskins on despite the roasting temperature. Then I walked back to the field gate.

"You still can't go in."

"Why not this time?"

"You haven't got rubber gloves on."

"I've never worn rubber gloves."

You've got to now - new rules." Had he not been so serious in his delivery then I would have thought that he was having a laugh.

"I don't have any so what do we do now?" He looked challenged for a moment. Then he had a good idea.

"Hey you," he shouted at the vet "he doesn't have any gloves." The vet was my old friend Tanis Brough yet again. She walked over.

"We shouldn't keep meeting like this," I said greeting her, "people will talk." Poor Tanis was in fact severely ill. She had summer flu and was already running a temperature even before the heat wave conditions. She looked ready to drop. I realised the work she was doing non-stop, must be taking a hell of a toll on her physically as well as mentally. She should not even have been at work that day. Like so many others she would have been driven on by a sense of duty. A day off work whether through sickness or not would have led to feelings of guilt. I knew that she could not admit any weakness at this time and I felt sorry for her.

Tanis told me that I actually did need gloves and that we should have had a directive sent to the office from DEFRA. If we had then I had not seen it. To speed things up Tanis gave me a pair of her own gloves. The man with the clipboard eyed me suspiciously as I walked through the gate.

The sheep I had to value were spread throughout some parkland. They had to be gathered and brought down to the roadside pens for slaughter. We all mucked in and successfully brought the sheep into the pens. The slaughter crew was the Penrith team I worked with down at Orton some weeks earlier.

I made my valuation, wrote up the forms and presented them to Nicky Richards who was waiting over the hedge on the roadside. He could not enter the premises because he was to return to his own holding. He accepted my figures and I gave him his copy of the form. As I moved back to the sheep the slaughter had already begun. Tanis wanted a re-count of the sheep because she thought we might be one short. To help the slaughter men I jumped into the pen to herd together some of the sheep that were still alive. By the time we finished my waterproofs were covered in blood. I realised that I should thank the clipboard man for making me put my oilskins on. Had I just used my paper protective suit in this instance I might have got blood on my clothes. In the end the count was right and all was well.

Eventually I was finished. I wished Tanis all the best and told her to keep her pecker up. She looked thoroughly miserable poor girl. Then I

221

walked out of the field but clipboard man was not there.

"Ah well," I thought, "he must have gone for a fag or a lie down or both." I decided not to waste my time waiting for him. I drove off without signing out. Maybe this was a childish action but I felt that whichever role someone was engaged in on a foot and mouth cull, they should act with courtesy and politeness. In this case it had not happened.

'If they want me they can bloody well come and find me' was my attitude. Looking back it was probably the wrong one.

I put it behind me and was soon back at home putting the children to bed and then getting out into my garden. A far better way to put my time in I thought.

August was always supposed to be the month of summer holidays, golden days and warm evenings. For auctioneers the end of the month would mark the commencement of the 'back-end' sales. This is the glorious autumn period when the hill farmers bring their stock to market having tended their calves and lambs throughout the summer months. We know it as the harvest of the fells. This year some of the fells had been harvested early. The difference this year was that the produce had been picked en mass and thrown away to be buried or burned. This year's back-end sales would be so very different. For the first time in over 130 years, there would be no auction sales in Cockermouth market. My god would we all miss it.

50

TO WOODFOOT AT LAST

Wednesday 8 August
Total national cases: 1937

Blue Box restrictions were operational around Thirsk covering almost 400 square miles. There were other heavily restricted areas still in operation at Settle and Penrith. The Penrith spur restrictions were to last until well into November. Those farmers that had escaped FMD were wondering how they might be able to turn their tups onto the fells to serve the ewes in the autumn. Without that operation they would have no lambs the following year. The restrictions that were imposed would make it impossible for the tups or any other livestock to be moved around the farm. What farmer would not be tempted to break the law in that situation? They would be bankrupted without stock to sell the following year.

Meanwhile the Lakeland Veterinary Association was making public claims that they were not being allowed to take blood samples from living sheep. DEFRA was insisting that if there was any doubt whatsoever about a diagnosis in sheep then they should be slaughtered immediately without recourse to further blood tests. This was felt to be a particularly dangerous tactic because there were several reasons why a sheep could have lesions in and around the mouth. Common ones in Cumbria were obviously the effects of orf, eating gorse bushes, thistles, salt licks and there were others.

I have heard that some vets have admitted that with hindsight sheep which were diagnosed with foot and mouth at the time, probably only had orf at worst. This reminded me of an incident in June when I was contacted by a farmer north of Cockermouth. A routine inspection of his sheep had apparently revealed FMD in several of his ewes. He was highly distressed when he called me

"It's bloody orf Adam. I've farmed sheep all my life and I know what it is." He went on to explain that a young Scandinavian vet had come to the farm and pronounced that the sheep definitely had foot and mouth because there were lesions around the mouth of the animals.

"Do something," the farmer pleaded and put the phone down.

I contacted DEFRA SVS at Carlisle and by luck managed to speak to a person that I had talked to several times before. I begged her to find out who the vet was. I told her that the farmer was adamant she was wrong and that the vet appeared to have had very little previous knowledge of sheep

"If she is a first timer," I said, "please please get a second opinion. If this goes on record as an infected premises you will wipe out any chance we have of a new market at Cockermouth."

Some time later the farmer contacted me. He told me that DEFRA had indeed taken a second opinion which was that the sheep had orf not foot and mouth. The first vet was indeed a rookie on her first visit to a farm. She may well have been delighted to find a case on her visit, but the ramifications of her mistake could have been horrific. The sheep were saved but for some reason the farmer's small herd of cattle had already been slaughtered by DEFRA before the second opinion took place.

Later I suggested to DEFRA that the inexperienced vets should always be second-guessed on their first 'discovery' of FMD clinical signs. I do not know whether this was ever made policy. Many farmers were usually so shocked on being told that they had foot and mouth, they never bothered to argue for a second opinion. In this case it was a damn good job we did argue.

Nick Richard's worst nightmare had come true. His cattle at Woodfoot had finally contracted the disease. In a way it was expected and as such was a relief when it finally happened. Even so it was not a pleasant time at all. Wednesday 8 August was miserable damp sort of a day, the rain seemed to be able to seep into your waterproof clothing somehow.

Nicky's cattle were in fields on the east side of the Bampton road. We walked down a lane to see them. We could not get too close because there were some excitable Limousins amongst them. Even so I got a good look at the cows and calves over the hedge. I made my valuation and then we walked back up the lane to the roadside. Knowing the volatile nature of the cattle, the vet had elected to bring in a marksman to shoot the animals. He was the brother of one of my regular customers at Cockermouth Market. Quietly he drove his van into the field and sidled right up to the animals. They never flinched. Carefully he put his rifle through the open van window and placing the muzzle of the gun almost to the head of the beast he pulled the trigger. One by one the animals fell where they stood. There was no panic and no pain. In a matter of minutes the cows and calves were all dead. It was exemplary work and so far removed from the horror stories that were being reported in the press of people taking pot shots at animals and chasing them like lunatics in other areas.

Back at the farm Nicky and I toured the remaining livestock and my job was wrapped up fairly quickly. It was raining hard now and the vet had not come back. The light was beginning to fade when we finally completed the paperwork and I was able to leave.

It was a sad day for the Richardsons who had waited in vain to beat the disease. Sadly it had got them in the end. Like so many others though, they would return to farming again in the future.

This was to be my last infected premises valuation of the summer. Had I known it then I would have gone home and cracked a bottle of bubbly (if I had one) but that is not to say that it was all over. Far from it for the disease raged onwards ripping through the hill country south of Hexham. Soon the 'blue box' in that area had been extended to include the whole Alston area. 30 farms had been affected there. Disinfectant spraying stations were springing up on roads leading into the 'blue box'. For the people in those areas who were not that far from the original source of the infection, the nightmare was only beginning.

The continued status of West Cumbria as being disease free allowed me to spend three consecutive days at home with my family by way of a summer holiday. It was to be the only break I would get that year. I enjoyed the time in the garden with my wife, daughter and baby boy. We walked up and down the village most days. We could not walk onto local farmland or onto the Greystoke Castle estate which was of course shut to the public. This annoyed Olivia for we had often walked up to the bridge just inside the main gate on the estate. Olivia used to spend many minutes peering under the bridge looking for Mr Troll who lived there. He never ever showed himself and now Olivia was disappointed that we could not go up to the bridge for another look.

My few days' break did some good. I did not know then that it was the calm before the storm, as the back-end rush would soon begin, bringing with it a new range of challenges and problems. I was lucky to have a break, for there were many other valuers at that time in the east of Cumbria and beyond, who were not so fortunate.

51
REMEMBER SEPTEMBER

Sunday 30 September
Total national cases: 2030

It may seem a little obtuse to recall all of the month of September in one chapter. Had I been continually involved in the fight against FMD then of course it would have been different. Thankfully neither I nor any of my colleagues were involved at this time. Yet still there were many new cases springing up and of course those forgotten contiguous farms being taken out as well. Summer was breathing its last but foot and mouth had not.

Early in the month the Allendale valley south of Hexham had many losses on more than thirty farms. Such was the threat of further spreading the disease that most of the disinfection points at the edges of the Hexham 'blue box' were manned continually day and night. An isolated case popped up in Yorkshire. There was another 'hotspot' remaining in the Orton/Tebay area of Cumbria.

All the while healthy stock on unaffected farms was prevented from essential movements. Difficult welfare cases were being created through no fault of the farmers. They were not allowed to move their stock either off the farm for sale or even around the farm to fresh pasture. Crazily there still remained cases of sheep on bare pasture with nothing to eat when a few yards down the road the farmer would have a green and fresh pasture overgrown with grass and yet he was not allowed to move stock to it.

The roll-back programme of blood testing continued on a zonal basis. All manner of people were employed by DEFRA to take the bloods. There were vets, field officers and even DEFRA clerical staff. A farmer friend of mine from the Threlkeld area told me that during one blood testing session a rather overweight field officer had tried several times without success to get a needle into a sheep's neck vein. Eventually the vein collapsed with the number of hits it had received. The wound had to be cauterised to stop the animal bleeding to death. The farmer refused to let the man carry on so in desperation they turned to the DEFRA clerk who was recording the samples. She had only had rudimentary training on oranges. Thankfully they must have been ripe blood oranges for she found that she could hit the vein straight away.

The farmer asked later why DEFRA would not allow local vets to do more of these jobs? I did not know the answer. I believe that some practice vets were employed in this role but it obviously was not exclusive. It led to bitter resentment.

The Government had by now brought in the revised AWS in August to purchase stock from farmers who could not move it or sell it in the normal manner. The set rates of payment were far below previous market values. I had attended several stakeholder meetings in the summer and fought for higher rates of payment for my customers. It did not happen. Most farmers took the price without complaint any way. They were just glad to be able to get the stock off the farm before all of their winter grazing and stored fodder was used up before winter had even started. Even worse, the auction companies that would so well have served the scheme were cut out totally. Farmers could either take the animals to the slaughterhouse themselves or have the abattoir send a wagon. Many livestock vehicles went through Cockermouth and travelled all the way to Carlisle to get to the nearest abattoir killing AWS stock. I wonder who undertook the bio-security risk assessment on that one?

However we were not despondent. The board of directors had taken a brave decision to proceed with the development of the new mart at Cockermouth. This even though FMD was still breaking out within the county and without the knowledge of just what stock would be available for sale when we finally opened. I do not think that many of our farmers stopped to think about what a momentous leap into the unknown the Lakeland Livestock Centre represented.

By now my work was split between project managing the development which was due to start in early October and travelling around farms with customers trying to negotiate deals on available stock. It was as I have said before tough going.

On Thursday September 11 2001 I attended a development meeting in the boardroom at Mitchell's headquarters. Our chairman came in with news that two planes had crashed into the World Trade Centre in New York.

The rest is history and the ramifications around the world were (and still are) enormous. Suddenly mother Earth looked a fragile place to live. Any lingering thoughts in the public eye about FMD were long gone. It was history.

The final reported case of FMD occurred at Little Asby near Appleby on 30 September. It was case number 2030. No one knew at the time how significant this case would be. One disease-free month later foot and mouth was officially over although my valuation work was not yet finished. The world was still coming to terms with what had happened in New York. We were also trying to come to terms with what had happened in our world since February.

52
Friday Night Horror

Friday 12 October
No new cases this month

Friday night after supper I pulled my chair up in front of the fire opened a tin of beer and began to watch the live game of Rugby League on the TV. The kids were in bed and I had had a really good day. I had done several on farm deals and for once both sides seemed satisfied in the day's proceedings. I was chilled out.

The phone rang and a gentlemen introduced himself as a DEFRA representative. It was 9.30pm. He told me that I was required to do an FMD valuation of sheep and cattle at Pica near Whitehaven in the morning. I burst out laughing and suggested that it was an excellent wind up and for a minute I had been seriously taken in.

"This is no joke," came the reply. He gave me the address and telephone number of the affected farm. I knew the people only vaguely. They were smallholders who had only recently begun to farm, but they were certainly real enough. I was told to proceed to the farm in the morning first thing.

I put the phone down and sat back in my chair looking at the ceiling. What the hell was going on? Could it be true? Who would know? I decided to ring one of my company's directors, Jackson Hodgson, himself a vet.

He answered the phone and I recounted the tale. He swore and swore again.

"Leave it with me," he said, "I'll get back to you." The phone went dead.

I sat and waited. Sure enough Jackson rang back. "It's true," he confirmed, "the stock has to be slaughtered but they have not got foot and mouth. Some have been found anti-body positive. They must have been in contact." That was all Jackson could tell me and I thanked him. Then I rang the farmers and found out that they gave me the full story. They had purchased the sheep the previous autumn from Lazonby mart in the east of the county. They were Swaledale ewes of reasonable quality. They had run around the parks near Pica all summer. Only by having the regulation 'roll-back' blood test, as all flocks were required to do, had the anti-bodies been discovered. The sheep had even run with the family's cattle but they had never been ill. I wished them well and told them I would see them in the morning.

As I lay in bed that night I kept thinking over and over again, "How many more will there be?" This was as cruel an end to the whole foot and mouth campaign as could be. West Cumbria had survived relatively intact compared to the rest of the county and was now to lose out whole-sale as a result of failed blood tests. We were building a bloody big mar-ket in which there might be nothing yet to sell. I was mad rather than miserable.

Next morning I arrived early at the farm to be met by the vet. He was a South African I had worked with before and I liked his style. I also met a man who I knew as a meat buyer and who had been seconded by a rival firm of auctioneers to undertake livestock valuations. Now he was work-ing for DEFRA in the role of 'invigilator'. His job was to eavesdrop on the valuation to make sure I was not inflating the figures and in doing so cheating DEFRA.

In the end I was pleased he was there for the farmers had obviously been briefed as to what the sheep should be worth. The difficulty was that the figures they had been told bore no resemblance to any of the val-uations I had ever done. An argument started and it looked like it might degenerate rather quickly. The farmers clearly thought I was trying to put one over on them when nothing could have been further from the truth. I assured them that I was there to try and give them the best set-tlement I could within the bounds of good practice. Eventually between the invigilator and myself we were able to convince them that the valua-tion was a damn good one.

The cattle were clearly not ill and never had been even though they had summered with the sheep. The vet's best guess was that the sheep prob-ably had FMD before they came to the farm and had recovered. Now that was frightening.

"Oh yes," said the vet "it is possible that foot and mouth might have been in Cumbria at the end of last year. We probably will never know." He was right for we probably never will.

Soon the job was done and we stood on the roadside completing the paperwork. There was a junction further up the road. I was amazed just how many farmers' vehicles pulled up to that junction, stayed a while then moved off in the direction away from the farm. Some went around two or three times. The word had spread and everyone was anxious. The sight of vets and slaughtermen was not what West Cumbria wanted to see.

That night at home I opened another can of beer and set off to drink it. The phone rang. It was another farmer from the same area. He was very upset as one of his housed cattle had clinical signs of FMD. His own vet had called for DEFRA blood tests. The result would be through in the morning. I assured him that if I was needed I would be there first thing. Another can of beer was poured down the sink. This was getting too much to bear again.

The farmer rang again in the morning. He was laughing. The blood tests were negative.

"Eeh Adam lad," he said "it really got to me last night." I felt like saying that I had had that for six months but it would not have been fair at all. The truth was that we were both delighted that all was well. We lived to fight another day.

Thankfully out of the thousands of blood tests that were done in Cumbria at the end of foot and mouth, remarkably few were anti-body positive.

One week later I was invited to undertake a valuation under the animal welfare (disposal scheme). The animals to value were pedigree Angora goats of which I had limited experience. However with comprehensive comparable evidence, the valuation was not difficult. It was just such a shame that the animals could not be moved from their Lake District farm, nor others brought in. Their only way out was to slaughter.

My final valuation in the whole crisis was only four miles from Cockermouth on Wednesday 31 October, Halloween night even if it did not register at the time. There were 80 or so sheep in one batch. Two blue-faced Leicester breeding rams had failed the blood tests and were anti-body positive to foot and mouth. All of the other sheep were clear. As I completed the forms the sheep already lay dead in the pen. It was the last pen of dead sheep that I would have to witness at a foot and mouth valuation. If only I had known it at the time.

By the end of the year it was doubtful that there would be any more valuations for the blood testing was complete. We had worried that the fell sheep would be found anti-body positive and yet again whole flocks would be lost. It did not happen and the foot and mouth crisis was over.

We stood watching our new market going up on the outskirts of Cockermouth. Here was hope. Here was the future. The difficulties of the FMD crisis and the dreadful time we had subsequent to it would soon be behind us. Now at last we could look forward to the new challenge even if the sickening memories were to linger on.

53
Time to Move On

Recounting some of my experiences during the foot and mouth crisis has been a cathartic yet wholly unsatisfactory experience. Many nights I sat at my computer tapping away, reliving so many of the dreadful days. It has not always gone down so well at home but I found that once I started to write I could not stop: I had to finish what I had started. My wife did not read one sentence of the book until it was finished. Then she sat down and read it in one sitting. For although we went through the crisis together she had no idea of what I had been through. After all that, she had been there for me from start to finish but I had told her so little of what actually happened. It was my way of dealing with it. Having read the book, she cried.

I always said that I would never be bitter about what happened in Cumbria in the year 2001 but writing these few short chapters opened up a lot of home truths about the whole disaster. I know that my experiences are nothing but the smallest tip of the iceberg. In that respect I cannot possibly have adequately conveyed the scale and enormity of the FMD disaster in Cumbria, and remember there were many more counties that suffered the same consequences to a lesser degree yet so many more people who suffered to a greater degree.

So what was the true scale of the disaster? How does one even begin to measure it?

The facts are as follows:- 2,030 infected premises of which more than half were in Cumbria, also an estimated 8,500 contiguous, direct and dangerous contact farms which lost everything. Added to that are an unknown number of fell farms losing vital replacement animals on away-wintering farms. The total number of animals that died as a result of the FMD epidemic and the resultant culling policies is staggering. It is believed that up to 11 million animals may have lost their lives. Only three animals in every 10,000 were actually infected. 13% of the entire UK sheep flock was wiped out, as were 6% of the total cattle breeding herds.

The total cost of fighting the outbreak is estimated to be over 8 billion pounds. The net effect on the farmers, rural communities and anyone employed within the dreadful battle has yet to be quantified. How the hell did it happen? Was there not a better way? Did so many animals have to die? Was it worth it? Who is responsible for such devastation? So many unanswered questions that should have been resolved long before now.

Within the introduction to this book I asked the question about who was really responsible for letting the people of Cumbria down so badly. It was a rhetorical question for deep down I already knew the answer but had never confronted it. My writings brought it all back to me. It was not the fault of the farmers, neither the auctioneers nor anyone else connected with the movement of farm animals throughout this great nation.

Why did it take so long to realise the truth? Why did people not listen to vets on the ground? People like Phil Watson, the DEFRA vet who knew from the start what had to be done and what would happen if it was not? Why did they believe that computer models would work to predict the spread of the disease? The questions are endless and the truth is so very easy to see with hindsight.

I feel proud of my company's small role. We did our best for our farmers. We never shirked the task and never gave up, even when we felt that we could sink no lower. Earning money for ourselves was never the issue. Our only thoughts were to help our friends and customers and in doing so maybe save our own existence.

One of the greatest disappointments to come out of the FMD crisis is the unjustified and enduring bad image that has been created of auction marts. Some would have us believe that the mart is a dangerous, disease-ridden, den of iniquity where animals are abused and punted from sale to sale. A visit to our new market opens the eyes of many of the uninitiated. A true farmers market like ours is the lifeblood of the farming community. That is why so many buyers travel long distances to buy our produce both for meat and as breeding animals. That is why they all came back as soon as they possibly could. And what is wrong with that?

The Government's veterinary advisors believe that animals travelling around the country to abattoirs or to farms are a disease risk because outbreaks like FMD will happen again. If this is true then it is because the rules regarding the importation of raw meat products and other foodstuffs are flouted.

After FMD, just when we are looking for help, guidance and maybe a touch of confidence building reassurance, the farmers of England's famous Lake District are being made to feel like lepers. We are slowly but surely being cast aside, strangled by European policies, national leg-islation and greedy supermarket multiples, day by day undermining the wonderful produce we should be so proud to call British.

Should demand rise, supply fall and the price of our beef, lamb or milk rise a by a penny or two, then off they all go abroad to buy the cheaper, often inferior, far less traceable food until they can pull the British price back again. Of course the other countries, especially our friends in the European Union don't mind a jot. They can take a cheaper price because they are so much better supported by their own Governments.

I have not forgotten the supermarket multiples within this country pro-nouncing during FMD that they would not buy meat from animals vac-cinated for FMD within the UK. Yet many of them were and still are buying meat from countries that do have such a vaccination policy. Of course we all know that it makes no difference whether meat or milk comes from vaccinated animals but where was the support for us when we needed it most from our major buyers?

So our general public continues daily life, blissfully unaware of the true effects of FMD and what has been forced upon farmers in the after-math. The economic and the social havoc that it has created is a disgrace. But this is not the fault of the British people. For we are being seduced by clever packaging and low prices that hide the origin of the food we eat. It also hides the deterioration of our own farming heritage and coun-tryside.

"So what?" I hear you cry, "they had it good once." We all had it good once but now the industry is dying. The young farmers cannot make a living on the same farm their fathers and grandfathers were born on. Two farms become one, four farms become two and so on. "Economies of scale," you argue "must be a good thing." Well yes if you don't mind the disappearance of a few dry stone walls, natural meadows and thicket hedges. For the truth of the matter is that if the farmers die out then so will the countryside. The beautiful place we live and work in called the Lake District is dying. FMD galvanised the process and so very little is being given back to us to regenerate what really needs to be regenerated.

Britain needs its farmers to produce food. We will all realise this in time of drought, flood, pestilence or war. History has proved it time and time again. If you cannot feed your own people then others will make great boun-ty from it.

Few people can say that they live in an ideal world but it is an interesting concept. Especially when times have been difficult. My ideal world goes something like this:

Firstly keep me and my family healthy and happy. Secondly keep our farmers prosperous and supportive. Thirdly, educate the people of Britain to have pride in their farmers, buy local produce and cast aside the imported food that puts money (in large amounts) only into the pockets of the greedy supermarkets. Fourthly, teach the leaders of this country to respect the rural way of life and those of us who are proud to be part of it. Fifthly, give us a rural ministry that supports and leads rather than fights and obstructs. Sixthly, make us all proud to be a British nation again.

It is a six point plan, all of which is achievable. Do not get me wrong, I am not anti-European in any way. I envy many of our brothers and sisters over the water. For they have a fervent nationalistic pride. They are French and German and Spanish first and Europeans second. What is wrong with that?

I am proud to be Cumbrian, English, British and European. I am proud to be a part of the farming community. Even my small role as an auctioneer of Lake District beef, lamb and all other things agricultural, plays a part in keeping the Lake District alive. Had FMD endured, then all of the livestock in Cumbria would have been destroyed. We came very close but we survived. It should never have come to that. The sad thing is that the farmers of Lakeland will never give in. The old cliché has never been more true: "Farming is not a job, it's a way of life."

If only a fairy godmother could wave her magic wand. People would flock to the Lake District, enjoy our lakes and valleys and mountains and buy our wonderful lamb and beef and milk too. It need not be a dream. It can be achieved. Who will help us? Who will support us to make the dream come true? We don't need hand-outs. All we need is recognition that what we have is good, what we do is for the best, and what we have created is worth maintaining.

We need rural policy makers who can deliver with common sense, understanding and support towards rural communities. In time the rural policy makers whose goal is to persuade farmers to dispose of even more livestock through 'environmental' schemes, will suddenly discover that the fells have become overgrown and are not delivering the habitats that they expected would be created. Whilst I accept that I am not really qualified to make this statement, there are many of my customers who have farmed the Lake District for generations who openly state these worrying concerns. Many of the old sheep hefts may disappear. It is happening now. Hundreds of years of tradition, viable farming and land management is in danger following FMD. Did our fells look any different 300 years ago? I only wish there were people alive to tell us now.

We should be proud that there are breed lines of both sheep and farmers that can be traced back that far. Now more than ever, the continuation of those breed lines are under immense threat. Why is it so difficult for some to see that farmers, whatever they produce, must be allowed to make a competitive living?

So what of the farmers, the lifeblood of the countryside, the backbone of England? What has been left of them in the mess that was scattered about after FMD? Slowly they are recovering. I am not talking about their businesses, more their psychological well being. Studies are being undertaken by academics to find out the true toll of FMD in terms of its effect on farmers, their families and the communities. I know because I have tried to give an honest input as to what effect the whole sorry affair has had on me as an individual.

I cannot speak for every farmer who suffered during the FMD crisis, but I can tell you about some of my customers. For there are many for whom a discussion about 'the day you came to value' is altogether too painful. Even now there are farmers who are reduced to tears should I stray too close to the subject. Most of the time I try not to mention it. Sometimes I talk about it without thinking. It just comes out. Maybe it is me addressing my own weaknesses. Often though I have to change the subject, not through my own inner reactions but the effect I can see it has on the other person.

How difficult and yet how great it was to help our farmers restock their farms. What a triumph over adversity. The old British bull dog spirit - 'Don't let the buggers get you down'. But so many farmers did get down and struggled hard to fight back up again. The memories are still there.

Even after restocking there are farmers who are struggling to bond with their new animals. They knew the old cows, their mothers and grandmothers. They knew the individual personalities and traits of the old stock. Overnight this knowledge was wiped out. It will take several generations of breeding before the new herd will again become so familiar. These are the hard facts of restocking and regenerating farms. It is not all plain sailing even though we sighed with relief as each farm was able to bring stock back in. Now there are fresh problems to deal with such as TB which appears to have been brought into the county in large amounts during the restocking process.

Of course there were many farmers who did not lose stock during FMD. A friend of mine on a tenanted farm was not allowed to sell or move his stock and had to ask his bank manager for an addition of another £50,000 to add to his already extensive overdraft facility. He is struggling to pay it off. How grateful he was to receive a small donation from a charity fund that helped many farmers in the same position. It was only a couple of thousand pounds but it helped to keep food on the table for his children. It proved to him the fact that somebody did care. When he was able to, he paid some of the money back by way of charitable donation. He did not have to but he had pride. He did not want a free handout but was mighty glad when there was some support at the time he most needed it.

FMD brought out the best and the worst in farmers. To those customers who backed my colleagues and me to the hilt I give grateful thanks. A few words of encouragement meant everything at that time. To those farmers who promised to back the new auction and have done so without fail, again we are in your debt. We valued your stock as dearly as we could within the bounds of professionalism. We were proud to do so. It was both a great honour and a great burden.

To those farmers who treated the dreadful job of valuation as a tender process by ringing several valuers to see who would be prepared to go the furthest, shame on you! Likewise the valuer who was prepared to bid for it.

To those farmers who scarcely gave their valuer a thought after he had done the job and moved on to the next customer, spare him a thought for he went through his own living hell working for you.

To those brave auctioneers who did the job so well, with professionalism and honour I salute you for few farmers or indeed the general public will ever know what you had to go through personally. Likewise the vets, slaughtermen, hauliers, pyre builders and all the rest of the troops in the fields of Cumbria. More often than not we were a team and we can be very proud even if our peers will not acknowledge it.

To so many farmers the loss of their animals was akin to the loss of family members. Believe me the pain and bitterness remains deeply embedded in hearts and minds. Money could not make up for the suffering endured by Cumbrian people.

It is my opinion that Ministers should be helping us, nurturing our industry back to health and above all else, showing respect for the countryside, the rural way of life and its guardians, the farmers. The gulf that exists between the farmers and their ministry has never been as wide. It is 'them and us' and it has to change.

I believe that all the weak scientific reasoning behind our industry's over-regulation is no justification to hide behind. Current policies are designed only to minimise cost and expenditure when diseases such as FMD return and we know they will because the disease is not being fought at the point of entry. How many prosecutions have been made against illegal meat importers? Or would the authorities still rather penalise the farmer who dares to break post-FMD regulations just to keep his business afloat? Is it not cheaper to train a sniffer dog and its handler than a team of vets, field officers, 'rural' DEFRA policemen and all the other support roles?

Take hold of the responsibility, stand up for your countryside and you may just gain the respect of the people. Now is the time to build bridges. Now is the time to be proud of our farmers and our food. Now is the time to put FMD firmly behind us, learn the lessons that will prevent, not cure such a dreadful disease outbreak in the future. Now is the time for us all to move on.

54
THE DREAM COMES TRUE

Friday 24 May 2002
The Lakeland Livestock Centre opens

It is Friday morning and we are standing at the loading docks within the brand spanking new Lakeland Livestock Centre. It is a fantastic site. You can see down the Lorton Valley to the steep and foreboding west face of Grassmoor. The Buttermere valley is only a few miles distant. To the east stands Skiddaw in plain view, a huge and rounded mass of slate. There cannot be many more auction marts built in such a stunning location.

I did not sleep much last night. Excited? Oh yes! Nervous? Like never before! Today marks the culmination of more than seven years' work. Only those who have played a part can truly know the highs and lows we have been through to get here. The new market has been a labour of love for most of the directors. So many times we thought we were not going to make it and so many times we found a way to keep the dream alive. Then at last when it all seemed to fall in to place, we were beaten down again. But this time it was not planning permission or failed grant applications, nor was it BSE or a general fall in meat prices. This time it was far worse, this time it was foot and mouth. So we struggled on last year valuing our customers livestock for the cull. In doing so we watched our own future going down the drain. Somehow we survived. What miracle ensured that most of the livestock in West Cumbria stayed healthy? We will never know. It doesn't matter now because we have made it and the dream is going to come true.

It's quite cold at the loading docks even for early summer. The yard staff have their clean oilskins on. There's going to be some sweat lost today when things warm up. Overseeing the day are Trading Standards, MLC and DEFRA. The rules and regulations to operate our market are unbelievably complex. We have had to spend several thousands of pounds on extra bio-security measures in recent days to satisfy the requests from these Government bodies. Indeed DEFRA only gave us our licence to operate at 8 o'clock last night. I thought we would have to cancel the sale at the eleventh hour. It would have been a disaster. At last they gave us the go ahead so there's no stopping us now. Tanis Brough is the DEFRA vet charged with responsibility on the day. I worked with her so many times during FMD, it is quite fitting that she is here now. She has a difficult job to do in making sure we all obey the stringent rules imposed by her employers. Sometimes enthusiasm and excitement gets the better of people. Our farmers are just so happy to be here and so are we. Tanis keeps us on our toes.

We have a huge entry of 700 cattle on the catalogue. Every available pen is full, it is magnificent. What support from the farming community, they all want to be a part of it. Of course there will be some cattle that do not turn up. Because of the large catalogue some will be saved for another day. Other farmers have decided to sell their cattle at home despite entering them for our sale. This is disappointing on such a special occasion. However the vast majority of farmers choose to support us to the hilt.

The first vehicle pulls around the side of the market building. It is Sharp's wagon from Silecroft. They back onto the loading docks, the ramp is down and the first cattle enter the market. Then the flood gates open as vehicle after vehicle arrives. Within minutes the whole mart is a hive of activity. It looks and feels like a proper livestock auction.

Soon the prize show judging is taking place. As this happens I move around the market greeting farmers who are looking to buy cattle. My nerves are jangling. I'm sure my fellow auctioneer Alisdare feels the same but he's like me, all smiles, riding on a high.

The judging is over. Ian Richardson from Greenlands Farm has won. It is bang on start time so I go to the rostrum and call for the first pen of cattle. The whole of the public seated area is crammed full of folk. They have come from all over, there is not even any standing room. BBC Look North want an interview - Judy Ingham came to see us when we sold all of the old pens in the town centre market last August. I promised her that we would see her in the new place and she remembered! I tell her that the livestock auction is so much more than a business centre. It is the lifeblood of the farming community. The social side of the mart is as important as the business its self. The farmers have missed their market during foot and mouth as much as we have. Some farmers have come to support us on the day even though they have nothing to sell. It is a carnival atmosphere and just what we wanted.

The first lot is in the ring, a cow with calf at foot from Harry Harper of

Commongate farm. Neither of us dwell on the fact that he is the first farmer to sell in the mart and I am the first auctioneer. Will anyone remember in 100 years time? Let us hope the market is still going strong then.

Our chairman Peter Greenhill says a few words of introduction. The PA level is not quite right. Everything is new and I worry that the sound will not be good enough around the ring. It sounds poor from the rostrum but clear as anything around the ring. Peter finishes his speech and I put the headset on and pick up my selling stick. It has been in a cupboard gathering dust for so long.

I introduce the first lot and check the information on the digital display board. We've never had one of these before, it's all new again but it looks great. A proper modern auction.

A good cow and calf, I look closely at her. Should be worth a thousand or so. I've been to other sales recently and I know what the cattle have been making. This is make or break time. Our prices have to be as dear as the other markets. There is pressure on me but I cannot do any more.

I ask a thousand and drop back to £800 but I don't have a bid. Silence all around the ring. You could hear a pin drop. Play safe Adam; don't mess about at the start. I come down way low to £600 to get a starting bid. Now we're off and running, hit the gas Adam. Within a few bids we are up to £1000 and still going. Thank God, the bids keep coming. Take your time on the first lot and don't rush. Soon we are at £1220 and all bidding has finished.

"Bang" the hammer falls and the buyer is our old friend Willie Miller from High Aikton. He tells me later he was determined to buy the first lot but he doesn't want a big thing made of it. There is a huge round of applause. The Lakeland Livestock Centre is now up and running.

No time to dwell on this as the next lot is in the ring. I take a deep breath for now the business really starts. I need to get the trade going fast, not take too long to get the hammer down but make sure the cattle are up to the price. It is 15 months since I was last a proper auctioneer. Since then we have been to hell and back. It is like riding a bike and within a few lots I am in to my stride. What fun it is, I am having a great time. There are plenty of good cattle and plenty of buyers, everyone wants a piece of the action.

There is something far more important than the prices. How is the market running outside? We have spent years planning and designing the layout. Many hours have been spent pouring over the penning scheme and we have visited so many other auctions up and down the country looking and learning. We think we have got layout right, today we find out, for if there is a fault then a farmer will find it.

In between lots I spy our yard foreman James. There is pressure on him and his staff as they have to make this sale run smoothly but again everything is brand new. The whole system from unloading to reloading at the end of the day is new. Add to that the fact that the market is crammed to overflowing and you can see that it is a difficult situation. I ask him if it is working OK. "Like a dream," he replies with a smile. Thank God we've got it right!

I have been selling for two hours. I do not want to stop but it is Alisdare's turn to sell as we agreed. The voice is a muscle and ours are out of training, so two hours on and two off should give us both a nice little stint at the end. In the end Alisdare bangs on really well, he too is enjoying it.

I move around the ring meeting customers old and new. We have friends who have made the trip up from Milton Keynes and Warwickshire. They are keen to support even though they say how they will miss the old market. They do however like the new place for it really works well. This is the best bit of the whole thing for everyone is commenting about what a good market it really is. We are all elated.

The sale has finished. The office is awash with sellers wanting cheques and buyers wanting to pay their bills. It's been a long hard day for all for the office staff as well. They too are out of practice in running a sale. Also they have had to learn to use new computer software as well. This happens to be the biggest sale we have had for many years but everyone involved in the sale had risen to the challenge and succeeded.

Alisdare and I are standing on the rostrum. The adrenaline rush for us both is over. We can analyse the day later but for now we have a glowing sense of satisfaction. We are both back doing what we should be doing, selling livestock through the ring - it is a good feeling.

The office is quiet now, many of the cattle have been loaded up and taken to their new homes. A few will lair over until the following morning. The yardmen have already started the clean up operation. Our shiny new concrete floor is awash with the muck of an auction full of cattle. Silly as it seems, it actually smells right, it is a proper auction.

Alisdare and I call the men over and dish out some cans of beer. We sit and drink them and look back at the day. It went very well indeed, as good as could have been expected, we are proud and relieved. Back in the office there is a sale report to do but I decide to leave it until morning. We are still too busy talking about the day. It is 8 o'clock already, thirteen hours have flown by. Last night I said to Paula that I would be glad to see Friday night, now it is here.

Almost reluctantly we shut the office down for the night. None of us really want to go home just yet. I decide to stop off at my local for a quick one, for months I have been keeping them updated as to our progress. When I walk in to the Boot and Shoe I get some stick because they have already seen my ugly mug on the telly. "You looked like a kid at Christmas," they said. Indeed that is a very good analogy for every member of our staff must have felt that way today. Our team worked very well and we are very proud.

"Here you are," says Paul the landlord handing me a brimming pint of 'Jennings' Cumberland ale, "seems like you might have earned that one."

"Cheers all," I toast "and here's to the Lakeland Livestock Centre, at last…."

GLOSSARY

Away Wintering A very common type of grazing agreement where young sheep bred on hard high fell farms are sent away to lowland and less harsh farms to over winter before returning to the fell the following year.

AWS Animal Welfare Scheme. Devised by MAFF to collect and dispose of livestock trapped on farms unaffected by FMD.

Blue Box A DEFRA control zone around an FMD hotspot designed to regulate the movement of animals and vehicles within that area.

DEFRA Department of Environment, Food and Rural Affairs. The successor to MAFF, created following the General Election in June 2001.

Gimmer Lamb A young female sheep.

Gimmer Hogg As above after weaning from its mother.

Gimmer Shearling A female sheep over one year of age having been shorn for the first time.

Heafed/Hefted An in-bred trait within sheep flocks on the open fell that ensures acclimatisation and territorial instinct to a particular area of the fell.

Herdwick The indigenous sheep breed of the Lakeland fells.

Kendal Rough The indigenous sheep breed of the Kendal and East Cumbrian fells.

IACS Integrated Administration and Control System. An annual return made by both arable and livestock farmers through which the claiming of agricultural subsidies is facilitated.

Lairage/Lair over A grazing or penning facility in which to keep and maintain livestock before or after sales within a livestock market pending removal from the market.

Limousin Popular breed of beef cattle within the UK originating from France.

MAFF Ministry of Agriculture, Fisheries and Food - the predecessor of DEFRA.

Mule Commonly a cross-bred sheep created by crossing the Blue Faced Leicester ram with a Swaledale ewe and known as the North of England Mule.

Suckled calf Young beef calf prior to or at the time of weaning.

Swaledale A prolific fell sheep common to many northern counties of England.

More books from Hayloft

Yows & Cows, A Bit of Westmorland Wit, Mike Sanderson
(£7.95, ISBN 0 9523282 0 8)

The Herdwick Country Cook Book, Hugh & Therese Southgate
(Hardback, £29.95, ISBN 0954071182/ Paperback, £14.95, ISBN 0954071174)

From the High Pennines, A History of the Alderson Family,
Marmaduke Alderson, (£10.00, ISBN 190 452 4079)

The Maddison Line, A Journalist's Journey around Britain, Roy Maddison
(£10.00, ISBN 1 9045240 6 0)

Pashler's Lane, A Clare Childhood, Elizabeth Holdgate
(£10.00, ISBN 095 4207203)

The Long Day Done, Jeremy Rowan-Robinson
(£9.50, ISBN 1 9045240 4 4)

Odd Corners in Appleby, Gareth Hayes
(£8.50, ISBN 1 9045240 0 1)

The Ghastlies, Trix Jones and Shane Surgey
(£3.99, ISBN 1 9045240 4 4)

A Journey of Soles, Lands End to John O'Groats, Kathy Trimmer
(£9.50, 1 9045240 5 2)

Changing the Face of Carlisle, The Life and Times of Percy Dalton, City Engineer and Surveyor, 1926-1949, Marie K. Dickens
(£8, ISBN 0 9540711 9 0)

From Clogs and Wellies to Shiny Shoes, A Windermere Lad's Memories of South Lakeland, Miles R. M. Bolton
(£12.50, ISBN 1 9045240 2 8)

A History of Kaber, Helen McDonald and Christine Dowson,
(£8, ISBN 0 9540711 6 6)

The Gifkin Gofkins, Irene Brenan
(£2.50, ISBN 1 9045240 1 X)

A Dream Come True, the Life and Times of a Lake District National Park Ranger, David Birkett
(£5.50, ISBN 0 9540711 5 8)

Gone to Blazes, Life as a Cumbrian Fireman, David Stubbings
(£9.95, ISBN 0 9540711 4 X)

Changing Times, A History of Bolton, Barbara Cotton
(£12.50, ISBN 0 9540711 3 1)

Better by Far a Cumberland Hussar, A History of the Westmorland and Cumberland Yeomanry, Colin Bardgett
(Hardback, £26.95, ISBN 0954071123/ Paperback, £16.95, ISBN 0954071115)

Northern Warrior, the Story of Sir Andreas de Harcla, Adrian Rogan
(£8.95, ISBN 0 9523282 8 3)

A Riot of Thorn & Leaf, Dulcie Matthews
(£7.95, ISBN 0 9540711 0 7)

Military Mountaineering, A History of Services Expeditions, 1945-2000,
Retd. SAS Major Bronco Lane
(Hardback, £25.95, ISBN 0952328216/Paperback, £17.95, ISBN 0952328267)

2041 - The Voyage South, Robert Swan
(£8.95, 0 9523282 7 5)

Riding the Stang, Dawn Robertson (£9.99, ISBN 0 9523282 2 4)

Secrets and Legends of Old Westmorland, Peter Koronka & Dawn Robertson
(Hardback, £17.95, ISBN 0 9523282 4 0)
(Paperback, £11.95, ISBN 0 9523282 9 1)

The Irish Influence, Migrant Workers in Northern England,
Harold Slight (£4.95, 0 9523282 5 9)

Soldiers and Sherpas, A Taste for Adventure, Brummie Stokes.
(£19.95, 0 9541551 0 6)

North Country Tapestry, Sylvia Mary McCosh (£10, 0 9518690 0 0)

Between Two Gardens, The Diary of two Border Gardens,
Sylvia Mary McCosh (£5.95, 0 9008111 7 X)

Dacre Castle, A short history of the Castle and the Dacre Family,
E. H. A. Stretton (£5.50, 0 9518690 1 9)

Little Ireland, Memories of a Cleator Moor Childhood, Sean Close
(£7.95, ISBN 095 4067 304)

A Slip from Grace, More tales from Little Ireland, Sean Close
(£10.00, ISBN 095 4067 312)

Antarctica Unveiled, Scott's First Expedition and the Quest for the Unknown Continent, David E. Yelverton (£25.99, 0 8708158 2 2)

You can order any of our books by writing to:
Hayloft Publishing Ltd., South Stainmore, Kirkby Stephen,
Cumbria, CA17 4EU, UK.
Please enclose a cheque plus £2 for UK postage and packing.
or telephone: +44 (0)17683) 42300
For more information see: www.hayloft.org.uk